CIVIL WAR

Revised Edition

CIVIL WAR

Revised Edition

MICHAEL GOLAY

JOHN S. BOWMAN
general editor

CHELSEA HOUSE
PUBLISHERS
An imprint of Infobase Publishing

Civil War, Revised Edition

Copyright © 2011, 2003, 1992 by Michael Golay

Chelsea House, Inc.
An imprint of Infobase Publishing
132 West 31st Street
New York NY 10001

Library of Congress Cataloging-in-Publication Data

Golay, Michael, 1951–
Civil War / Michael Golay ; John S. Bowman, general editor.—Rev. ed.
p. cm.—(America at war)
Includes bibliographical references and index.
ISBN 978-0-8160-8190-5 (acid-free paper) 1. United States—History—Civil War,
1861–1865—Juvenile literature. I. Bowman, John Stewart, 1931– II. Title. III. Series.
E468.G65 2010
973.7—dc22   2009050494

Chelsea House books are available at special discounts when purchased in bulk quantities for businesses, associations, institutions or sales promotions. Please call our Special Sales Department in New York at (212) 967-8800 or (800) 322-8755.

You can find Chelsea House on the World Wide Web at http://www.chelseahouse.com

Text design by Erika K. Arroyo
Cover design by Takeshi Takahashi
Composition by Hermitage Publishing Services
Cover printed by Bang Printing, Brainerd, Minn.
Book printed and bound by Bang Printing, Brainerd, Minn.
Date printed:November 2010
Printed in the United States of America

10 9 8 7 6 5 4 3 2 1

This book is printed on acid-free paper.

Contents

Preface

The causes, course, and consequences of the Civil War continue to engage scholars and students of the history of the United States. This book aims to contribute to the examination of this resounding event and to call attention to its major themes. Contemporaries evidently had a clearer understanding of the causes of the Civil War than did succeeding generations. In his second inaugural address in March 1865, Abraham Lincoln asserted that some 4 million African Americans held in slavery in prewar America constituted "a peculiar and powerful interest" around which gathered the conflicts and contradictions of a nation founded on principles of equality. "All knew that this interest was somehow the cause of the war," Lincoln went on. "To strengthen, perpetuate, and extend this interest was the object for which the insurgents would rend the union even by war." The question of slavery receded for later generations, becoming a contributory cause merely, especially in popular accounts of the war, subordinate to the real issue—the constitutional principle of states' rights.

But surely Lincoln was in the right of it. Disputes over federal and state powers, controversies over tariffs and aid to manufacturing interests, diverging ways of life in the increasingly urban and industrial North and the traditional and agrarian South: Surely these could have been resolved or at least defused short of civil war. Yet, as Lincoln also remarked on the steps of the Capitol in Washington that cold and gray March day, "Both parties deprecated war, but one of them would *make* war rather than let the nation survive, and the other would *accept* war rather than let it perish, and the war came."

The conflict that opened with the Confederate bombardment of Fort Sumter on April 12–14, 1861, soon gained a furious momentum. It proved, in the end, to be the most destructive war in U.S. history. From the first major battle at Bull Run to the climactic skirmish around Appomattox Court House, four years of fighting claimed

620,000 men on both sides—a death toll exceeding that of the United States in the 20th century's two world wars, the Korean War, and the Vietnam War *combined*. Tens of thousands of men were maimed. The conquering Union armies left the South a ruined land. The material cost approached $20 billion. Southern wealth declined a catastrophic 43 percent, a figure that does not include the "market value" of former slaves. What had been, per capita, the nation's richest region became the nation's poorest—and remained so for a century.

The war changed the nation in ways great and small. First and foremost, it left to be settled later the question of the freed blacks' place in American society. Beyond emancipation, the Union did little or nothing for former slaves. The war destroyed the notion of the American union of states as a voluntary compact—after 1865, the United States was indissoluble. It stimulated industrial development and accelerated the evolution of ever more powerful corporations. Four years of bitter warfare coarsened American life. The war even introduced into common use a new adjective, *shoddy*, which became a synonym for what many saw as the cheapness and vulgarity of American business and public life. Political corruption flourished as never before in the

The battle at Bull Run, or Manassas, in Virginia, on July 21, 1861, was the first major battle of the Civil War. *(Library of Congress)*

aftermath of 1861–65. The presidential administration of the victorious Union general-in-chief Ulysses S. Grant (1869–77) became a byword for graft.

Then, too, a sort of revulsion against the idea of human improvement seemed to sweep the country, replaced by the chilly and mechanical notion that nature should be left to take its course. Political thinkers would dub this "Social Darwinism"—the survival in society of the fittest. After all, argued those who advocated a retreat from reform, the urge to betterment in antebellum America fed the movement to abolish slavery, and abolitionism helped ignite rebellion and war.

So the postwar generations forgot about the "peculiar institution" of slavery. As the decades passed, Lincoln's insights into the causes of the war were, if not rejected, then at least relegated to a secondary place. In a provocative essay published in 2001, "The Enduring Legacy of the South's Civil War Victory," the historian David Brion Davis attributes this neglect of what had been the leading feature of antebellum national life to what he styles the South's ideological victory in the Civil War. "Though the South lost the battles, for more than a century it attained its goal: that the role of slavery in America's history be thoroughly diminished, even somehow removed as a cause of the war," he wrote. "The reconciliation of North and South required . . . a distorted view of slavery as an unfortunate but benign institution that was damaging for whites morally but helped civilize and Christianize 'African savages.'"

More recent scholarship has sought to redress the imbalance. The renewal of emphasis on slavery has also opened a wide-ranging discussion of the issue of reparations for descendants of slaves—payment as a token of apology for the 250 years that African Americans were held in bondage. Some reparations advocates calculate the bill as high as $1.5 trillion. Randall Robinson lays out the argument for reparations fully in his book *The Debt: What America Owes to Blacks* (2000). This vexed question has touched off a vigorous debate in academic circles as well as in national newspapers and magazines. Is compensation a validation of victimhood, blaming history for the social ills of the present? Or is it a just recompense for the crimes of history?

"When a party unlawfully enriches himself by wrongful acts against another, the wronged party is entitled to be paid back," Robinson writes. With the exception of land, slaves represented the nation's greatest prewar capital asset, as Davis points out. And Robinson notes the painful irony that enforced and unpaid black labor helped build the Capitol from which Lincoln delivered those imperishable lines in the second inaugural, offering malice toward none and charity for all. "This was the house of Liberty," writes Robinson, "and it was built by slaves."

However the reparations issue plays out, it is clear that "slavery's centrality in American history," in Davis's phrase, has been firmly reestablished. Union conduct of the war soon reflected the reality of slavery as the leading cause of the conflict. Lincoln could not escape its looming presence. "My paramount object in this struggle is to save the Union, and is *not* either to save or to destroy slavery," the president famously told the newspaper editor Horace Greeley in 1862. "If I could save the Union without freeing *any* slave I would do it, and if I could save it by freeing *all* the slaves I would do it, and if I could save it by freeing some and leaving others alone, I would also do that."

With his Emancipation Proclamation of January 1, 1863, Lincoln attempted a delicate balancing act—the decree, which the president justified as a war measure, freed slaves only in the rebellious states where Union power could not yet reach. But Lincoln, even had he sought to, could not escape the logic of events. As the war became harder, his view of its significance expanded. How otherwise to rationalize and accept the carnage of the battles at Fredericksburg (18,000 casualties), Chancellorsville (30,000 casualties), and Gettysburg (50,000 casualties)?

So by the end of 1863, Lincoln's words to Greeley were a dead letter. At the dedication of a new national cemetery for the dead of Gettysburg in November, Lincoln redefined the meaning of the war—and defined it for future generations if they chose to understand him. In his brief speech, Lincoln moved beyond the objective of mere restoration of the Union, calling on the nation to dedicate itself "to the great task remaining before us—that from these honored dead we take increased devotion to that cause for which they gave the last full measure of devotion; that we here highly resolve that these dead shall not have died in vain; that this nation, under God, shall have a new birth of freedom; and that government of the people, by the people, for the people, shall not perish from the earth." Lincoln's words, then and later, have been taken as a plea for the reaffirmation and extension of the founding principles of the United States.

The conduct of the war reflected the suffering and pain of this new birth. The inexorable General Grant and the implacable General

Sherman practiced new techniques of total war—a calm acceptance of terrible battlefield casualties on Grant's part, and a carrying of the hardships of war to the South's civil population on Sherman's part.

"No general yet found can face the arithmetic," Lincoln mused after the Battle of Fredericksburg in December 1862, "but the end of the war will be at hand when he shall be discovered." Grant was that man, and he stared down the numbers—60,000 killed, wounded and missing, *more men than his adversary mustered at the outset of the campaign—* from the Wilderness to Petersburg in the spring and early summer of 1864. Historians now generally agree that Sherman spoke more fiercely than he acted. Still, he carried the war to Southern civilians in an unprecedented way. "War is cruelty and you cannot refine it," he explained to the citizens of Atlanta as he prepared to make refugees of them in September 1864. By the end of the year, Grant's and Sherman's methods had won full acceptance in the North. Lincoln swept to reelection over an opponent—the "soft-war" former Army of the Potomac commander George B. McClellan—whose platform called for

Wounded soldiers recovering in Carver Hospital in Washington, D.C. *(National Archives)*

negotiations with the rebellious states and an armistice. Remarkably, thousands of Union soldiers voted in what amounted to a referendum on whether to continue the war to a victorious conclusion—and voted overwhelmingly for Lincoln.

David Brion Davis remarked that historians of the future will be asked to explain "the remarkable recent upsurge of interest in slavery and the Civil War." Many of the hundreds of new scholarly and popular books published each year on the war reflect this upsurge. It is reflected, too, in the broad appeal of the 1990 Ken Burns television documentary *The Civil War* (reissued in 2002); the 1989 feature film *Glory*, which recounts the exploits of the black 54th Massachusetts regiment during the siege of Charleston in 1863; and the 1993 television film *Gettysburg*, based on Michael Shaara's best-selling 1974 novel, *The Killer Angels*.

The hold of the Civil War on Southerners' imagination and the puzzling phenomenon of the widespread popularity of Civil War reenactments are examined in Tony Horowitz's lively *Confederates in the Attic* (1998). Horowitz introduces the book with an epigram from the author Shelby Foote: "Southerners are very strange about that war." And Charles Frazier's novel *Cold Mountain* (1997), the tale of a Confederate deserter based on a story handed down in the author's family, became a surprise best-seller.

On the scholarly front, a number of books focus on the role of African Americans in their own emancipation. In *Free at Last: A Documentary History of Slavery, Freedom and the Civil War* (1992), the editor Ira Berlin provides an abridged version of a massive compilation of letters and other documents by and about African Americans. Editor Edwin Redkey collects letters of African-American soldiers in *A Grand Army of Black Men* (1992). Both books provide a solid primary-source foundation for an understanding of the black experience of the war and emancipation. Two more recent studies of emancipation throw light on the complex question of slavery and disunion: Allan Guelzo's *Lincoln's Emancipation Proclamation: The End of Slavery in America* (2004) and Richard Striner's *Father Abraham: Lincoln's Relentless Struggle to End Slavery* (2007).

For drama, scope, color, and appeal, it will be difficult for anyone to improve upon Shelby Foote's magnificent *The Civil War: A Narrative* (1958–74; revised 1990). Recent books cover some of the same ground as Foote, but perhaps with a more scholarly and less literary slant. One such is Russell Weigley's *A Great Civil War: A Military and Political*

History, 1861–1865 (2000). This work emphasizes the interrelation of military and political strategy. *The Longest Night: A Military History of the Civil War* by David J. Eicher (2001) delivers just what its title promises: a chronological account of campaigns and battles, with slight social or political background. For a detailed study of the Confederacy's main army, turn to *General Lee's Army: From Victory to Collapse* (2008). A more specialized study is *The Hard Hand of War: Union Military Policy toward Southern Civilians, 1861–1865* (1995), which tracks the evolution of Northern policy from the limited aims of McClellan to the hard war of Grant and Sherman. George S. Burkhardt's *Confederate Rage, Yankee Wrath: No Quarter in the Civil War* (2007) addresses similar themes.

Recent biographies offer reassessments of major Civil War leaders. David Herbert Donald's *Lincoln* (1995) presents the 16th president as a man more controlled by events than directing them, a controversial view. A flood of new studies of Lincoln as a political and military leader anticipated and then celebrated the 200th anniversary of his birth in 2009. A sampling includes Michael Burlingame, *Abraham Lincoln: A Life* (2008); Eric Foner, ed., *Our Lincoln: New Perspectives on Lincoln and His World* (2008); Doris Keans Goodwin, *Team of Rivals: The Political Genius of Abraham Lincoln* (2005); and James M. McPherson, *Tried by War: Abraham Lincoln as Commander-in-Chief* (2008). Alan T. Nolan dulls the aura of Robert E. Lee in *Lee Considered* (1991), in which he assesses the commander of the Army of Northern Virginia as a timid strategist (he never lifted his gaze beyond the Virginia theater) and a clumsy, even reckless tactician wasteful of his troops' lives. Thomas Emory's *Robert E. Lee: A Biography* (1995), however, is an admiring account of the Virginia icon. A lively short biography of Lee is Roy Blount, Jr.'s *Robert E. Lee: A Penguin Life* (2003). And Tom Carhart's *Lost Triumph: Lee's Real Plan at Gettysburg—and Why It Failed* (2005), although not solely designed to defend Lee's decision on the third day at Gettysburg, offers a most detailed and rational explanation for that fateful day.

In *Ulysses S. Grant: Triumph over Adversity, 1822–1865* (2000), Brooks D. Simpson treats the Union commander as an enigmatic character, ruthless on the battlefield but magnanimous in victory. Two recent studies of Sherman's life offer contrasting views. John F. Marszalek's *Sherman: A Soldier's Passion for Order* (1993) presents the scourge of legend as a soldier far less ruthless than he appears in the popular image. In *Citizen Sherman: A Life of William Tecumseh Sherman* (1995),

Michael Fellman portrays the general as a "furious" self-doubter who found his true vocation and "moral affirmation" through the approved violence of war. A recent assessment of the Grant-Sherman partnership is Charles Bracelen Flood's *Grant and Sherman: The Friendship That Won the Civil War* (2005).

The pages of this book cover the history of the Civil War from causes to consequences. The military history of the conflict is, of course, set forth, but at least as important is the examination of the war's political and social aspects. In addition to the main narrative text, the book has proven to be especially valued for its supplementary elements: the many interesting illustrations, the maps custom designed to make events particularly clear, the glossary, the recommended reading and Web sites, and, above all, the many sidebars, with their brief essays on subjects that often explore the more personal aspects of the war.

And now in this revised edition, there are several new features to complement these already proven contributions to clarifying this war for many readers. Beyond updating the recommended reading list and Web sites, the volume has added many color illustrations. It has a special new sidebar, "A Just War?" designed to inspire debate on the pros and cons of this war. Finally, it has a completely new chapter on the weapons and tactics employed during the war, highlighting these elements while placing them in the broader context of warfare in this era.

But while reading it is well to keep larger issues in mind: the meaning Lincoln read into the sacrifice of the Civil War generation, and how nearly America has approached the new birth of freedom he envisioned. Just a month before an assassin's bullet claimed him as one of the last of the terrible war's direct casualties, Lincoln interpreted the national tragedy as a judgment on America for the sin of slavery.

"Yet, if God wills that it continue until all the wealth piled by the bondsman's two hundred and fifty years of unrequited toil shall be sunk, and until every drop of blood drawn with the lash shall be paid by another drawn with the sword, as was said three thousand years ago, so still it must be said 'the judgements of the Lord are true and righteous altogether.'"

The Civil War ended abruptly with Robert E. Lee's surrender at Appomattox five days before the murder of Abraham Lincoln. Yet the struggle for the war's meaning continued on through Reconstruction and through a century of racial segregation added onto those two and a half centuries of unrequited toil. It continues still to this day.

Prologue
A NATION DIVIDES

Union troops in and around Centreville, Virginia, broke camp at two o'clock in the morning. Under a bright full moon, they put away the remains of their breakfast of hard bread and coffee, doused their camp-fires, and formed in columns of four along the Warrenton Turnpike. Burdened with muskets, full knapsacks, extra ammunition, blankets, and canteens, they moved with a clatter that surely must have roused the dozing rebels ahead. Three miles down the turnpike, in defensive positions in the wooded bluffs on the far side of a sluggish stream called Bull Run, a Confederate army waited this Sunday morning of July 21, 1861.

Union forces under Gen. Irvin McDowell had been concentrating since early June near Washington, D.C., only 30 miles east of Centreville. For weeks, pressures had been mounting for a campaign against the 11 Southern states that had seceded from the Union in the winter and early spring of 1861. Impatient congressmen and aggressive news-paper editors urged President Lincoln to send the army into Virginia to crush the rebellion. By the end of June they were clamoring for a Union advance on Richmond before the congress of the new Confederate States of America could convene there on July 20. "Forward to Richmond!" Horace Greeley's influential *New York Tribune* trumpeted. "The Rebel Congress Must Not Be Allowed to Meet!"

General McDowell protested that his troops were not ready to fight. He had 34,000 men, but they were militia, mostly—untrained volunteers grouped by hometown, county, and state. They were the most amateur of soldiers, awkward at drill, and they tended to ignore orders they did not like or understand. Their officers were amateurs, too. They were men of high standing at home—judges, storekeepers, and schoolteachers—but they knew little of war.

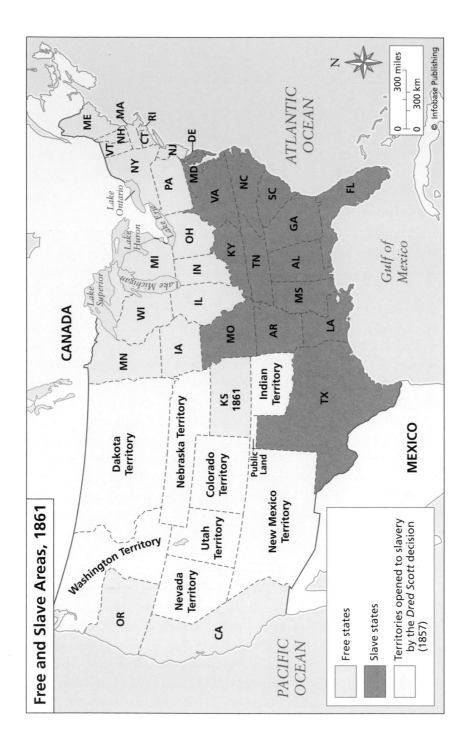

Free and Slave Areas, 1861

The 23,000 Confederates drawn up on an eight-mile front along Bull Run north of the town of Manassas were no better prepared. Their commander, Gen. Pierre G. T. Beauregard, had concerns about his troops' training and equipment. He even worried whether the rebels, who dressed, marched, and talked much like the Yankees, would be able to tell friend from foe.

"You are green, it is true," the president had told McDowell, "but they are green, also; you are all green alike." So Lincoln and his cabinet ordered McDowell to attack.

The Union army waiting in the moonlight early that Sunday morning had left Arlington, Virginia, across the Potomac from Washington, five days earlier, on Tuesday, July 16. A light breeze ruffled the silken regimental flags. Mounted officers in gold braid cantered up and down the long columns of troops. Some of the troops were gaudily uniformed, as though for a parade: the New York Fire Zouaves in their red shirts, gray jackets and knickers, and red fezzes; the 79th New York Highlanders in Scots plaid; the 1st Minnesota in red flannel shirts and black trousers. The midsummer sun burned down, though, and soon the brilliant shirt fronts were dark with sweat. These civilian soldiers were unused to marching. Hot, choked with dust, and footsore, they managed only seven miles that first day.

General McDowell decided to rest and resupply his army, giving the Confederates time to reinforce theirs. McDowell had hoped that Confederate forces in the Shenandoah Valley, 60 miles to the west, could be prevented from joining Beauregard. But McDowell's delays enabled Gen. Joseph E. Johnston to use the railroad to move his Shenandoah regiments to Bull Run in time for the battle.

That morning of July 21, McDowell sent his main assault column of 14,000 men on a long flank march to the north of the Confederate positions. A second column of 10,000, commanded by Brig. Gen. David Tyler, was to attack the Confederates at the arched stone bridge that carried Warrenton Turnpike over Bull Run. The flanking columns would cross two miles upstream and fall upon the rebel left flank. If all went well, the flanking column would roll up the Confederate left like a blanket. If reinforcements were needed, McDowell had another 10,000 troops in reserve in defensive positions around Centreville.

General Tyler's force moved off toward the stone bridge on time, but the crush of traffic and other confusions delayed the flanking column. Finally the column moved out, the men struggling with their 50 pounds of gear through thick underbrush and over rough, broken ground. After a 12-mile march, the column forded Bull Run at 9:30, two and a half hours behind schedule.

Tyler had opened fire at daybreak, but at such a feeble rate that the Confederate commander opposite him, Col. Nathan G. Evans, did not take the attack seriously. Soon reports were coming in of a large Federal crossing to the north. Evans found confirmation in a dust cloud rising into the sky. He left a small force to hold Tyler at the stone bridge and hurried two regiments of infantry across country to meet the assault.

Finding Evans's troops in front of them, the Federals moved obediently to the attack. The leading 2nd Rhode Island Volunteers were confused, though, and unable to see much through the smoke and dust. A brisk return fire stopped their assault almost as soon as it started. Fresh Federal troops soon arrived, however, and two artillery batteries, 11 big guns in all, began pounding away at the Confederate line.

By now General Beauregard had seen the dust cloud. He sent Shenandoah brigades under generals Barnard Bee and Thomas J. Jackson marching north to help Evans. Bee's troops joined Evans in the front line, but the Federal assault gained weight and confidence. The Confederates retreated gradually over rising ground toward a hill that took its name from the Henry farmhouse near the crest. Here the Virginians of Jackson's brigade, crouching behind their muskets just below the brow of the hill, awaited the Federal advance.

Down at the stone bridge, Tyler had stepped up his attack. Nearby, Union general William Tecumseh Sherman's brigade splashed across Bull Run and into the battle. Some of Tyler's troops followed. Under this pressure the rebel line sagged, then broke. The defenders turned and fled up the slopes of Henry House Hill to safety.

By noon the Federals seemed close to victory. The ladies and gentlemen who had driven down from Washington to watch the battle that hot, sultry Sunday expected a decisive result. Though smoke enshrouded the battlefield more than a mile away, they had heard encouraging news from Union officers who had become separated from the fighting and joined their party. The picnickers, among them more than a dozen U.S. congressmen, spread their lunches on the ground and waited for final word of the rebel defeat.

General McDowell had reason for confidence. Both his columns had crossed Bull Run and driven the rebels up Henry House Hill. Many of the 6,100 Confederates there were rattled and disorganized. They milled around dejectedly as bullets whizzed overhead. The Federal batteries were firing effectively too.

Prospects doubtless looked bleak to the Confederates. Beauregard himself rode up to the front line to steady the rebels to meet a new Union attack. A shell exploded nearby, killing his horse; uninjured, he found a new mount and moved up and down the line, shouting encouragement. General Bee also galloped about, trying to rally his men. Through the haze he caught sight of Jackson's brigade waiting calmly for the next Yankee charge. Standing in his stirrups, waving his sword in Jackson's direction, he shouted out the words that were the beginning of an American legend.

"Look! There is Jackson standing like a stone wall! Rally behind the Virginians!"

A moment later General Bee tumbled from his horse, mortally wounded. But Jackson's men had delivered a hot volley of fire into the Federal advance. Jackson's brigade held the line along Henry House Hill, and the Union attackers stumbled back down the slope in disorder.

By midafternoon McDowell had regrouped and prepared a final assault. He had 10,000 men in four brigades, plus fresh troops in reserve. Two Federal batteries had moved into the front line and were

Confederate general Thomas J. Jackson became known as "Stonewall" Jackson because of the way he held his ground "like a stone wall" against the Federal attack at the Battle of Bull Run, July 21, 1861. *(Library of Congress)*

firing furiously into the rebels. One of their shells hit Henry House, killing its mistress, 84-year-old Judith Henry, an invalid who had refused to leave her bed even as the battle swirled outside.

Avenging Mrs. Henry, J. E. B. Stuart's Virginia cavalry swept across the turnpike and charged into the Federal artillery. Then a blue-clad Virginia regiment came in close behind Stuart. Mistaking these troops for friends, the Union gunners paused. The rebels opened fire. Within seconds, battery commander Charles Griffin recounted, "Every cannoneer was cut down and a large number of horses killed, leaving the battery perfectly helpless."

The Federal attacks continued, but became increasingly ragged. Johnston's troops streamed in from the west, and they were fed immediately into the battle. At about 3:30, the Federals surged forward in a final effort to take Henry House Hill. Again they were stopped. As they fell back, Beauregard ordered a counterattack. Jackson's men and a fresh brigade rose and stood along the crest of the hill. Suddenly an eerie, high-pitched wail rolled up and down the Confederate line. Though the rebel yell would soon become all too familiar, the Federals were hearing it here for the first time.

"There is nothing like it on this side of the infernal region," a Yankee veteran remembered after the war. "The peculiar corkscrew sensation it sends down your backbone can never be told. You have to feel it."

The attackers had been marching and fighting for 14 hours. They were hot, tired, and in shock; the dead lay all around and they could hear the moans of the wounded. Now the rebels had sent up their demonic shriek and come swarming down the hill. It was too much. The Federals fell back, slowly at first, then faster and faster. Damaged vehicles blocked a main line of escape. Supply wagons, gun caissons, and the pleasure carriages of the Washington gentry were all entangled in a monumental traffic jam. Rumors spread among the troops. "Black horse cavalry!" they shouted to one another. "The cavalry is on us! Get along, get along!"

As panic spread, the retreat became a rout. Soon provisions, knapsacks, greatcoats, muskets, blankets, and canteens littered the green Virginia countryside. The soldiers called out their grim news: "Turn back, turn back! We are whipped!" Some men cut horses from their harness and rode off bareback. On horseback, in wagons, and on foot, the stricken army fled through the evening down the dusty turnpike toward Washington.

The winning Confederates were nearly as disorganized as their opponents. "Both armies were fairly defeated," the Yankee general Sherman said later. "Whichever had stood fast, the other would have run." Because the Union broke first, the spoils went to the rebels. They captured nine battle flags, 28 cannon, 500,000 rounds of small arms ammunition, and New York congressman Alfred Ely, who had tried, without success, to conceal himself behind a tree.

After nightfall a steady rain began to come down, soaking the wounded, the dying, and the dead. Seven hours of battle had left 418 Federals dead and 1,100 wounded; 1,500 were missing or captured. The Confederates lost 387 dead and 1,500 wounded. The casualties were not heavy by later standards of what would be America's bloodiest war. Still, they were heavy enough to shock the North into a recognition that a long, hard struggle lay ahead. In the South, the initial flush of victory soon faded. Bull Run had not guaranteed Southern independence, though it would be many months before the Union would again attempt to send an army into Virginia.

The beaten Federals returned overnight to Washington. Rain fell all day Monday. The fine uniforms of the Zouaves and the Highlanders were tattered now, and stained with blood and mud. They were "queer-looking objects," the poet Walt Whitman wrote, "strange eyes and faces, drench'd . . . and fearfully worn, hungry, haggard and blister'd in the feet." They had paid the toll for decades of political strife between the North and South, and especially for the irresolvable conflict over slavery. At Bull Run, as General Beauregard would write later, the political battles of a generation were at last fought with weapons instead of with words.

IRREPRESSIBLE CONFLICT

The Quakers of Christiana, Pennsylvania, had a reputation in the years before the Civil War for helping runaway slaves. A few miles south of the little town lay the border of Maryland, a slave state. The Quakers, long opposed on moral grounds to the ownership of people, would feed fugitives, allow them to rest, and give them clothes and a little money before sending them on to safety via the Underground Railroad. For two years, though, two runaways had been living and working in Christiana itself just beyond the reach of their Maryland owner, Edward Gorsuch. In September 1851, Gorsuch resolved to use the new federal Fugitive Slave Law to recover his property. On the morning of September 11, Gorsuch, his son and other relations, and three U.S. deputy marshals arrived in Christiana to capture the runaways and return them to Maryland.

The slave catchers found the fugitives at the farm of William Parker, a free black, protected by a party of more than 20 African-American supporters armed with clubs and guns. A deputy marshal read out warrants for the runaways' arrest. They refused to surrender. Two of Parker's Quaker neighbors appeared, studied the warrants, and noted that they were bureaucratically correct and properly sealed. Then, rejecting the federal authority, the Quakers advised Gorsuch and company to go home.

"I will have my property," Gorsuch replied furiously, "or go to hell!" From within the crowd a shot rang out, then another. Both sides began firing wildly. Gorsuch fell dead, and his son was seriously wounded. The slave catchers retreated in confusion. The runaways and their supporters disappeared into the countryside.

A Lancaster, Pennsylvania, newspaper likened this brief flaring of violence to civil war, and the encounter at Christiana did seem to foretell a decade of escalating conflict that would end with the nation divided and at war with itself. Attitudes toward slavery were hardening in the North and the South during the 1850s. No further spread of slavery could be permitted, many Northerners came to believe. Southerners were increasingly convinced there could be no safety for their "peculiar institution" within the Union.

Slavery was nearly as old as European settlement of North America. A Dutch trader brought the first slaves to America in 1619, and the institution spread throughout the colonies during the 17th and 18th centuries. Slavery gradually died out in the North, inefficient in an economy based on small farming, trading, and manufacturing. In the South, however, where the plantation system required a large unskilled labor force, slavery flourished. At the start of the American Revolution in 1776, three-quarters of the slaves were in the South. One by one, Northern legislatures outlawed slavery. By 1846 it had been abolished in every Northern state.

The U.S. Constitution protected slavery, and it did not become a political issue until 1818, when Missouri settlers applied for statehood. A New York senator proposed banning the import of slaves into Missouri, and the freeing of those already there. The proposal divided Congress along North-South lines, and the dispute delayed Missouri's application for nearly two years. Then, when Maine applied for admission to the Union in 1820, the Speaker of the U.S. House of Representatives, Henry Clay of Kentucky, arranged a compromise. Maine came in as the 12th free state, Missouri as the 12th slave state, preserving the sectional political balance. Additionally, the Missouri Compromise, as Clay's measure became known, prohibited slavery in territories north of an imaginary line extended west from Missouri's southern border.

The Missouri Compromise muted the slavery conflict for a quarter-century. Other issues remained, however, to divide the sections. Northerners sought high tariffs on imported manufactured goods to protect their fragile industries. Representatives of the new states west of the Appalachians pressed for federal spending on internal improvements, especially canal and road construction. Southerners traded tobacco and cotton for English goods, and so opposed tariffs. They objected, too, to paying taxes to support federal projects that would benefit the other sections.

These issues were debated endlessly through the 1830s and 1840s, but compromise solutions were generally found. Then, in 1846, the

Slaves were sold in the South on the auction block. *(Library of Congress)*

Mexican War reintroduced the slavery question. In a 16-month campaign, the United States won 10 major battles, and on September 14,
1847, American troops raised the Stars and Stripes over Mexico City.
In the settlement, Mexico ceded to the United States hundreds of thousands of square miles of virgin land in Texas, the desert Southwest, and
California.

The acquisition of this enormous territory threatened to upset the
balance between free and slave states. Already the North was growing
faster in wealth, population, and political weight. New free states would
further increase Northern power in Congress. Southerners could keep
up only by carrying slavery west into Texas and beyond. When Northerners rallied around Pennsylvania congressman David Wilmot's
proposal to ban slavery in the territories taken from Mexico, Southern
radicals countered with threats to pull their states out of the Union.

As he had done 30 years before on the Missouri question, Henry
Clay put together a compromise. After a summer of fierce debate, Congress approved its separate elements. The Compromise of 1850 brought

California into the Union as a free state. Settlers in New Mexico and Utah were themselves to decide for or against slavery when these territories were ready for statehood. To appease the South, a fugitive slave law would require federal magistrates and policemen to capture runaway slaves and return them to their owners.

The compromise achieved a temporary peace, but the sectional divisions continued to deepen. Two distinct cultures were emerging. By the 1850s, a dynamic new industrial system had begun to reshape the North and West. The South, with its plantations, small farms, and backwoods settlements, remained dependent on a few cash crops, especially cotton. Northern factories and farms were now producing goods for mass consumption. A farmer sold his crop for cash, and bought his harness, his farm tools, and the lamps, tables, chairs, and crockery that furnished his house, with the proceeds. The era of the small, self-sufficient farmer was ending.

Northern farmers invested in such products of Yankee invention as John Deere plows and McCormick reapers. Southerners, when they could afford them, invested in slaves. A Yankee farmer, taking a living from the stony Connecticut soil, might argue that careful management could make his 50 acres as productive as two or three times the acreage worked indifferently by slaves and exhausted by cotton. After all, that farmer might say, he toiled for his family and the future. A slave had little incentive except fear of the lash.

Southern cotton, it was true, dominated the world market. Annual cotton production nearly tripled between 1849 and 1859, and the United States produced more than three-quarters of the world's supply. "King Cotton" kept a few planters wealthy. These were the familiar figures of Southern legend: wealthy, fox-hunting landowners who lived like lords off the labor of their slaves. More thoughtful Southerners worried, though, that a one-crop economy was turning their region into an economic dependency of the North.

"We purchase all our necessities from the North," an Alabama newspaper noted glumly in 1851. "Our slaves are clothed with Northern manufactured goods, have Northern hats and shoes, work with Northern hoes, plows and other implements. The slaveholder dresses in Northern goods, rides in a Northern saddle, sports his Northern carriage, reads Northern books."

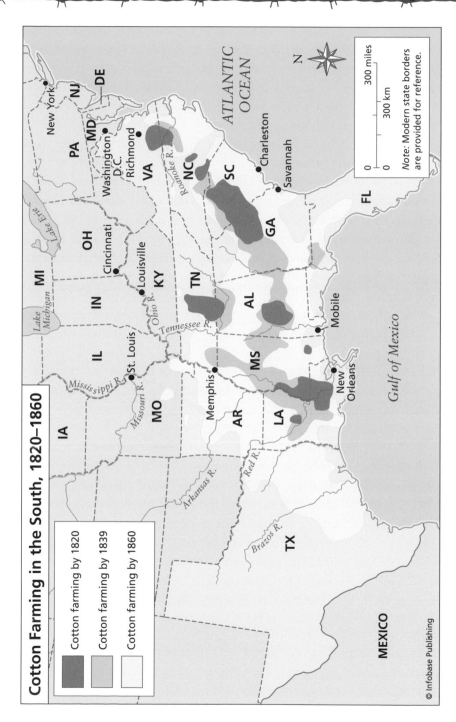

Cotton Farming in the South, 1820–1860

Cotton farming by 1820
Cotton farming by 1839
Cotton farming by 1860

300 miles
300 km
Note: Modern state borders are provided for reference.

ATLANTIC OCEAN

Gulf of Mexico

MEXICO

© Infobase Publishing

For the United States as a whole, the 1850s were years of tremendous growth and prosperity. By the end of the decade, its population had passed 30 million. Northern cities grew boundlessly. Four great railroad lines were completed across the Appalachians, linking the East and the Midwest, and by 1860 more than 30,000 miles of track had been laid. Fifteen lines led into booming Chicago alone; at an average speed of 30 miles per hour, the railroad train had cut the travel time from New York to Chicago from three weeks to two days. By the end of the decade, the telegraph connected even the smallest towns to the outside world. News of a great debate in Congress could be transmitted hundreds of miles in seconds, and published in newspapers the next day.

All this furious activity widened the gap between rich and poor. To some observers, crowded, disease-ridden slums in Northern cities seemed as inhuman as any filthy slave quarters on a Georgia plantation. But the Northern system produced far more wealth than the Southern, however unevenly it was shared. By 1860, there were 110,000 factories in the North and only 18,000 in the South. New York State alone produced twice as many manufactured goods as the entire South. Of those 30,000 miles of railway, 22,000 were in the North. The North had six times as many engineers as the South, and three times as many merchants. Southerners dominated the military, but Northerners were the leaders in literature, medicine, and education.

Still, much remained to bind North and South, even as political and economic forces combined to pull them apart. White male Americans shared a broad democratic political heritage. Northerners and Southerners spoke the same language and most held some variant of Protestant Christian belief. They were overwhelmingly of British ethnic origin, though Irish and German immigrants had been streaming into the eastern cities since the 1840s. And sometimes sectional differences could work to the nation's advantage. The South's export cotton crop brought cash that paid for U.S. imports. The Midwest fed the South; the East provided manufactured goods and commercial expertise to the other sections.

Over it all, though, loomed the conflict over slavery. "On the subject of slavery," the Charleston, South Carolina, *Mercury* declared, "the North and the South are not only two peoples, but they are rival, hostile peoples." Small but influential numbers of Northerners increasingly viewed slavery as an absolute moral evil, one that must not only be checked but also destroyed. "Instead of an evil," South Carolina senator John C. Calhoun countered, slavery was "a positive good . . . the most safe and stable basis for free institutions in the world." As the debate intensified, the ground for compromise narrowed. "If this union, with all its advantages, has no other cement than the blood of human slavery, let it perish," said New Hampshire senator John P. Hale.

Hale spoke for a minority in the 1850s, but two decades of agitation for the abolition of slavery had inflamed Northern opinion. The abolition cause had no more fierce and uncompromising leader than William Lloyd Garrison, who used his newspaper *The Liberator* to campaign for the immediate freeing of the slaves. "I am in earnest," wrote Garrison in the first issue of *The Liberator* on January 1, 1831. "I will not equivocate—I will not excuse—I will not retreat a single inch—and I will be heard."

Born in Newburyport, Massachusetts, in December 1805, Garrison was the son of a drunken immigrant sailor who soon deserted the family. Raised by his mother, he trained first as a shoemaker, then as a cabinetmaker. He disliked both trades, and in 1818, he became an apprentice printer. He began writing political articles almost at once. By 1829, he had become a convert to the antislavery cause. Two years later, he founded *The Liberator* in Boston, and in 1833, he established the American Anti-Slavery Society.

A pacifist, Garrison believed that agitation, political action, and civil disobedience would sooner or later force slavery to collapse. Although he opposed violence, he fought furiously with the weapons available to him. "I do not wish to think or speak or write with moderation," he said. "I will be as harsh as truth and as uncompromising as justice." Garrison judged abolition more important than preservation of the Union. In March 1854, in protest against the authorities' capture of a fugitive slave in Boston, he publicly burned a copy of the U.S. Constitution. Because it protected slavery, he told his rapt audience, it was "a covenant with death and an agreement with hell."

The Fugitive Slave Law, by provoking such confrontations as the Christiana shootout of September 1851, actually seemed to work in the abolitionists' favor. Although only some 330 slaves were returned to their masters under the law, each individual instance seemed to many Northerners an insult to the nation's founding principles and an affront to moral law. In February 1851, federal agents arrested an African American in southern Indiana and returned him to an owner who claimed he had fled as a slave 19 years before. They led him away as his wife and children watched helplessly. In January 1856, when federal agents closed in on a fugitive named Margaret Garner, she killed one of her children and tried to kill another rather than allow them to be returned to slavery. Such stories were widely reported, and they began to work a revolution in Northern attitudes. Wrote one Yankee: "We went to bed one night old-fashioned, conservative, Compromise Union Whigs, and waked up stark mad abolitionists."

Beyond creating such tragedies as Garner's, the Fugitive Slave Law had this unforeseen effect: It apparently moved a 40-year-old Cincinnati matron named Harriet Beecher Stowe to write *Uncle Tom's Cabin.* Cincinnati lay across the Ohio River from Kentucky, a slave state, and Stowe, the daughter and wife of Presbyterian ministers with abolitionist sympathies, had a direct exposure to the trials of the escapees and the lengths to which their masters would go to reclaim them.

"Hattie," a sister-in-law wrote Stowe, "if I could use a pen as you can, I would write something that will make this whole nation feel what an accursed thing slavery is." Stowe read the letter to her children, then stood up and pledged: "I will if I live."

Uncle Tom's Cabin dramatized the evils of slavery in three major characters: Tom, taken from his family in Kentucky and sold into the Deep South; Eliza Harris, who fled, her son in her arms, across the Ohio River ice floes; and the sadistic slave owner Simon Legree. The novel undermined Southern justifications for slavery by presenting its black characters as fully human, with feelings and ambitions that were savagely repressed by the slave system. Published on March 20, 1852, it sold 305,000 copies in the first year alone and made countless converts to the antislavery cause. By the outbreak of war, more than 1 million copies had been sold. (When Stowe called on President Lincoln at the White House in 1862, the president reportedly remarked, "So this is the little lady who made this big war.") For millions of Northerners, the novel and its many dramatizations for the stage exposed slavery in all its ugliness and brutality.

Even though *Uncle Tom's Cabin* exaggerated and sentimentalized some slave conditions for propaganda effect, much in the novel was true. Slaves were frequently sold away from their families. Some studies have shown that as many as one in every four slave marriages was broken by the sale of husband or wife. The sale of young children was also common. Usually slaves would change hands at auctions, where they would be put on display for potential buyers. "The customers would

This illustration depicts Uncle Tom and Eva, two characters in *Uncle Tom's Cabin,* the 1852 novel by Harriet Beecher Stowe that greatly influenced many Americans' views about slavery. *(Library of Congress)*

feel our bodies," one slave remembered, "and make us show our teeth, precisely as a jockey examines a horse."

The 1860 census counted nearly 4 million slaves. One-quarter of white Southern families owned slaves—about 385,000 households in all. In South Carolina and Mississippi, half the families owned slaves;

in Virginia, one-third; in Maryland and Missouri, only one-eighth. Nearly 90 percent of slave owners had fewer than 20 slaves. The planter aristocracy so closely associated with popular notions about the old South consisted of about 10,000 families, only one-third of which owned more than 100 slaves.

Slaves worked year-round, six days a week, usually with Sundays free. Their routines followed the rhythms of the planting year. In January and February they finished processing and shipping the cotton; they cut wood and repaired fences; they cleared new fields and plowed. March and April were planting months, when slaves sowed cotton or corn and started vegetable gardens. From May through August, they worked daily in the fields, weeding, shaping, and hand-tending the cotton crop. The harvest ran from September through the end of the year. Slaves picked the cotton, separated the tough seeds from the white fiber, and baled the crop for shipping. All through the year, year after year, the basic tools available to the slaves were the hand, the hoe, and the plow.

"We get up before day every morning and eat breakfast before day and have everybody at work before day dawns," Arkansas slave owner

Cotton plantations such as this one in Mississippi required large numbers of laborers, and this need was met by enslaved African Americans. *(Library of Congress)*

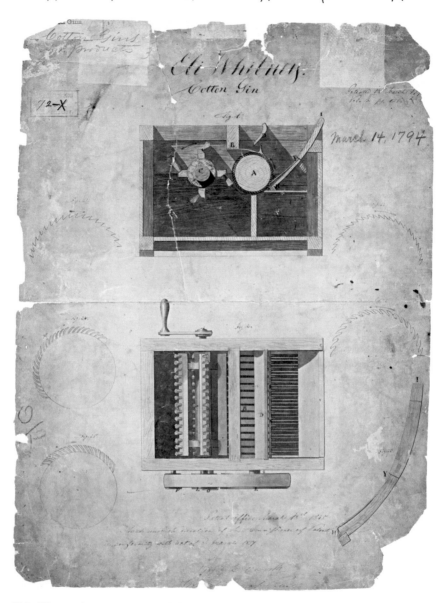

This illustration accompanied the application for a patent for the cotton gin, filed by its inventor, Eli Whitney, on March 14, 1794. By allowing for a faster and easier processing of cotton, the device actually increased the need for more slaves to work in the fields. *(Library of Congress)*

Gustavus A. Henry wrote in 1860. "I am never caught in bed after daylight nor is anybody else on the place, and we continue in the cotton fields when we can have fair weather till it is so dark we can't see to work, and this history of one day is the history of every day."

Black slaves such as Solomon Northrup had their own views of all this. Northrup had lived many years as a freedman before he was kidnapped and sold into slavery on a Red River plantation in northern Louisiana. The demand for cotton had drawn planters to this hot, dank, swampy, malarial country. Their slaves, Northrup among them, cleared thousands of acres of scrub and pine forest for planting. The rich soil yielded fabulous profits—planters there were "making oceans of money," as one Louisianan noted. By one estimate, a successful planter would take profits of $250 a year and more on each prime field hand.

"The slaves are required to be in the cotton field as soon as it is light in the morning," Northrup recalled, "and with the exception of ten or fifteen minutes which is given them at noon to swallow their allowance of cold bacon, they are not permitted to be a moment idle until it is too dark to see, and when the moon is full, they often times labor until the middle of the night."

Some masters permitted slaves to sing or whistle as an accompaniment to work. Others enforced silence and discipline with prods and whips of chain and leather. Thirty lashes could make a bloody jelly of a person's back. To prevent infection, a slave driver might drench the wounds with buckets of seawater. Victims of this treatment found the pain all but impossible to describe. At the mere memory of it, one slave wrote, "The flesh crawls upon my bones."

Many slave owners were careful of their slaves' welfare, just as many Northerners were careful of their livestock and farm machinery. After all, a field hand cost a thousand dollars or more to replace. But slaves were too often overworked and underfed, and they were at great risk of disease. Malaria, yellow fever, typhus, and tuberculosis were endemic in some parts of the South. Though they occasionally were permitted to cultivate their own garden plots, the slaves' diet more often consisted almost entirely of corn and fatty pork. They dressed in cheap, flimsy clothes, and children went barefoot even in the winter. Fewer than five of every hundred slaves lived beyond the age of 60.

This was the institution Southerners wanted to carry into the new states of the western prairie. Their effort to extend slavery into the Nebraska Territory touched off an explosion that ended the uneasy truce following the Compromise of 1850, wrecked the old political party system, and led to anarchy and violence in Kansas.

It started innocently enough. In January 1854, Illinois senator Stephen A. Douglas, chairman of the Committee on Territories, reported

FANNY KEMBLE AND SLAVERY

Seeking an escape from the stage, the English actress Fanny Kemble married Charles Butler, a Philadelphia grandee with extensive plantation holdings in the Sea Islands of Georgia. Kemble's choice proved disastrous. A first-hand view of the "peculiar institution" from which her husband's fortune derived fired her latent abolitionism and ultimately destroyed her marriage.

The notion that she lived in idleness and luxury off the sweat of African-American slaves repelled and fascinated Fanny Kemble, and she finally persuaded her husband to allow her to spend the winter of 1838–39 on his Butler Island estates. She returned to the great house after her first visits to the slave settlements to confront her husband, who saw no reason to apologize for his ownership and exploitation of human beings. But she found she could do nothing to lighten the physical burdens of the slaves or the moral burdens of the masters.

"These discussions are terrible," she wrote of her efforts to force the issue with Charles Butler; "they throw me in perfect agonies of distress for the slaves, whose position is utterly hopeless; for myself, whose interventions in their behalf sometimes seem to me worse than useless; for Mr. Butler, whose share in this horrible system fills me by turns with indignation and pity."

Kemble returned to Philadelphia to write a passionate account of her experience with slavery in the Georgia rice country. She and Butler were divorced in 1849. Because her husband had custody of their two daughters, she withheld publication until the girls were grown. Hoping to influence British public opinion against slavery, she saw her *Journal of a Residence on a Georgia Plantation* into print in England in 1863.

on a bill to organize the Nebraska Territory, which included what is now Kansas, for statehood. The bill stalled because of the old slavery dispute. Douglas, a 41-year-old Democrat, decided to try to break the deadlock. The Little Giant, as admirers called the five-foot-four-inch Douglas, gained Southern support for a Northern transcontinental railroad route by offering an amendment to the Kansas-Nebraska Bill that would let the settlers themselves decide the slavery question. This "popular sovereignty" clause infuriated many Northerners, who demanded an outright ban on slavery. Then Douglas went a step further. Boldly, even recklessly, he agreed to an amendment repealing the Missouri Compromise, which had established slavery's northern boundary.

Douglas, who had presidential aspirations, genuinely hoped he could work a deal that would settle the slavery question peaceably. Even so, he must have been aware of the tremendous risk he ran. "I will incorporate it in my bill," he said of the Missouri Compromise amendment, "though I know it will raise a hell of a storm."

The Kansas-Nebraska Act passed the Senate in March and the House in June. Although Douglas himself had predicted it, he seemed baffled by the fury with which Northerners reacted to the new law. In direct response to Kansas-Nebraska, antislavery Democrats, Whigs, Free-Soilers, and others opposed to slavery expansion came together over spring and summer 1854 to form the Republican Party. And the Kansas-Nebraska Act drew Abraham Lincoln of Springfield, Illinois, a lawyer and former state legislator and U.S. representative, out of five years of political retirement.

Lincoln, 45 years old in 1854, reentered public life to campaign for Illinois congressman Richard Yates, an opponent of the Kansas-Nebraska legislation. Douglas himself returned to Illinois for the congressional recess to defend his record. He argued that the measure would appease Southerners but would have no practical effect. Popular sovereignty actually would work against slavery expansion, he said, because soil and climate conditions on the prairie made slavery unprofitable. "You come right back to the principle of dollars and cents," Douglas said.

On October 3 the Little Giant presented his case to a large crowd at the Illinois State Fair in Springfield. The next day Lincoln rose to challenge him. The Kentucky-born Lincoln had seen slavery up close, and it repelled him. Nevertheless, he opposed the abolitionist call for emancipation, and favored leaving slavery alone in the states where it existed. But he argued brilliantly against permitting it to expand.

"Slavery is founded in the selfishness of man's nature, opposition to it in his love of justice," Lincoln told his state fair audience. "These principles are in eternal antagonism, and when brought into collision so fiercely as slavery extension brings them, shocks and throes and convulsions must ceaselessly follow. Repeal the Missouri Compromise; repeal all compromises; repeal the Declaration of Independence; repeal all past history—you still cannot repeal human nature. It will still be

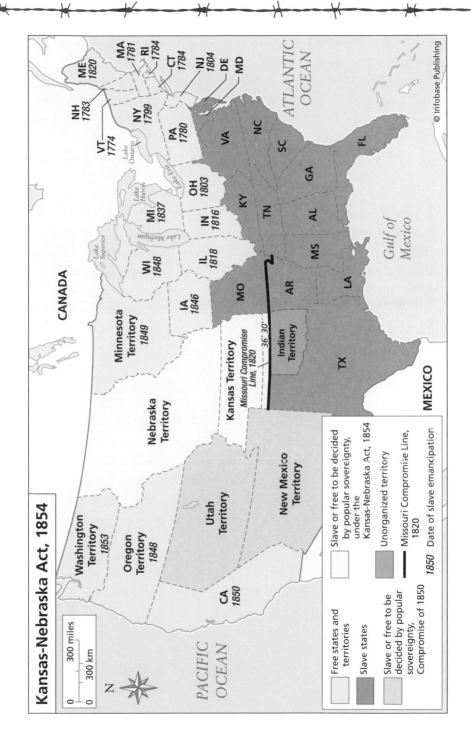

Kansas-Nebraska Act, 1854

© Infobase Publishing

CANADA

ATLANTIC OCEAN

Gulf of Mexico

MEXICO

PACIFIC OCEAN

MA *1781*
RI *1784*
CT *1784*
ME *1820*
NJ *1804*
DE
MD
NH *1783*
NY *1799*
PA *1780*
VA
NC
SC
GA
FL
VT *1774*
OH *1803*
KY
TN
AL
MI *1837*
IN *1816*
MS
WI *1848*
IL *1818*
MO
AR
LA
IA *1846*
Indian Territory
TX

Lake Ontario
Lake Erie
Lake Huron
Lake Michigan
Lake Superior

Minnesota Territory *1849*

Nebraska Territory

Kansas Territory

Missouri Compromise Line, 1820
36°30'

Washington Territory *1853*

Oregon Territory *1848*

Utah Territory

New Mexico Territory

CA *1850*

N

0 ——— 300 miles
0 ——— 300 km

Legend	
Free states and territories	Slave or free to be decided by popular sovereignty, under the Kansas-Nebraska Act, 1854
Slave states	Unorganized territory
Slave or free to be decided by popular sovereignty, Compromise of 1850	Missouri Compromise Line, 1820
	1850 Date of slave emancipation

the abundance of man's heart that slavery extension is wrong, and out of the abundance of his heart his mouth will continue to speak."

Douglas had been right. He had raised a storm. Soon the Massachusetts Emigrant Aid Society, an abolitionist group, began sending settlers into Kansas. In response, proslavery settlers, many of them from just across the border in Missouri, poured into the territory. These Border Ruffians, as they called themselves, helped the proslavery faction win a rigged election in March 1855.

An investigation showed that nearly 5,000 of the 6,300 votes cast had been fraudulent, and Free Staters—antislavery settlers, some of whom were emigrants sponsored by abolition organizations—refused to recognize the result. They elected their own governor, voted to outlaw slavery, and applied to Congress for admission as a free state. Small-scale civil war broke out. Both sides carried on intermittent warfare, with ambushing, stealing of horses, and burning of crops. In May 1856, a Border Ruffian detachment rode into Lawrence, Kansas, a Free State town, and burned the hotel, ransacked a newspaper office, and plundered stores. In retaliation, a few days later, Massachusetts-born John Brown led a midnight raid in which five proslavery Kansans were murdered in cold blood.

All across the North newspapers played up the tragedy of Bleeding Kansas. Then, in the autumn of 1856, an energetic new governor came out from Washington. Backed by a force of U.S. Army regulars, John Geary brought order to the prairie. As after the Compromise of 1850, an eerie quiet settled upon the land. The truce lasted for less than a year, broken this time by the U.S. Supreme Court.

Dred Scott, a Missouri slave, had sued for his freedom on the grounds that his master had taken him into the free territories of Illinois and Wisconsin. The law explicitly prohibited slavery in both places, so Scott argued he should be free. The Supreme Court rejected Scott's claim in early 1857. Chief Justice Roger Taney wrote that slaves were not citizens of the United States, and so had no right to sue in U.S. courts. Taney went on to declare the Missouri Compromise void, because Congress had no right to interfere with private property—in this case, with slavery.

The decision outraged abolitionists and moderates alike. "A judicial lie," one Republican newspaper editor called the decision. Lincoln disputed the ruling, but believed it wrong to resist the Court. Douglas, however, tried to turn the Scott ruling to his advantage. The Court had vindicated Kansas-Nebraska's repeal of the Missouri Compromise, he said. Besides, Douglas went on, the decision did not prohibit the settlers from barring slavery, only Congress. So popular sovereignty would still apply.

By 1858, Lincoln and Douglas had been arguing the slavery issue for four years. Now the voters would judge them, for the new Republican Party chose Lincoln to challenge the Little Giant in the Senate election of 1858. Both men agreed that slavery remained the central issue. Douglas still believed that some sort of legislative compromise could be found. But Lincoln knew the slavery issue would continue to build to a final crisis.

The two men spoke night after night for four months, across Illinois, in the big Chicago halls, in dusty squares in the prairie towns, in hot, airless tents at county fairs. Douglas traveled around the state in a private railcar decorated with banners and bunting. Lincoln rode with the plain people in the same train. It was no accident that Lincoln, taking advantage of his better-known opponent's ability to attract a crowd, always seemed to be rising to speak just as Douglas had finished. So Douglas agreed reluctantly to a series of debates.

Stephen A. Douglas narrowly defeated future president Abraham Lincoln in the 1858 Illinois senate elections. During the campaign, they participated in seven high-profile debates over the question of whether or not the institution of slavery should be allowed to expand in new U.S. territories. *(National Archives)*

The two argued themselves hoarse in seven Illinois towns. The speeches varied little from place to place. Douglas accused Lincoln and the Republicans of abolitionism. Lincoln repeated that the Republicans would leave slavery alone where it existed, but oppose any expansion. The debates attracted huge crowds: 10,000 for the first debate in Ottawa, 15,000 at Freeport, 12,000 at Charleston. Douglas accused Lincoln of favoring racial equality, a potent charge in the Illinois of 1858. Lincoln urged his hearers to "discard all this quibbling about . . . this race and the other race being inferior . . . and unite as one people throughout this land, until we shall once more stand up declaring that all men are created equal."

Senatorial elections were then decided in the state legislatures. Lincoln actually won the popular vote, but lost narrowly in the legislature. Still, the campaign against Douglas had made him a national figure among the newly organized Republicans, already in search of a presidential candidate for 1860. The campaign gave Lincoln a platform, too, for a solemn prophecy that would echo down the years:

"'A House divided against itself cannot stand,'" Lincoln told a Republican convention in Springfield in June 1858. "I believe this government cannot endure permanently half slave and half free. . . . It will become all one thing or all the other. Either the opponents of slavery will arrest the further spread of it, and place it where the public mind shall rest in the belief that it is in the course of ultimate extinction, or its advocates will push it forward till it shall have become alike lawful in all the states, old as well as new, North as well as South."

As Lincoln spoke, another sort of prophet had begun to plot a blow against slavery. Some said old John Brown was insane. Sane or not, his moment had come.

PURGED WITH BLOOD

John Brown moved into a farmhouse across the Potomac River from Harpers Ferry, Virginia, on July 3, 1859. He had rented the place under an assumed name, Smith, for here he intended to touch off a great slave revolt and he needed time to plan, unrecognized and undisturbed. Over the next few weeks, Brown's little army gathered—five whites, including two of his sons, and 17 blacks. As summer advanced, the recruits drilled while John Brown studied accounts of irregular warfare and of slave uprisings. In late September, the weapons arrived in boxes labeled "farm equipment": 198 Sharps rifles and 950 pikes (wooden shafts with metal points). With these Brown would seize the U.S. Arsenal at Harpers Ferry, collect the guns and ammunition stored there, and sweep south along the Appalachian ridge, inciting rebellion among Virginia's slaves. "I expect to effect a mighty conquest," he had written, "even though it be like the last victory of Samson."

Fifty-nine years old in 1859, Connecticut-born John Brown was an unsuccessful farmer, wool trader, and livestock dealer. He had managed a tannery and speculated in land. None of these ventures had turned out well; the records show Brown failed in at least 15 businesses in four states. Over the years, he drifted with his enormous family (Brown had 20 children by two wives) from small town to small town in Ohio, Pennsylvania, Virginia, New York, and Massachusetts.

Brown had little schooling, but he knew his Bible. Deeply religious, he believed that God intervened directly in human affairs. He had a boundless devotion to the antislavery cause. Like Samson pulling the temple down on his enemies, he would destroy slavery. "Without the shedding of blood there is no remission of sin," Brown said, quoting the Old Testament Book of Hebrews, and he meant it literally. By the early 1850s he was calling for armed resistance to the federal enforcers

In 1859, John Brown instigated and led a short-lived and small-scale uprising of slaves at Harpers Ferry, in what became West Virginia. *(National Archives)*

of the Fugitive Slave Law. "Whenever he spoke, his words commanded earnest attention," the escaped slave, abolitionist, and author Frederick Douglass wrote. "His arguments seemed to convince all; his appeals touched all; and his will impressed all."

As he grew older and more obsessed, Brown seemed to take on the fierce, fanatic appearance of the biblical warriors he so admired. One of his sons said he looked like an ax. Some likened him to an eagle—"or another carnivorous bird," as another son noted. "With an eye like a snake, he looks like a demon," wrote Mahala Doyle. But Mrs. Doyle had a grievance against Brown. He and his guerrilla band had murdered her proslavery husband and sons along Pottawatomie Creek in Kansas in May 1856.

Now, in the late summer of 1859, Brown and his followers were preparing to strike at Harpers Ferry. The "Secret Six," a group of New England abolitionists, supplied money for arms and helped him plan the attack. The Shenandoah River joined the Potomac at Harpers Ferry, and hills surrounded the drab little town on all sides. Though he had spent the summer among his books on warfare, Brown had overlooked many details, neglecting even to scout escape routes out of Harpers

Ferry. The town was a strategic trap, according to Frederick Douglass—who refused to join the conspiracy. He wrote Brown: "You'll never get out alive."

Dozens of promised recruits failed to show up. However, Brown was inspired by his avenging mission and decided to act anyway. "One man and God can overturn the universe," he said. So, leading 16 men, he set out from the farmhouse at dusk on the damp, moonless evening of October 16. Two men cut the telegraph wires into the town. Others guarded the railroad bridge over the Potomac. Brown himself led the main party up to the arsenal's main gate. Brown said to the lone watchman there: "I came here from Kansas, and this is a slave State; I want to free all the Negroes in this State; I have possession now of the United States armory, and if the citizens interfere with me I must only burn the town and have blood."

Brown sent out a patrol, which soon returned with a few hostages. The express train for Baltimore rumbled over the bridge shortly after midnight; Brown detained it for a few hours, then let it go. The train crew soon spread the alarm of a slave uprising in Harpers Ferry, and by dawn, militia forces were mustering. Already Brown's force and the townspeople were exchanging fire, and Brown soon had his wish: Blood was being spilled. One of the first raiders to die was Dangerfield Newby, a free black whose wife remained in slavery in Virginia. "Dear Dangerfield," she had written not long before, "come this fall without fail, money or no money I want to see you so much: that is one bright hope I have before me."

Excited by the conflict, the townspeople started drinking early and continued throughout the day. The harder they drank, the more viciously they fought. They shot down one of Brown's sons as he walked out of the armory waving a flag of truce. Later, they dragged a captured raider from the jail and lynched him. As the firing increased, Brown's force retreated into the armory firehouse for a last stand. That night a force of U.S. Marines, commanded by Lt. Col. Robert E. Lee of the army, arrived in Harpers Ferry. The marines stormed the firehouse the next morning, capturing Brown and eight other survivors. Eight of the raiders, including Brown's two sons, had been killed.

News of Brown's raid outraged many Southerners. In Virginia, mobs poured into the streets calling for Brown's death. In the North, the reaction was mixed at first. Many approved of Brown's aims, but opposed his means. Abolitionist leader William Lloyd Garrison called

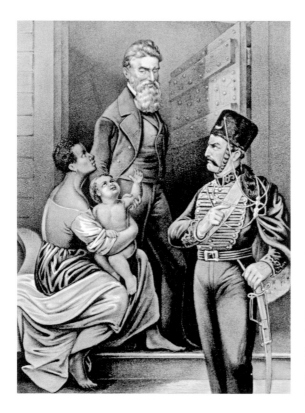

In this idealized illustration, John Brown is shown being led to his execution by a U.S. Army officer while an African-American mother with her infant look on admiringly. *(Library of Congress)*

the attack "misguided, wild and apparently insane." Virginia moved quickly to try Brown on charges of treason, murder, and fomenting insurrection. The trial opened in Charles Town on October 25. Brown, wounded during the final assault on the arsenal, had to be carried into the courtroom on a stretcher.

"I believe that to have interfered as I have done, in behalf of His despised poor, is no wrong, but right," Brown told the court. "Now, if it is deemed necessary that I should forfeit my life for the furtherance of the ends of justice, and mingle my blood further with the blood of my children and with the blood of millions in this slave country whose rights are disregarded by wicked, cruel and injust enactments, I say, let it be done."

Brown's calm eloquence at his trial won over many Northerners, but the court's verdict was guilty. The sentence, death by hanging, was to be carried out on December 2, 1859. Suddenly Brown was elevated from murderer and renegade to martyr. Ralph Waldo Emerson, the New England philosopher and essayist, predicted that Brown would "make the gallows as glorious as the cross." The abolitionist minister

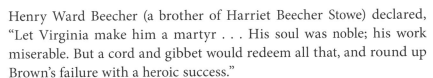

Henry Ward Beecher (a brother of Harriet Beecher Stowe) declared, "Let Virginia make him a martyr . . . His soul was noble; his work miserable. But a cord and gibbet would redeem all that, and round up Brown's failure with a heroic success."

Awaiting his end, Brown understood this perfectly. "I have been whipped," he wrote his wife from the Charles Town jail, "but am sure I can recover all the lost capital occasioned by this disaster; by only hanging a few moments by the neck; and I feel quite determined to make the utmost possible out of a defeat."

The sun shone on the morning of December 2. Troops lined the street leading from the jail to the hanging ground. Brown sat atop his own oak coffin in the wagon that carried him slowly to the field where the scaffold had been set up. Looking all around, he seemed to see certain things for the first time. "This *is* a beautiful country," he marveled, staring at the far-off Blue Ridge, hazy in the mild sunlight. Then he handed his jailer a note. "I John Brown am now quite certain that the crimes of this guilty land will never be purged away but with blood."

Brown went to the scaffold alone. There was a delay while the troops marched ceremonially back and forth. He waited in silence, white linen hood over his head, rope knotted around his neck, for eight terrible minutes. Finally the hangman sprang the trap and the floor fell away beneath Brown's feet.

Although it hardly seemed possible at this point, the Harpers Ferry raid and its aftermath pulled North and South even further apart. In the North on the day of the hanging, church bells tolled, salutes were fired and memorial sermons were preached. Meanwhile, Southerners charged that the North had sanctified a thief, a killer, and a traitor. "The Harpers Ferry invasion has advanced the cause of disunion more than any [other] event," a Richmond newspaper claimed. "Thousands of men . . . who a month ago scoffed at the idea of a dissolution of the Union . . . now hold the opinion that its days are numbered."

Hysteria spread through the South as many Southerners believed a slave rebellion had been narrowly averted. Southerners associated such violence with the new Republican Party, calling its adherents Black Republicans with a mixture of fear, hatred, and contempt. As 1860 began, the political parties began preparing for the presidential campaign later in the year. Republicans hastened to distance themselves from the Harpers Ferry episode. William H. Seward of New York, a Republican presidential candidate, called Brown's execution necessary and right. Likewise, Abraham Lincoln could not find any justification for lawlessness and murder. But he had a stern reply to Southern cries for secession. "It will be our turn to deal with you," he told the secessionists, "as old John Brown has been dealt with."

By spring 1860, however, the Southern radicals—or fire-eaters, as they were called—had stopped listening. They heard neither threats nor offers of compromise. Many fire-eaters, including the leaders, Robert Barnwell Rhett of South Carolina and William Lowndes Yancey of Alabama, were influential in the Democratic Party. They planned a coup attempt for the Democrats' presidential nominating convention, which opened in Charleston, South Carolina, on April 23.

Rhett and Yancey convinced several Southern delegations to bolt if the convention refused to endorse a series of proslavery platform proposals. When Northern delegates rejected the proposals overwhelmingly, Yancey led 50 Southerners in a walkout that left the convention with too few delegates to choose a nominee. Those remaining voted to reassemble in Baltimore in June. There the same issues were raised. Again the Southerners walked out, this time to set up a rival convention. Northern Democrats went on to nominate Stephen A. Douglas.

William Lowndes Yancey of Alabama led 50 Southern delegates in a walkout of the Democrats' 1860 presidential nominating convention after Northern delegates refused to endorse a series of proslavery platform proposals. *(Library of Congress)*

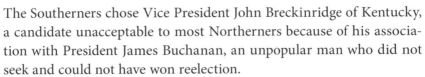

The Southerners chose Vice President John Breckinridge of Kentucky, a candidate unacceptable to most Northerners because of his association with President James Buchanan, an unpopular man who did not seek and could not have won reelection.

With the Democrats broken into warring Northern and Southern halves, the Republicans sensed their opportunity. In May 1860, their convention opened in Chicago in a vast wooden hall called the Wigwam. Senator Seward was the clear favorite. But Seward had been the first to speak of an "irrepressible conflict" between North and South, and that made him sound radical on the slavery issue. Lincoln, whose Illinois associates had been quietly promoting him for several months, hoped he might be a compromise choice. "My name is new in the field," Lincoln said, "and I suppose I am not the first choice of a very great many. Our policy, then, is to give no offense to others—leave them in the mood to come to us, if they shall be impelled to give up their first love."

Seward led by a wide margin after the first ballot. But Lincoln's floor managers worked aggressively on his behalf, offering cabinet posts, judgeships, and other patronage in return for delegate pledges. After the second ballot, Seward's advantage had been cut to only a few votes. On the third ballot, with the shift of four Ohio votes, Lincoln became the Republican nominee.

The 10,000 delegates in the Wigwam celebrated madly, while another 20,000 frenzied Republicans swarmed in the streets outside. "Imagine all the hogs ever slaughtered in Cincinnati giving their death squeals together, [and] a score of big steam whistles going," wrote one reporter, straining to describe the scene. Lincoln's operatives telegraphed the news to him at home in Springfield. "Just think of such a sucker as me being president," an awestruck Lincoln said.

Lincoln had been presented to the convention as a symbol of the frontier, of the farm, and of hard work and success. He was Honest Abe; he was the Rail Splitter. Lincoln had been expert with an axe—he had split rails, thousands of them. He really had been born in a log cabin, on February 12, 1809, near Hodgenville, Kentucky. His family had moved from one subsistence farm to another in Kentucky and Indiana. The life was hard, cold, mean, deprived. His formal education consisted of several weeks in a "blab" school in Indiana, so called because the pupils were required to study out loud. Lincoln summed up his early years in a comment to his campaign biographer in 1860.

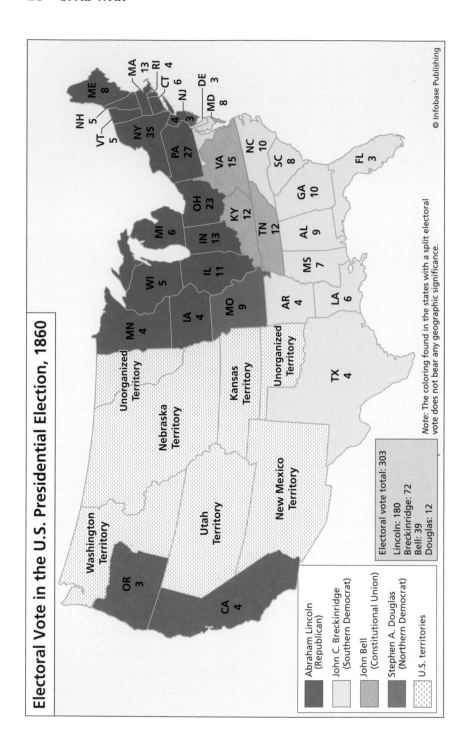

Electoral Vote in the U.S. Presidential Election, 1860

MA 13
RI 4
CT 6
NJ 4
DE 3
MD 8
MA 13
NH 5
ME 8
VT 5
NY 35
PA 27
VA 15
NC 10
SC 8
FL 3
OH 23
KY 12
GA 10
MI 6
IN 13
TN 12
AL 9
WI 5
IL 11
MS 7
IA 4
MO 9
AR 4
LA 6
MN 4
TX 4
OR 3
CA 4

Unorganized Territory
Nebraska Territory
Kansas Territory
Unorganized Territory
Washington Territory
Utah Territory
New Mexico Territory

Electoral vote total: 303

Lincoln: 180
Breckinridge: 72
Bell: 39
Douglas: 12

Note: The coloring found in the states with a split electoral vote does not bear any geographic significance.

© Infobase Publishing

Abraham Lincoln (Republican)
John C. Breckinridge (Southern Democrat)
John Bell (Constitutional Union)
Stephen A. Douglas (Northern Democrat)
U.S. territories

"It can all be condensed into a simple sentence and that sentence you will find in Gray's 'Elegy'—'The short and simple annals of the poor.'"

The family moved in 1830 to Illinois, and Lincoln soon struck out on his own. He failed as a storekeeper, but managed to repay his debts from his earnings as a postmaster. He served in the militia in the Black Hawk Indian war of 1832. He studied law, receiving his license to practice in 1836. He served four terms in the Illinois legislature and, from 1847 through 1849, in the U.S. Congress as a Whig. By then he had become the familiar Lincoln: very tall, thin and bony, with a sad, leathery face, coarse black hair and, in his voice, the nasal twang of the Midwest. His constituents, clients, and friends in Illinois found him forceful, honest, and affable too—a man who could delight an audience with a comic story.

There were other sides to Lincoln. Although many knew and admired him, he had few intimates. Prone to depression, he would withdraw into himself for weeks at a time. "Melancholy dripped from him as he walked," his law partner William Herndon wrote. And he was driven. He worked ceaselessly on his own behalf, certain he would be called to greatness. "That man who thinks Lincoln calmly sat down and gathered his robes about him, waiting for the people to call him, has a very erroneous knowledge of Lincoln," Herndon said. "He was always calculating, and always planning ahead. His ambition was a little engine that knew no rest."

By autumn 1860, his ambitions were soon to be realized. As was traditional, Lincoln remained in Springfield while his allies campaigned for him. Southern rights nominee Breckinridge and John Bell of Tennessee, the choice of a small party of former Whigs called the Constitutional Unionists, stayed home too. Only Douglas, the Little Giant, took to the road, moving restlessly from place to place telling audiences that only he could preserve the Union. He carried a strong antisecession message into the South, pleading with crowds in Tennessee, Alabama, and Georgia to accept the outcome of the vote, whatever it might be.

In effect, the choice fell between Lincoln and Douglas in the North, Bell and Breckinridge in the South. Some 4.7 million votes were cast on November 6, 1860. Breckinridge won 11 slave states. Bell carried the border states of Virginia, Kentucky, and Tennessee. Although he polled

President Abraham
Lincoln, photographed in
1864 *(National Archives)*

the second-highest vote total, Douglas won only Missouri. Lincoln carried all the Northern states except New Jersey, where he and Douglas
ran even. He carried none of the 15 slave states, and in five of those
states he drew not a single vote. With only 40 percent of the total vote,
Lincoln would be a minority president.

Many in the South immediately repudiated the result. In secessionist South Carolina, the *Charleston Mercury* called Lincoln a "free soil
Border Ruffian, a vulgar mobocrat and a Southern hater." Within six
weeks of the election, the breakup of the Union had begun. It started in
the South Carolina port city of Charleston, on December 20, where ral-
lies, fireworks, parades, and bands preceded a 169–0 convention vote
in favor of an ordinance dissolving "the union existing between South
Carolina and the other states."

Mississippi, Florida, Alabama, Georgia, and Louisiana followed in
the next few weeks. On February 1, 1861, Texas joined in secession. The
border states, including Virginia, hesitated. Buchanan, serving out the

last months of an ineffective presidency, followed a policy of inaction. In his final message to Congress, Buchanan had firmly denied a state's right to secede. In almost the same breath, however, he said the federal government lacked the authority to "coerce a state into submission which is attempting to withdraw."

COUNTERREVOLUTION IN CHARLESTON

For the Southern nationalist radicals known as "fire-eaters," Abraham Lincoln's election in November 1860 was cause in itself for secession. His victory, with 40 percent of the ballot and not a single electoral vote from a slave state, raised Southern fears of Northern conspiracy to a fever pitch. The rise of the "Black Republicans" meant disaster for the South.

"I see poison in the wells of Texas—and fire for the houses of Alabama," South Carolina congressman Lawrence M. Keitt warned. "How can we stand it? *It is enough to risk disunion.*"

So South Carolina led off what historian James McPherson has dubbed "the Counterrevolution of 1861." The secession convention gathered in Columbia, the state capital, on December 17 with the object of ending relations with the government "known as the United States of America." But a smallpox outbreak drove the delegates to Charleston, where they reassembled in St. Andrew's Hall two days later against a backdrop of marching bands, militia troops on parade, and crowds of citizens waving the state's palmetto flag.

The presiding officer, David F. Jamison, the owner of 70 slaves, brought down the gavel on the convention on the afternoon of December 20, 1860. The delegates approved the secession ordinance on a vote of 169 to 0. "The union now subsisting under the name of 'The United States of America' is hereby dissolved," their declaration read. Thirty years before, South Carolinian John C. Calhoun had argued that union was voluntary and that states could nullify laws their citizens found objectionable. Now Calhoun's political heirs advanced his theory to the next stage.

Two weeks later, Mississippi enacted an ordinance of secession and the other Deep South states followed South Carolina's lead. By Lincoln's inauguration day, the fire-eaters had called the Confederate States of America into being.

As the winter advanced, the nation seemed to shuffle blindly toward disaster. "So far as civil war is concerned," a Georgia editor wrote, "we have no fear of that in Atlanta." South Carolina senator James Chesnut volunteered to drink all the blood shed as a result of the secession crisis. Even Lincoln at first characterized the withdrawal of the seven Southern states as mere bluster.

By February, however, Southern intentions had become uncompromisingly clear. Representatives of the seven states, meeting in Montgomery, Alabama, organized a provisional government and adopted a states' rights constitution. On February 16, they inaugurated Jefferson Davis, a Mississippi planter and former U.S. senator, as president of the new Confederate States of America. The border states remained loyal—neutral might be a better word, for they made their loyalty conditional on the North's continued inaction. In December, president-elect Lincoln had quietly asked the U.S. Army commander, Winfield Scott, to prepare to defend federal forts in the breakaway states, or to recapture them if they had been surrendered. But Davis, accepting the

Photograph of Jefferson Davis, president of the Confederacy, ca. 1860 (National Archives)

Confederate presidency, had warned against any federal use of force. "The South is determined to maintain her position, and make all who oppose her smell Southern powder and feel Southern steel," he said.

As the rebel government formed, Lincoln set out for his own inaugural in Washington. Leaving Springfield, Illinois, on February 11, he took a roundabout route by special train, stopping frequently to deliver short, campaign-style speeches. He said little of substance, however. In trying to avoid offending the wavering states of the upper South, he merely succeeded in sounding confused and uncertain. There was danger, too. He arrived in Washington amid rumors of assassination plots and threats of violence.

Inauguration Day, March 4, 1861, broke gray and cold, with a stiff breeze. By midday, however, clouds had given way to sunshine. Lincoln, wearing a new black suit, black boots, and a stiff white shirt, and carrying a tall hat and a gold-headed cane, left the Willard Hotel for the Capitol at noon. Foot soldiers lined his Pennsylvania Avenue route, and cavalry guarded the intersections. Sharpshooters were posted on rooftops, and two batteries of artillery had unlimbered on the Capitol grounds.

In his inaugural address, Lincoln promised, as he had before, not to interfere with slavery where it existed. He asserted that secession was unlawful. He vowed to use federal authority to "hold, occupy and possess the property and places belonging to the government," and to collect taxes and customs duties. "In your hands, my dissatisfied countrymen, and not in mine, is the momentous issue of civil war," Lincoln said, pitching his voice to carry far beyond the Capitol and into Jefferson Davis's Confederacy. "The government will not assail you. You can have no conflict without yourselves being the aggressors."

Lincoln ended his speech with an appeal to a common and hallowed past that he believed should transcend any issue that might divide North and South. "I am loath to close," the new president said. "We are not enemies, but friends. . . . Though passion may have strained, it must not break our bonds of affection. The mystic chords of memory, stretching from every battlefield and patriot grave to every living heart and hearthstone all over this broad land, will yet swell the chorus of the Union when again touched, as surely they will be, by the better angels of our nature."

Given time, Lincoln hoped, the secessionists would hear at least an echo of those mystic chords. He hoped, too, for time to organize his government, bind the wavering states firmly to the Union, and allow

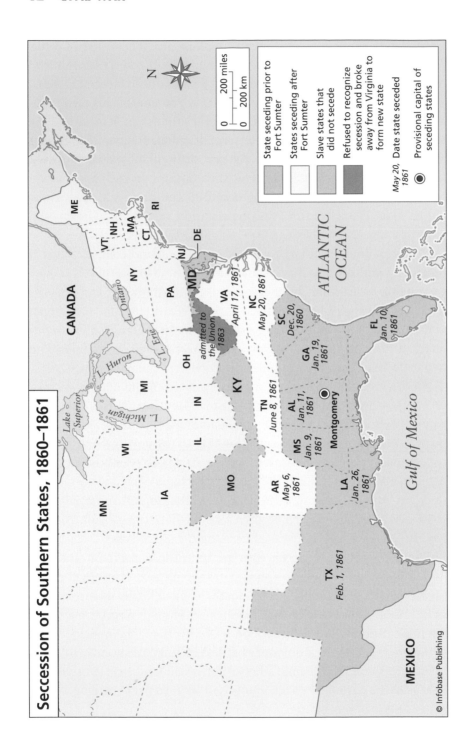

Seccession of Southern States, 1860–1861

Legend:
- State seceding prior to Fort Sumter
- States seceding after Fort Sumter
- Slave states that did not secede
- Refused to recognize secession and broke away from Virginia to form new state
- *May 20, 1861* Date state seceded
- ● Provisional capital of seceding states

0   200 miles
0   200 km

N

CANADA

Lake Superior
L. Michigan
L. Huron
L. Erie
L. Ontario

MN
WI
IA
MI
IL
IN
OH
ME
VT
NH
MA
CT
RI
NY
PA
NJ
DE
MD

MO
KY
admitted to the Union 1863
VA April 17, 1861
NC May 20, 1861
SC Dec. 20, 1860
TN June 8, 1861
AR May 6, 1861

AL Jan. 11, 1861
GA Jan. 19, 1861
MS Jan. 9, 1861
● Montgomery
LA Jan. 26, 1861
TX Feb. 1, 1861
FL Jan. 10, 1861

ATLANTIC OCEAN
Gulf of Mexico
MEXICO

© Infobase Publishing

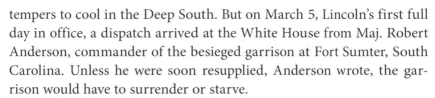

tempers to cool in the Deep South. But on March 5, Lincoln's first full day in office, a dispatch arrived at the White House from Maj. Robert Anderson, commander of the besieged garrison at Fort Sumter, South Carolina. Unless he were soon resupplied, Anderson wrote, the garrison would have to surrender or starve.

The Fort Sumter crisis had been building for months. The fort, on an artificial granite island in Charleston harbor, had been unfinished and empty when South Carolina voted to secede. The 80 U.S. troops in Charleston were stationed in Fort Moultrie, an indefensible outwork a mile away from Sumter. On the night of December 26, 1860, six days after the secession vote, Anderson secretly moved his small force from Moultrie into Sumter. South Carolina authorities, claiming all federal property in the state, demanded he leave. On January 9, South Carolina artillery fired on a ship carrying supplies for the garrison and drove it away.

An unofficial truce followed, lasting several weeks. It ended when the Confederates cut off Anderson's access to the markets of Charleston. So a hungry, anxious Anderson pressed the new president for a decision: resupply or withdrawal. General Scott advised withdrawal. In early April, however, Lincoln approved a plan to carry provisions into Sumter, and he so informed South Carolina governor Francis Pickens. No troops or weapons would be landed, Lincoln promised, and the supply ships would be unarmed. To stop the operation, the Confederates would have to fire upon defenseless men.

The Stars and Stripes flying over Fort Sumter were maddeningly visible from Charleston, and pressure built there for an attack. Only a few voices urged caution. Firing on Sumter would "inaugurate a civil war greater than any the world has yet seen," warned Robert Toombs, the Confederacy's secretary of state. "And so we fool on, into the black cloud ahead of us," Charleston resident Mary Boykin Chesnut wrote in her diary. Her husband, James Chesnut, had resigned from the U.S. Senate and now served as an officer on the staff of Gen. P. G. T. Beauregard, the Confederate commander in Charleston. On April 11, Chesnut and two others rowed out to Fort Sumter to present a surrender demand to Major Anderson.

"If you do not batter us to pieces, we shall be starved out in a few days," Anderson replied. Hearing a hint that the Confederacy might

This illustration depicts Federal troops inside Fort Sumter during the bombardment on April 12, 1861, the event that is regarded as the start of the Civil War. *(Library of Congress)*

be able to take the fort without firing a shot, Chesnut returned after midnight. This time, Anderson said he would be forced to evacuate on April 15 unless he received new orders or supplies from the government. Beauregard considered this a conditional promise. He thus ordered the Confederate batteries into action. At 4:30 A.M. on April 12, 1861, a mortar shot burned a red trail through the gray dawn, signaling the start of a full-scale bombardment. Over the course of two days, 4,000 rounds fell on Fort Sumter. The only casualties were two Federals killed and one wounded when a powder keg exploded as Anderson fired off a ceremonial salute at the surrender.

Lincoln issued a proclamation the next day mustering 75,000 militia for national service. Soon the Northern regiments were streaming into Washington. Southerners were on the march too, and the fractured nation moved off toward the killing ground of Bull Run.

ON TO RICHMOND

The Northern states responded enthusiastically to President Lincoln's call for volunteers, but mustering, equipping, and transporting the troops took time. By the third week of April, Washington had become a loyal island in a rebel sea. Within two days of Lincoln's call, the state of Virginia, just across the Potomac from the capital, had taken the first steps toward secession. In Maryland, which bordered Washington on three sides, secession sentiment ran high. The legislature there seemed ready to fall in with the Confederacy. Alarm spread in Washington. Government workers formed militia companies, and sandbags and barricades went up around the city's public buildings.

The states of the Upper South defied Lincoln's call for troops. "Tennessee will not furnish a single man for the purpose of coercion, but fifty thousand if necessary for the defense of our rights and those of our Southern brothers," Governor Isham G. Harris vowed. "I am left no other alternative but to fight for my section," said another Tennessean, the 1860 presidential candidate John Bell. "Lincoln has made us a unit to resist until we repel our invaders or die." On April 17, Virginia delegates to a secession convention voted 85-55 to leave the Union. Over the next two days, Virginia troops seized the U.S. arsenal at Harpers Ferry and the Gosport Navy Yard near Norfolk. Arkansas, North Carolina, and Tennessee soon followed Virginia into rebellion.

The 6th Massachusetts Regiment responded first to Lincoln's call. The troops arrived in Baltimore on April 19. The rail line did not pass through the city in 1861, so the 6th had to leave the cars at the Northern outskirts and march across town to meet the Washington train. On the way, a secessionist mob attacked the regiment with bricks, paving stones, and pistols. The troops fired on the crowd. Twelve townspeople and four soldiers were killed. After the riot, the mayor of Baltimore ordered bridges destroyed to prevent the passage of Union troops, and

On April 19, 1861, troops from Massachusetts passing through Baltimore on their way to defend Washington, D.C., were attacked by a mob that favored the Confederacy. *(Library of Congress)*

secessionists severed telegraph lines linking Washington to the North. For several days, the capital was cut off from the rest of the country.

"I don't believe there is any North," a gloomy Lincoln told officers of the 6th Massachusetts in the besieged city on April 24. "The [New York] Seventh Regiment is a myth. Rhode Island is not known in our geography any longer. You are the only Northern realities."

Soon, though, the Northern regiments broke the siege. Railway workers and mechanics in the ranks of the 8th Massachusetts repaired equipment and reopened the line to Washington. To Lincoln's relief, the 7th New York arrived on April 25. By the end of April, 10,000 troops were available for the defense of the capital and Federal forces bound Maryland firmly to the Union.

The Confederates were mobilizing, too. Earlier, on March 6, the new Confederate government had authorized an army of 100,000 men for 12 months. Many state militia regiments were sworn into Confederate service. More than 300 regular U.S. Army officers, about one-third of the officer corps, resigned and made their way south. When Virginia seceded, some of the best regular soldiers, including Robert E. Lee, Thomas J. Jackson, and J. E. B. Stuart, chose their state over the nation. Lee refused Lincoln's offer of command of the Union field army. "I must side with or against my section," Lee wrote to a Northern friend. "I cannot raise my hand against my birthplace, my home, my children." At the end of April, Lee became commander in chief of the Virginia forces. In May, he joined the Confederate army as a brigadier general.

In both North and South, complaints of inefficiency, shortages, and corruption accompanied the formation of the armies. "Twenty-four hundred men in camp and less than half of them armed," Indiana governor Oliver P. Morton wrote to Lincoln's secretary of war, Simon Cameron. "Why has there been such a delay in sending arms? Not a pound of powder or a single ball sent us, or any sort of equipment." Confederate cavalrymen and gunners were required to supply their own horses, and many soldiers brought their own weapons when they enlisted.

Robert E. Lee refused President Lincoln's offer of command of the Union field army and instead became commander in chief of the Virginia forces and then brigadier general in the Confederate army. *(National Archives)*

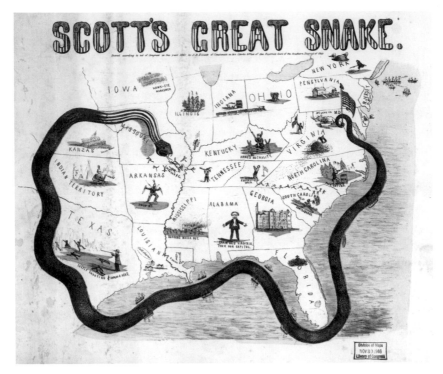

This cartoon map illustrates Gen. Winfield Scott's plan to crush the Confederacy by isolating it economically. It became known as "The Anaconda Plan" because it aimed to strangle the South like a giant snake. *(Library of Congress)*

While the troops were being mobilized, the leaders planned strategy. The Confederacy, which could win by not losing, would fight a largely defensive war. The North, however, needed to defeat and occupy the rebellious states. The Union commander in chief, the ailing, elderly U.S.-Mexican War hero Winfield Scott, proposed a strategy of blockade and penetration along the coasts and down the Mississippi River. Such a strategy would slowly strangle the Confederacy—thus its nickname, "The Anaconda Plan." Scott fretted, though, that Northerners' impatience would spoil his plan before it could show results. "They will urge instant and vigorous action, regardless, I fear, of the consequences," Scott predicted—correctly, as it turned out.

Early Union successes in the fighting along the borders cheered the anxious Northern public. Energetic action by Federal forces in deeply divided Missouri managed to keep that state tenuously within the Union. Lincoln's policy of avoiding confrontation in Kentucky gave pro-Union sentiment a chance to build there. Kentucky governor

RAISING THE ARMIES

Everyone expected a short war. The Confederate states had to build an army from the ground up, and the peacetime U.S. Army—16,000 men, most of them in frontier detachments—lacked the size, strength, and leadership to quell a major rebellion. So volunteers—citizen soldiers—would fight the Civil War. Thousands would die needlessly as they and their volunteer officers learned the soldier's art in the hard school of war.

Both North and South turned first to existing militia companies. Most of these units were more social than military and assigned a higher priority to drinking and companionship than drilling. By early 1861, South Carolina had 5,000 militiamen in service. The Confederate Congress on March 6 authorized an army of 100,000 volunteers for 12 months' service. Mobilization allowed Southern individuality to express itself fully. Cavalrymen and cannoneers supplied their own horses; many men brought their own weapons; and soldiers of all arms turned out in a bewildering variety of martial attire. In many Southern regiments, the men elected their own officers.

With the fall of Fort Sumter in April 1861, President Lincoln issued a call for 75,000 volunteers for 90 days of federal service. Massachusetts militia units were the first to respond—and the first Union troops to suffer casualties. In July, Congress authorized 1 million volunteers for three-year enlistments. Like Southerners, Northern volunteers paraded in an array of styles and colors: Vermonters showed off green trim, Iowans wore gray, and Minnesota volunteers donned rustic red flannel shirts. Perhaps the most colorful were the various Zouave regiments, both Union and Confederate; they wore the gaudy uniforms of the Algerian Zouaves who served in the French colonial armies and prided themselves on their disciplined drill. As in the South, too, many regiments were organized by county, city, town, and even ethnic background—the Irish 69th New York, for example.

Voluntarism implied enthusiasm for a cause, but commitment, however sincere, hardly made up for lack of training and equipment. "Col. Roberts has showed himself to be ignorant of the most simple company movements," a Pennsylvanian wrote home. "There is a total lack of system about our regiment. . . . We can only justly be called a mob & one not fit to face the enemy."

Beriah Magoffin refused calls for troops from both Lincoln and Davis. Thousands of Kentuckians slipped south into Tennessee to fight for the South, however, and federal authorities ignored Kentucky's profitable trade with the South in horses, mules, food, and even weapons. By late spring, however, Kentucky seemed secure for the Union. In a special election on June 20, Unionists polled 70 percent of the vote and won five of Kentucky's six congressional seats.

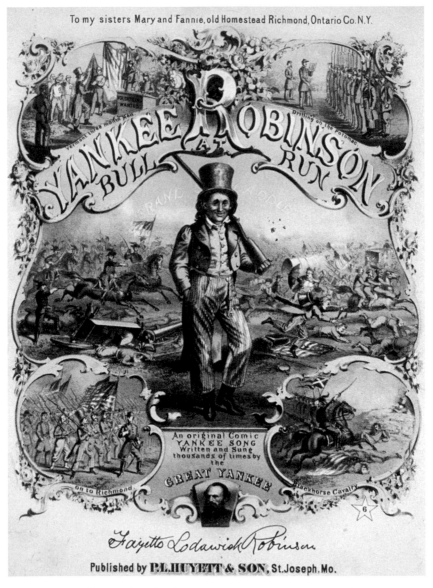

Despite the suffering that the Civil War would inflict on both sides, publishers would issue music such as this, titled "Yankee Robinson at Bull Run." *(Library of Congress)*

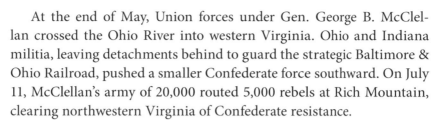

At the end of May, Union forces under Gen. George B. McClellan crossed the Ohio River into western Virginia. Ohio and Indiana militia, leaving detachments behind to guard the strategic Baltimore & Ohio Railroad, pushed a smaller Confederate force southward. On July 11, McClellan's army of 20,000 routed 5,000 rebels at Rich Mountain, clearing northwestern Virginia of Confederate resistance.

The Battle of Rich Mountain gave the North its first great hero in General McClellan. President Lincoln, Congress, and the Northern press soon would place complete confidence in him. Expectations were high. In the South as well as the North, most people believed early in 1861 that a short, sharp campaign would end the war. In May, a Confederate civilian reported that the trains "were crowded with troops, and all as jubilant as if they were going to a frolic, instead of a fight." Wrote a New York volunteer from his camp outside Washington: "I and the rest of the boys are in fine spirits . . . feeling like larks." Few then shared Robert E. Lee's grim vision. "I foresee that the country will have to pass through a terrible ordeal," Lee wrote darkly, "a necessary expiation perhaps for our national sins."

The ordeal began in earnest on July 21, 1861, along muddy, sluggish Bull Run in northern Virginia. There Confederate forces under General Beauregard repulsed a series of Union attacks, then sent the beaten and confused Northerners running in panic all the way back to Washington. Roughly 800 died on this first great battleground, and thousands more were wounded. The North's bid for a decisive encounter ended in a bloody rout.

"The fat is all in the fire now and we shall have to crow small until we can retrieve this disgrace somehow," John Nicolay, one of Lincoln's secretaries, wrote two days after the defeat.

Lincoln chose McClellan to repair the Union losses. "Circumstances make your presence here necessary," the president telegraphed to McClellan in western Virginia. "Come hither without delay." Four days after Bull Run, Lincoln authorized the enlistment of 1 million volunteers to serve three years. McClellan turned at once to the task of organizing and training this mass of men.

"I found no army to command, [but] a mere collection of regiments cowering on the banks of the Potomac, some perfectly raw, others dispirited by the recent defeat," McClellan wrote of his first days on the job. "The city was almost in condition to be taken by a dash of a regiment of cavalry."

Gen. George B. McClellan was the first great hero for the North after he led the Union troops to victory at the Battle of Rich Mountain, Virginia, in July 1861. *(National Archives)*

Thirty-four years old in 1861, George Brinton McClellan accepted command of the new Army of the Potomac as though it had come to him by right. Born into a wealthy Philadelphia family, he had known nothing but success. At 14, he entered West Point by special permission. By age 20, he had served with distinction in the U.S.-Mexican War. By age 31, he had resigned from the army and become vice president of the Illinois Central Railroad. He reentered military service as a major general of volunteers a few days after the surrender of Fort Sumter. McClellan took full credit for the Union success in western Virginia. Now, in the aftermath of Bull Run, Northerners hailed him as a savior.

Handsome and self-assured, of medium height and powerful build, with a reddish mustache and thick auburn hair, McClellan seemed well cast in the deliverer's role. There was a touch of glamour about this military paragon, especially when he galloped from camp to camp on his big bay horse, Daniel Webster. "People came from afar to see him at the head of a brilliant staff, to which counts and princes from abroad were attached," the journalist Carl Schurz wrote. "He was the 'Young Napoleon,' the pet of the nation."

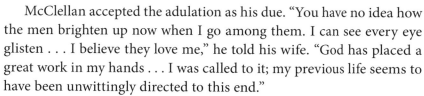

McClellan accepted the adulation as his due. "You have no idea how the men brighten up now when I go among them. I can see every eye glisten . . . I believe they love me," he told his wife. "God has placed a great work in my hands . . . I was called to it; my previous life seems to have been unwittingly directed to this end."

In August and September, new troops were arriving in Washington at the rate of 10,000 a week. Huge tent cities appeared on the hills and meadows outside the capital. A brilliant organizer, McClellan established a rigorous training routine for these clumsy volunteers. There were squad drills before breakfast, regimental drills before lunch, full dress regimental parades at the end of the day. The general saw to the removal of incompetent or corrupt officers. He ordered improvements in the troops' food and clothing. Gradually, sometimes painfully, the frequent, repetitive drilling turned the recruits into soldiers.

As the regiments took on the soldierly qualities he admired, McClellan formed them into brigades, then divisions, and showed them off in reviews and parades. On November 20, the general would mass the entire Army of the Potomac, more than 100,000 men marching under their regimental banners, for a grand review on a field outside Washington. Impressed, the politicians prodded McClellan. When, they asked, would he take this fine army into the field in pursuit of the rebels?

Praise for McClellan's military thoroughness had turned to criticism of what looked like excessive caution. McClellan never seemed to have enough men or enough guns; the army's training was never quite complete. A Democrat, he complained that powerful Republican politicians were undermining him. And he consistently overestimated the enemy's strength. In late summer the Confederates, still encamped at Manassas, near Bull Run, pushed pickets to within sight of Washington. McClellan resisted pressure to chase them away. "I am here in a terrible place," he wrote in August. "The enemy have from 3 to 4 times my force—the Presdt. [President] is an idiot, the old general [Scott] in his dotage—they cannot or will not see the true state of affairs." In fact, McClellan had more than twice as many men as Gen. Joseph E. Johnston, the Confederate commander.

Summer turned into a dry, mild autumn, and still McClellan failed to lead his troops into battle. Meanwhile, Johnston and the other Confederate commanders were subjected to similar pressures for action. "We are resting on our oars, while the enemy is drilling and equipping

500,000 or 600,000 men," wrote the Richmond diarist John B. Jones, a clerk in the Confederate War Department. But Johnston faced problems as serious as McClellan's, perhaps more so. If Northern troops chafed under military discipline, Southerners could be positively anarchic. "The order was read out at dress parade the other day that we all have to pull off our hats when we go to the colonel or the general," a private in a Georgia regiment wrote. "You know that is one thing I won't do. I would rather see him in hell before I will pull off my hat to any man and they just as well shoot me at the start."

McClellan's inaction gave Johnston ample time to convince his soldiers to take orders, even to salute. After a bloody clash at Ball's Bluff north of Washington in late October, McClellan sent the Army of the Potomac into winter quarters. There would be no offensive until the spring. The general's once-admiring public began to lose patience. "'Young Napoleon' is going down as fast as he went up," one Indiana Republican wrote.

By early in the new year of 1862, Lincoln had tired of McClellan's delays, excuses, and complaints. The general had been ill with typhoid, and while he was still recovering, the president called a White House conference of cabinet members and senior generals. "If General McClellan does not want to use the army," Lincoln told them, "I would like to borrow it, provided I could see how it could be made to do something." The generals discussed various ideas, including an advance on Richmond, which had become the permanent Confederate capital in mid-1861. Word got back to McClellan. Alarmed, he told Lincoln that he had a plan for action. He would not, however, say what it was.

The president waited for details, but received none. Out of patience, he ordered McClellan on January 27 to launch an attack on Johnston at Manassas by the third week of February. Under pressure, McClellan finally let Lincoln in on his plan. He would transport the army by ship down the Potomac, across Chesapeake Bay, and up the Rappahannock River to Urbanna, Virginia, 60 miles northeast of Richmond. The move would bypass the Confederates at Manassas. When McClellan marched on Richmond, Johnston would be forced to rush south to defend the rebel capital.

Lincoln, worried about the defense of Washington, had doubts about the operation. Nevertheless, he allowed his order for an attack on Manassas to lapse. Johnston, meanwhile, told Confederate president Davis in mid-February that his positions were vulnerable, and that he would soon withdraw his army of 42,000 to a new defensive line on the Rappahannock halfway between Manassas and Richmond. By March 7, the Confederates, having set fire to tons of stores they could not carry away, were retreating southward. The smell of burning bacon alerted Union scouts to the move, and at last McClellan put his army in motion. The first regiments entering Manassas found smoldering fires, abandoned trenches, and a few "Quaker" guns. These were logs cut and painted to look like cannon, one of the deceptions that had convinced McClellan that Johnston's forces were as strong as his own.

The withdrawal forced McClellan to drop his plan for a move up the Rappahannock. Instead, he proposed taking the army to Fortress Monroe, Virginia, 70 miles from Richmond at the head of the peninsula formed by the York and the James rivers. McClellan would march rapidly up the peninsula and fight a decisive battle near the capital. The first troops boarded the transports on March 17. In three weeks, 400 vessels made the 200-mile transit from Washington to Fortress Monroe, carrying 121,500 men, 15,000 animals, 1,150 wagons, 44 batteries of artillery, and 74 ambulances.

The Peninsular campaign opened on the sunny morning of April 4, 1862, when three of the six corps of the Army of the Potomac set out from Fortress Monroe. The next day the rains came. The peninsula, 50 miles long and 15 miles wide at its widest, was low, sandy, wooded country. The downpour filled the streams and swamps and turned the roads to mud. Wagons sank up to their axles, and struggling through the knee-deep mud left the infantry exhausted.

As much as the weather, McClellan's caution slowed the army's progress up the lightly defended peninsula. When the Federals bumped into a weak defensive line at Yorktown and along the Warwick River, McClellan decided to bring up siege guns. Again the Confederates deceived him, not with Quaker guns this time but by marching the infantry in circles and having the bands play day and night, giving the impression that fresh regiments were arriving hourly. "It seems clear that I shall have the whole force of the enemy on my hands, probably not less than 100,000 men," McClellan wrote President Lincoln on April 7. In fact, the Confederates had 17,000 men. "No one but McClellan could have hesitated to attack," Johnston said after inspecting the Warwick River lines.

McClellan's elaborate preparations cost the army a full month. On May 3, as the Union forces were about to open fire, the Confederates

Thomas J. "Stonewall" Jackson, the Confederate hero of Bull Run, outmaneuvered Union forces in Virginia in May 1862 and stalled Union general McClellan's move on Richmond. *(National Archives)*

slipped out of their positions at Yorktown and fell back toward Richmond. As at Manassas, McClellan's blow had landed in the air. The Federals followed the retreating Confederates, but at such a deliberate pace that one of his generals referred privately to McClellan as the "Virginia Creeper."

By mid-May, however, McClellan's advance troops and skirmishers had crept to within a few miles of Richmond. For the final approach, he deployed his forces on both sides of the Chickahominy River, with the larger wing on the right, north of the river. Here he awaited the arrival of the 35,000-strong I Corps of Gen. Irvin McDowell, which had been left behind to protect Washington. Before McDowell could march, Gen. Thomas "Stonewall" Jackson—the Confederate hero of Bull Run—began to stir. Jackson's basic strategy was to "always mystify, mislead and surprise the enemy." Now, for a few weeks in May and early June, he put these principles into action in the Shenandoah Valley.

Jackson marched back and forth across the Blue Ridge Mountains and up the valley, covering more than 160 miles in two weeks. "We can

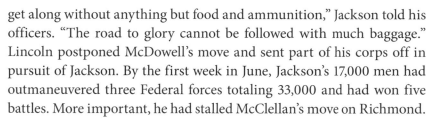

get along without anything but food and ammunition," Jackson told his officers. "The road to glory cannot be followed with much baggage." Lincoln postponed McDowell's move and sent part of his corps off in pursuit of Jackson. By the first week in June, Jackson's 17,000 men had outmaneuvered three Federal forces totaling 33,000 and had won five battles. More important, he had stalled McClellan's move on Richmond.

The "Young Napoleon's" forces were awkwardly astride the Chickahominy. The heavy rains had swollen the river to its highest level in 20 years, washing out bridges and disrupting communication between the two wings of the army. Johnston, well established in defensive positions around Richmond, attacked the weaker wing south of the river on May 31. Over two days, 84,000 Union and Confederate troops slugged it out in the thick woods and swamps near the village of Fair Oaks. At the end of the first confused and terrible day, the skies opened again. "It was a night of drizzling rain and inky darkness," a private in the Fifteenth Massachusetts wrote later. "All were wet to the hips, many had lost their shoes in the mud and the bodies of the dead and the wounded were lying on every side. You could not move without falling over them—the air was filled with shrieks and groans."

This miserable episode ended inconclusively. Among the 11,000 casualties was General Johnston, wounded in the chest and shoulder. On June 1, Robert E. Lee replaced him in command of what the Confederates now designated the Army of Northern Virginia. Lee broke off the Battles of Fair Oaks and Seven Pines and withdrew to Johnston's original defensive positions. Here he began to plan his own attack. First, he called Jackson's corps down from the Shenandoah Valley. Then, after a remarkable four-day reconnaissance in which 1,200 Confederate cavalrymen led by J. E. B. Stuart rode a circle around the entire Army of the Potomac, Lee decided to strike the Federals' exposed northern flank, where McClellan had hoped to link up with McDowell's corps. This time, the Union commander hit first. Giving up on McDowell, McClellan had shifted all but Gen. FitzJohn Porter's 30,000-strong V Corps south of the Chickahominy for the final advance on Richmond. On June 25, McClellan attacked at Oak Grove.

This action opened the weeklong series of engagements known as the Seven Days battles. McClellan called off the faltering Oak Grove attack on the evening of June 25, and Lee seized the initiative the next day, sending 60,000 men against Porter's isolated corps north of the Chickahominy at Mechanicsville. By now, McClellan's 75,000 Federals south of the river were facing only 27,000 Confederates. Lee gambled that McClellan would stay in place, awaiting the outcome of the battle to the north, rather than roll boldly over the thin rebel line and into Richmond. He guessed correctly. McClellan, his attention fastened on Confederate diversions at Garnett's and Golding's farms on June 27 and 28, left Porter to fight virtually alone.

Lee's attack at Mechanicsville failed, largely because of poor coordination between his divisional commanders. Jackson, unaccountably, seemed confused by his role and showed up several hours late. The blow staggered Porter's troops, but they held the line before falling back a short distance to stronger positions at Gaines's Mill. Union forces south of the Chickahominy remained passive as Lee pressed his attack the next day. The Federals were well protected by the morass of Boatswain's Swamp, however, and again the usually prompt Jackson turned up late to the battlefield.

Despite their generals' confusion, the Confederates fought ferociously. "Almost every moment I looked for our first line to give way,"

JACKSON AND SLEEP DEPRIVATION

General Lee tapped Thomas J. "Stonewall" Jackson to open the attack near Mechanicsville on June 26, 1862, the second day of the Seven Days battles east of the Confederate capital of Richmond. He ordered Jackson to launch an attack on the Federal flank early in the morning, but most of the day passed with no sign at all of the brilliant, eccentric, usually reliable Jackson.

So the battle began without him in the late afternoon, and it was a shambles for Lee's army. As it developed into a bloody repulse, Jackson lay inert a few miles to the north, within the sound of the guns. Why? What detained him?

Jackson had hardly slept on the march east from the Shenandoah Valley, and six weeks' furious campaigning there in the spring had worn him down. Historians thus have diagnosed sleep deprivation and stress fatigue as the explanation for his curious and uncharacteristic lack of vigor during the Richmond battles.

So far as is known, Lee never upbraided Jackson for his performance. And Jackson went on to distinguish himself at the Second Battle of Bull Run and the Battles of Antietam and Chancellorsville.

There were more than 17,000 casualties from two days of fighting in and around Mechanicsville, Virginia, on June 27 and June 28, 1862. Most of the casualties occurred on the battlefield here, at Gaines's Mill. *(Library of Congress)*

Union officer Edward Acton wrote not long after the battle. Still, Porter's regiments held their ground. "They would not give way," Acton went on. In fact, they rose from their rifle pits and counterattacked. By evening, though, Lee had all his divisions in place. A final attack an hour before dark sent Porter's corps reeling. That night, the Federals retreated across the river. The two days of fighting had cost more than 17,000 casualties, most of them at Gaines's Mill.

The battle at Gaines's Mill convinced McClellan to abandon the drive on to Richmond and order a general withdrawal southeastward to the James River. Lee would not allow him to leave quietly, however, attacking Federal rear guards at Savage's Station and White Oak Swamp on June 29 and 30. By July 1, the three Union corps covering the retreat had set up strong defensive positions at Malvern Hill, overlooking the James. Lee attacked anyway, sending his divisions across open fields toward the Union entrenchments. The results were disastrous. Writing years later, William W. Averell, a Federal cavalry officer, remembered looking downhill at the battlefield as the fog lifted early on the morning of July 2. "Our ears had been filled with agonizing cries from thousands . . . but now our eyes saw an appalling spectacle upon the slope down to the woodlands half a mile away," wrote Averell. "Over five thousand dead and wounded men were on the ground . . . enough were alive and moving to give the field a singular crawling effect."

The Seven Days battles ended in a strategic victory for the Confederates. Union forces had drawn close enough to hear the church bells of Richmond, but in a week of bloodletting Lee had driven them away. Still, Lee had hoped for more. "Under ordinary circumstances," he wrote, "the Federal Army should have been destroyed." Lee did not say it, but one extraordinary circumstance was the baffling performance of Stonewall Jackson. He actually fell asleep at several critical times during the Seven Days. Historians have speculated that Jackson may have been suffering from stress fatigue brought on by the rigors of the Shenandoah Valley campaign. Whatever the cause, his inertia cost Lee an opportunity to fatally wound his opponent.

After Malvern Hill, McClellan ordered a final retreat to Harrison's Landing on the James. Here the Union army, 100,000 strong, remained entrenched until August, when it reboarded the transports and sailed back to its starting point on the banks of the Potomac.

THE RIVER WAR

Three great rivers led into the heart of the western Confederacy. Union strategists aimed from the start to control the most crucial artery, the Mississippi, and to cut the Confederacy in two. By the autumn of 1861, they were also planning offensives along the second and third of these rivers, the Tennessee and the Cumberland. Troops, arms, and a flotilla of ironclad gunboats were assembling at Cairo, Illinois, where the Ohio River joins the Mississippi. East of Cairo, the Tennessee and the Cumberland flow into the Ohio at points only 12 miles apart. By late 1861, the Federals were established at the mouths of both rivers, and an obscure general named Ulysses S. Grant was preparing to move south.

The Confederate commander, Albert Sidney Johnston, had a 500-mile line to defend, stretching from the Appalachian foothills in eastern Kentucky beyond the Mississippi into southwest Missouri. He anchored his defenses on a system of strongholds and forts along the three rivers, with large concentrations of troops in the Kentucky towns of Columbus and Bowling Green. But he had only 70,000 men to hold this long line. As the Federals continued their buildup, Johnston sent a courier to Richmond with a plea for more regiments, weapons, and supplies. "Tell my friend General Johnston that I can do nothing for him," President Davis replied. "He must rely on his own resources."

The stronger Federals were hampered, however, by a divided command and the rivalry it created. Henry W. Halleck's area of responsibility ran from the Cumberland River westward into Missouri. Don Carlos Buell had charge of all of Kentucky east of the Cumberland. The two did not work well together, and Halleck schemed to obtain authority over Buell. President Lincoln urged his generals to join in an offensive against the overstretched Confederates. Like McClellan in Virginia a thousand miles to the east, they claimed they were ill-prepared. "I

The ironclad Union gunboat *Onondaga* monitors traffic on the James River in Virginia. *(National Archives)*

am not ready to cooperate," Halleck wrote the president on New Year's Day, 1862. "Too much haste will ruin everything."

Halleck had an important advantage in his campaign against Buell. He had Ulysses S. Grant, the general commanding at Cairo. Grant had a simple, direct military philosophy: "Find out where your enemy is, get at him as soon as you can and strike him as hard as you can, and keep moving on." He rarely complained, rarely asked for reinforcements, and was always ready to strike with whatever he had.

Thirty-nine years old in 1861, Grant was short, soft-spoken, and plain, sometimes seedy in appearance. A West Point graduate, he had resigned from the army in California in 1854 amid persistent rumors of drunkenness. The rumors remained unproven, but it was true that Grant was lonely, bored, and miserable on garrison duty. Civilian life did not improve his fortunes. Grant failed at farming and real estate. A friend in St. Louis got him a job collecting bills. He failed at that too. One year, he cut and sold firewood for a living. By 1860, he was supporting his wife, Julia Dent Grant, and their children by clerking at his father's leather goods store in Galena, Illinois.

Then the war came. In June 1861, Governor Richard Yates appointed Grant colonel in command of the 21st Illinois Infantry. He took the

regiment into Missouri, where it protected pro-Union citizens from
rebel guerrilla attacks. Grant's months with the 21st taught him an
important lesson in command. In July, he led the regiment in search of
a large force of irregulars under Col. Thomas Harris. "My heart kept
getting higher and higher, until it felt as though it was in my throat,"
he wrote, recalling the approach to the rebel camp. "I would have given
anything then to have been back in Illinois." He was not afraid, he said,

Probably issued for his presidential campaign in 1868, this print depicts
Ulysses S. Grant in front of the Capitol. Behind him is his favorite horse,
"Cincinnati." *(Library of Congress)*

just unsure of himself. He lacked, he went on, "the moral courage to halt and consider what to do." The 21st pressed on, climbing a last hill beyond which Grant expected to find the rebels drawn up in a battle line. They had vanished. "My heart resumed its place. It occurred to me at once that Harris had been as much afraid of me as I had been of him. This was a view of the question I had never taken before; but it was one that I never forgot afterwards."

Grant had a political patron prepared to overlook past failures and the rumors of heavy drinking that followed him east from California. Illinois congressman Elihu Washburne obtained a brigadier general's appointment for Grant, and on September 4, 1861, he took command at Cairo. "Be careful," Grant's father wrote after learning of the promotion. "You're a general now; it's a good job, don't lose it."

So Grant prepared to go south, drilling the regiments and collecting supplies in wet, muddy, fever-ridden Cairo. He sent troops to occupy Paducah, Kentucky, at the mouth of the Tennessee. A few weeks later, he took five regiments down the Mississippi by steamboat to a Confederate camp at Belmont, Missouri. In a short, sharp battle on the morning of November 7, the Federals routed the rebels there. But the Confederates counterattacked with 10,000 men ferried across the river from Columbus. They nearly surrounded Grant's force, and some of his officers counseled surrender. "We cut our way in," Grant told them, "and we could cut our way out just as well." The Federals scattered the enemy that blocked their way, reboarded their transports, and steamed back to Cairo.

In January, Grant began pressing for an attack up the Tennessee, which cut a long loop from its beginnings in the Great Smoky Mountains into northern Alabama, then flowed northward through Tennessee and Kentucky. Fort Henry, a half-finished Confederate strong point on low ground on the Kentucky-Tennessee line, guarded the river and a trestle bridge upstream on the Memphis & Charleston Railroad. Meeting Halleck in St. Louis, Grant proposed taking Fort Henry. However, much to Grant's dismay, Halleck objected to his suggestion. "I was cut short as if my plan was preposterous," said Grant. He returned to Cairo "very much crestfallen." Soon recovering his spirits, Grant wired Halleck on January 28 once again for permission to move on the fort. Halleck, needing a victory in his battle with General Buell, granted it this time. By the evening of February 3, 1862, Grant and 7,500 men were aboard transports steaming up the broad avenue of the Tennessee River.

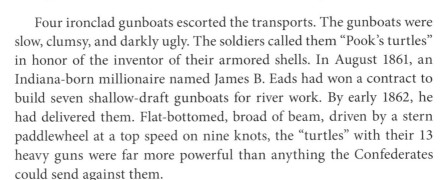

Four ironclad gunboats escorted the transports. The gunboats were slow, clumsy, and darkly ugly. The soldiers called them "Pook's turtles" in honor of the inventor of their armored shells. In August 1861, an Indiana-born millionaire named James B. Eads had won a contract to build seven shallow-draft gunboats for river work. By early 1862, he had delivered them. Flat-bottomed, broad of beam, driven by a stern paddlewheel at a top speed on nine knots, the "turtles" with their 13 heavy guns were far more powerful than anything the Confederates could send against them.

Andrew H. Foote, a 56-year old Connecticut Yankee and a saltwater sailor of long service, commanded the gunboats. Before 1861, his chief ambition had been to see the rum ration abolished in the fleet. He had equally strong religious convictions. Each Sunday, he led Bible school sessions for his gunboat crews. Foote and Grant, navy and army, teetotaler and suspected drunkard, believer and skeptic, liked one another in spite of their differences. And they worked well together, like, as Foote put it, "the blades of shears—united, invincible."

The transports landed the Union army a few miles north of Fort Henry on February 5, then returned downstream to Paducah for reinforcements. Heavy rains had turned the roads to mud, and the rising river threatened to flood Fort Henry before Grant could get there and take it by force. While his regiments struggled forward through the ooze, Grant ordered Foote to attack with the gunboats.

At midday on February 6, they approached Fort Henry in line abreast. Foote's flagboat, the *Cincinnati,* opened the bombardment. Though the floodwaters were two feet deep and rising inside the fort, the defenders returned a brisk fire. The rebel guns struck the *Cincinnati* some 32 times. One shot, a witness reported, "had the effect . . . of a thunderbolt, ripping her side timbers and scattering the splinters over the vessel. She did not slacken her speed, but moved on as though nothing had happened." Relentlessly the gunboats pounded the sodden fort, whose return shots glanced harmlessly off the boats' armored sides. After a two-hour exchange, and before Grant's troops could arrive, Fort Henry gave up. Foote sent a small boat to accept the surrender. It floated into the fort through the sally port.

Most of the garrison had slipped out the night before, marching 12 miles overland to Fort Donelson near the little town of Dover on the Cumberland River. Grant sent the gunboats south to destroy the rail bridge, cutting an important Confederate east-west link. Then he set

The Union gunboat *Fort Hindman* of the Federal Mississippi River fleet. These ironclad boats, designed by Samuel Pook, escorted troop transports and, because of their armored shells, were nicknamed "Pook's turtles." *(Library of Congress)*

to work preparing an assault on Donelson. Meantime, the loss of Fort Henry had forced Confederate general Albert S. Johnston to retreat southward from Bowling Green to Nashville. He decided to try to hold Fort Donelson, however. With reinforcements, 17,500 men were available for the defense.

Grant's army marched on February 12, leaving a garrison behind to hold Fort Henry. It was a fine, mild day and the troops, burdened with two days' rations and 40 rounds of ammunition, threw away their blankets and overcoats. The next day, Grant ordered a series of probing attacks on the outer Confederate defenses at Fort Donelson. These gained little, so he decided to wait for more men and for the gunboats, which had to return to Paducah, cut over to the Cumberland, then paddle 50 miles up the Cumberland to Dover.

By February 14, the gunboats were ready. This time, though, they faced strong opposition. The Confederates had nine big guns dug into the high bluffs commanding the river. From there, shellfire could be directed down onto the flotilla. One by one the gunboats were disabled and driven off. The *St. Louis* alone took 57 hits. Ashore, Grant settled in for a siege. Drizzle began to fall that night. The wind veered to the north, and the rain turned to sleet, the sleet to snow. The temperature dropped to 10 degrees. Men huddled together; some units marched

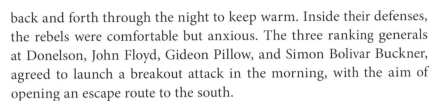

back and forth through the night to keep warm. Inside their defenses, the rebels were comfortable but anxious. The three ranking generals at Donelson, John Floyd, Gideon Pillow, and Simon Bolivar Buckner, agreed to launch a breakout attack in the morning, with the aim of opening an escape route to the south.

The rebels hit the half-frozen Federals with explosive force. Almost at once, the right-hand division under Gen. John A. McClernand began to give ground. He sent word for help. But Grant, in conference with Foote five miles downstream that morning, had left orders that no troop movements were to be made in his absence. He had not, he said later, expected a battle "unless I brought it on myself." So McClernand fought on alone. After a three-hour struggle in the blood-stained snow, the road south lay open to the Confederates. But General Floyd, the senior commander, hesitated. Unaccountably, he ordered the attackers back to their original positions, giving McClernand's disorganized division a chance to recover.

Grant arrived on the battlefield shortly after noon. What he found surprised but did not unnerve him. In what would become a characteristic attitude, he had thought far more about what he meant to do to his opponent than about what his opponent might do to him. Now he calmly set about repairing the damage. "The position on the right must be retaken," he told McClernand. "[The enemy] has attempted to force his way out, but has fallen back; the one who attacks first now will be victorious and the enemy will have to be in a hurry if he gets ahead of me." Grant then ordered a counterattack along the left of the line, which the rebels had thinned to reinforce the breakout on the right.

By evening all the lost ground had been retaken. Generals Floyd and Pillow fled the besieged fort in the night, leaving Buckner to arrange a surrender. Buckner and Grant had been friends in the old army. In fact, Buckner had lent Grant money for his return east when he left the service in 1854. He did not anticipate Grant's hard reply to his request for negotiations: "No terms except an unconditional and immediate surrender can be accepted. I propose to move immediately on your works." Buckner bristled at the note, calling it ungenerous. But he had no choice. On February 16, he surrendered the 13,000 men remaining in Fort Donelson.

Grant had won the biggest victory of the war so far. The collapse of Fort Donelson forced the Confederates to evacuate Nashville, with its important arms factories and textile mills, on February 23, and

The taking of Fort Donelson in Tennessee and the capture of the Confederate general Buckner was the first of Ulysses Grant's major victories. *(Library of Congress)*

the Mississippi River strong point at Columbus a few days later. In early March, Nashville became the first rebel capital to fall. Johnston's beaten and demoralized army retreated all the way to Corinth, Mississippi, a railroad junction a few miles south of the Tennessee line.

No sooner had Johnston got his army safely away than word came of new Confederate defeats in the West. With 16,000 men, Gen. Earl Van Dorn had planned to invade Missouri, occupy St. Louis, and threaten Grant's Cairo base from the rear. A small Union army under Samuel R. Curtis stood in his way, and the two forces clashed at Pea Ridge, Arkansas, on the morning of March 7. Fighting continued inconclusively through the day. The next morning, the battle resumed at Elkhorn Tavern, a few miles away. A Union charge broke the Confederate line, scattering the rebels and abruptly ending Van Dorn's invasion.

At the same time, the Federals under Gen. John Pope began their long-planned move down the Mississippi. In a series of actions, Union troops and gunboats breached the Confederate defenses at New Madrid, Missouri, and Island No. 10. The monthlong campaign climaxed with the opening of the Mississippi all the way to Fort Pillow, only 40 miles above Memphis.

By the third week of March, Grant's army had moved up the Tennessee to the village of Pittsburg Landing, only 20 miles north of Corinth. There Grant awaited the arrival of the slow-moving Buell, who was coming down from Nashville. Halleck had finally won his

ISLAND NO. 10

With a garrison of 7,000 men and 50 big guns, the defensive works at Island No. 10 and its environs in a great U-shaped bend of the Mississippi southeast of New Madrid, Missouri, gave the Confederates absolute control of the strategically vital river. Northern vessels could attempt to pass the rebel bastion only at unacceptable risk.

In spring 1862, as part of a general offensive down the Mississippi, Union general Henry Halleck prepared a joint army-navy operation to seize the stronghold and open another stretch of the river. While Flag Officer Andrew Foote's seven ironclad gunboats and 10 mortar barges bombarded the Island, the Army of the Mississippi under Gen. John Pope closed on the Confederate works from the Missouri bank. Pope arrayed his forces so as to control access to Island No. 10 on three sides, leaving the Confederates only a single tenuous supply (and escape) route through swamplands on the Tennessee side.

One of Foote's ironclads, the *Carondelet,* ran the gauntlet of Confederate guns on the stormy night of April 4 and, with Pope's foot soldiers, sealed off the swamp road. Pope crossed the Mississippi under the protection of the *Carondelet*'s guns and surrounded the island garrison. The Confederate surrender on April 7, 1862, opened the river to Union shipping as far south as Fort Pillow, 40 miles above Memphis, Tennessee. Pope scored important gains—among them three generals and 5,000 men taken captive—at virtually no cost to himself.

The victory at Island No. 10 made John Pope an instant national hero and he soon would be called to Virginia to command the Army of the Potomac—with results, at the Second Battle of Bull Run in August, gravely damaging to his self-esteem.

private war with Buell. Largely because of Grant's victories, he had been given command of all Union forces west of the Appalachians. Halleck ordered Grant, whose aggressive instincts he mistrusted, not to advance until Buell could join him. Then he, Halleck, would come down from St. Louis to take command of the combined army.

Reinforcements had been sent to Corinth, and Federal delays gave the rebels time to rest and refit. General Johnston and his just-arrived second-in-command, General Beauregard, the hero of Bull Run, now planned a campaign to regain Tennessee for the Confederacy. Once Buell arrived, Halleck would have 75,000 men, nearly double the Confederate strength. So Johnston resolved to attack Grant's army, encamped outside Pittsburg Landing around a log chapel called Shiloh, before the odds turned heavily against him.

The Confederates marched out of Corinth on the afternoon of April 3. However, they experienced monumental delays of men, horses, cannon, and transport wagons, and the attack, planned for April 4, had to be postponed. Despite the delay, Union forces were unaware of the Confederate approach. Frontline troops in Gen. William T. Sherman's division reported contact with rebel patrols on April 4 and 5, but

The battle at Shiloh church in southwestern Tennessee broke out on April 6, 1862, and raged throughout the day, taking a terrible toll of casualties on both sides. *(Library of Congress)*

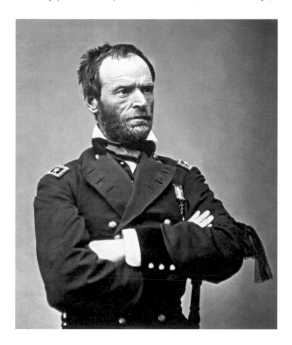

William Tecumseh
Sherman, 1820–
1891 (*Library of
Congress*)

Sherman dismissed this as unimportant. "I do not apprehend anything like an attack on our position," he told Grant.

Five of Grant's six divisions were encamped as though for training. (The sixth, under Gen. Lew Wallace, was five miles to the north, guarding a second river landing.) There were no trenches and no defensive line, for Grant did not want to dampen the men's offensive spirit by having them dig in. As at Fort Donelson in February, he did not expect a battle. "I have scarcely the faintest idea of an attack being made upon us," he wired Halleck.

At dawn on April 6, thousands of shrieking rebels hurled themselves from the woods near Shiloh church. Earlier, a patrol from Benjamin Prentiss's division had stumbled into the van of the Confederate army as it deployed for the attack, so the Federals had had at least a few minutes' warning. At the sound of firing, the divisions of Prentiss and Sherman left their breakfast and formed a makeshift battle line. Hearing the guns, Sherman rode forward to investigate. A volley sounded and his orderly fell dead from his horse. "My God, we're attacked!" Sherman called out, convinced at last.

Few men in Sherman's and Prentiss's divisions had been under fire before. Yet they absorbed the full force of the rebel assault. Sherman, especially, had a difficult morning. As the rebels swarmed into his line, the colonel of the 53rd Ohio shouted, "Fall back and save yourselves," then ran in panic to the rear. The colonel of the 71st Ohio also declined to participate in the battle. The 6th Iowa's colonel was drunk. Still, Sherman kept his division intact. It repulsed four rebel charges before withdrawing a half-mile to good defensive positions.

Grant had heard distant firing as he sat down to breakfast at his headquarters in Savannah, Tennessee, nine miles downriver. He left immediately for the battlefield. By the time he stepped off the steamboat, hundreds of soldiers, some wounded, all terrified, had streamed into Pittsburg Landing. Shocked and confused, they huddled under the bluffs for protection and screamed warnings to troops about to be fed into the battle. Grant placed two reserve regiments across the line of retreat to turn back stragglers. Then, sending staff officers to collect first-hand reports from the divisional commanders, he headed for the sound of the guns.

"Tell Grant if he has any men to spare I can use them," Sherman told one of the general's aides. "If not, I will do the best I can. We are holding them pretty well just now. Pretty well; but it's hot as hell."

Sherman, 42 years old, had led a brigade at Bull Run. Unlike so many at Shiloh, he already had "seen the elephant"—the soldiers' phrase for experiencing combat. But he was recovering from what today would be called a nervous breakdown. Preceding General Buell as commander of the Department of the Ohio, Sherman had faced General Johnston's forces in Kentucky in the autumn of 1861. Anxious and uncertain, he wildly overestimated the Confederate strength. Fearing attack at any moment and at every point, he asked for 200,000 men to hold off Johnston. Halleck removed him from command and gave him a minor job in Missouri. Sherman rested and collected himself. By midwinter, he had joined Grant as a divisional commander. Grant had full confidence in the high-strung, brilliant Sherman, and at Shiloh church the two men formed a partnership that would last to the end of the war.

At the front, Grant found Sherman holding his ground on the right: McClernand's division fighting hard behind Shiloh chapel; and Prentiss, after initial setbacks, in a strong defensive position along a sunken road, where by midday he had already beaten back several Confederate charges. Grant told Prentiss to hold this line "at all hazards." Engagements of greater or lesser ferocity were flaring all along the battlefront, a six-mile line from the Tennessee River on the Union left to Owl Creek on the right. Afterward, an Iowa soldier wrote that the firing was so intense where he lay that he actually could see musket balls whizzing thickly overhead, as visible as swarms of insects.

Along the sunken road, Prentiss obeyed Grant's order to the letter. Troops of the 31st Indiana repulsed several attacks, including one that had come within 10 yards of their position. As the rebels regrouped for yet another charge, the woods in front of the Indianans caught fire. A choking woodsmoke filled the air, mingling with the acrid smoke from the guns and, soon, with the stench of burning bodies.

The Confederates charged again and again into what they later called the Hornet's Nest. Prentiss's division stopped each assault. In the late afternoon the Confederates massed 62 field guns, the largest concentration of artillery in the war to date, to blast the defenders out of their position. The barrage came in "like a mighty hurricane," a lieutenant in the 2nd Iowa remembered, "sweeping everything before it." The thirteenth Confederate charge overwhelmed the Federals. His line collapsing around him, Prentiss surrendered the Hornet's Nest at 5:30 that afternoon.

His stand had given the four surviving Union divisions time to fall back and regroup along a strong line on a ridge overlooking Pittsburg Landing. There, Grant waited for an evening attack. It did not come. Confederate general Johnston had bled to death on the battlefield that afternoon when a musket ball severed an artery in his leg. His successor, Pierre G. T. Beauregard, called off the battle at sunset, then wired news of a great victory to President Davis in Richmond.

Grant had a different view of the situation. The first of Buell's troops had reached Pittsburg Landing. Lew Wallace's division, which had taken a wrong turn on the way to battle and wandered lost all day, turned up as well. So Grant had 25,000 fresh troops. Nevertheless, some of his staff advised retreat. The suggestion seemed to surprise Grant. "Retreat? No. I propose to attack at daylight and whip them."

With nightfall came thunder and lightning and torrents of rain that soaked the 2,000 dead and 10,000 wounded strewn over the battlefield. Their presence haunted the untouched. "Sickening sights fell before my eyes," a Mississippi private recalled. "I saw a large piece of ground covered with dead heaped and piled upon each other." From the river, Union gunboats fired at regular intervals into the rebel positions, adding to their confusion, discomfort, and terror.

Beauregard went to bed confident. "I thought I had General Grant just where I wanted him and could finish him up in the morning," he wrote afterward. Grant, on the other hand, had trouble sleeping. The log house he had used as a headquarters had been converted into a hospital. The moans, the smells, and the steady sound of the bonesaws drove him out into the night. Sherman found him later standing under a tree, hat pulled low, coat collar upturned, a cigar between his teeth, rain dripping off him.

"Well, Grant, we've had the devil's own day, haven't we?"

"Yes," Grant said. "Yes. Lick 'em tomorrow, though."

The Federals attacked in the morning, advancing over the dead and wounded from the day before. "Their groans and cries were heart-rending," a Union soldier recalled. "The gory corpses lying all about us, in every imaginable attitude, and slain by an inconceivable variety of wounds, were shocking to behold." The Federals pressed forward anyway, past Bloody Pond, red with the blood of the wounded who had crawled there to drink; past the peach orchard, over a carpet of shredded blossoms stained with blood; past the sunken road and the

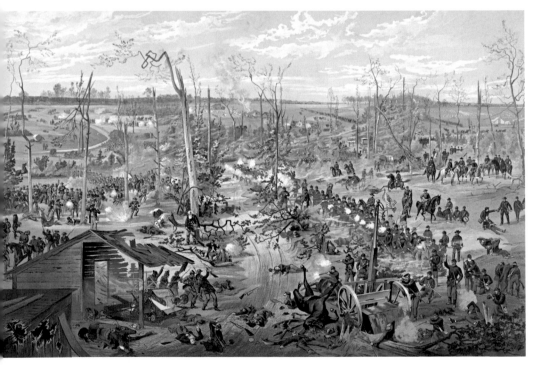

The Battle of Shiloh, or Pittsburg Landing, took place on April 6, 1862, and although the Federals held command of the battleground the next day, it was an extremely costly battle for both sides. *(Library of Congress)*

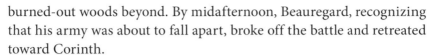

burned-out woods beyond. By midafternoon, Beauregard, recognizing that his army was about to fall apart, broke off the battle and retreated toward Corinth.

The 23,000 dead, wounded, and missing at Shiloh added up to considerably more than the total casualties of all the preceding Civil War battles: Bull Run, Wilson's Creek in Missouri, Pea Ridge in Arkansas, Fort Donelson—and all the rest. "I never realized the 'pomp and circumstance' of the thing called glorious war until I saw this," a Tennessee private wrote after Shiloh. "Piles of dead soldiers' mangled bodies . . . without heads and legs," Sherman wrote to his wife. "The scenes on this field would have cured anybody of war."

Still, the killing would go on. Johnston was dead, Beauregard would soon be relieved of his command, and Grant was in eclipse. Northern opinion turned on him after Shiloh. He had been unready; his army had been surprised; he had been miles from the battlefield when the fighting began (there was even a rumor that he had been drunk); many believed that only Buell's timely arrival had prevented a Union disaster. In Washington, a Pennsylvania congressman laid all these charges before President Lincoln, who replied, "I can't spare this man. He fights."

THE USES OF
SEA POWER

While the armies clashed violently in Virginia and along the midwestern river lines in 1861–62, the Union gradually brought the weapon of sea power to bear. Politicians and newspaper editors had scoffed at the elderly General Scott's Anaconda Plan, but soon the Federal strategies of encirclement and blockade had begun slowly strangling the Confederacy, which had few defenses against the North's overwhelming naval superiority.

As they grew in size and strength, Union maritime forces could strike at will along the Atlantic and Gulf coasts and on the rivers. By mid-1862, Union forces would gain command of most of the Mississippi. Seaborne assaults would give the Federals control of important harbors and anchorages in the Carolinas. The Union ironclad *Monitor* would fight its only battle, and revolutionize naval warfare. A Union fleet would steam up the Mississippi from the Gulf of Mexico and seize the city of New Orleans. Week after week, month after month, the Union blockade would go about its quiet business, denying the South imports of arms, munitions, medicines, and clothing and barring the export of cotton to pay for them.

Although Confederate blockade runners scored spectacular individual successes, the Federal warships cruising ceaselessly offshore would make their operations increasingly risky. Chances of capture, only one in 10 in 1861, would rise sharply to one in three by 1864. More than 800 ships penetrated the blockade during the first year of the war. This number represented a sharp decline, however, from the 6,000 vessels that had entered and left Confederate ports during the last year of peace.

The Confederates hoped to trade cotton for munitions and other materials of war. Recognizing the importance to the rebel war effort of

Fifteen officers stand on the deck of the USS *Monitor,* the Union navy's first ironclad. With its gun turret, it was described as looking like a "cheesebox on a raft." *(Library of Congress)*

the free flow of goods, President Lincoln banned trade with the secession states on April 16, 1861, and announced the blockade of Southern ports in two proclamations later in the month. The task was far beyond the capability of the peacetime U.S. Navy. To seal off 10 major ports and nearly 200 inlets, bays, and river mouths along 3,550 miles of Confederate coast, the Federals had about 40 warships fit for service, and a strength of 1,500 officers and 7,600 seamen. In the spring of 1861, Flag Officer Silas Stringham, the first commander of the Atlantic Blockading Squadron, had only 14 vessels to patrol 1,000 miles of coast from Hampton Roads, Virginia, to Key West, Florida.

Lincoln's navy secretary, the Connecticut newspaper editor and politician Gideon Welles, soon set in motion a tremendous expansion of the sea service. As General McClellan was doing in the Army of the Potomac, Welles studied the officer lists, combing out the lazy and incompetent. He began buying or leasing cargo ships, barges, ferries, tugs—any vessel large and seaworthy enough to be armed with a gun or two and assigned a blockade station. By mid-July, only three months after the outbreak of war, the blockade had begun to take hold. By the end of 1861, 76 ships of the old navy had been repaired and recommissioned, 136 ships had been purchased, and 52 new ships had been built.

Welles put most of these vessels to work shutting off the Confederacy from the rest of the world.

Blockade duty was dull, dreary, and uncomfortable. "Day after day, day after day, we lay inactive, roll, roll," the young Union officer Alfred T. Mahan wrote. For much of the time the crews were idle, except for the lookouts staring anxiously into the gloom or squinting into the glare of the sun on water. Over four years of war, about 150 warships were on blockade duty at a given time. Some 1,500 blockade runners were captured or destroyed from 1861 to 1865, yet best estimates are that, on average, a warship participated in only a dozen sightings and one or two captures a year.

For this tedious work, ordinary seamen earned $16 a month, but the chance for prize money kept them watchful. A blockader's capture would be turned over to the government prize court, which auctioned off both ship and cargo. For the capture of the blockade runner *Hope,* the captain of the tug *Eolus* received $13,000, and each crewman received $1,000. Over the full course of the war, the U.S. government awarded more than $10 million in prize money to the officers and men of the blockading squadrons.

By contrast, slipping through the screen of Federal warships was high adventure. "Nothing I have ever experienced can compare with it," wrote Thomas Tyler, a British merchant who made eight runs through the blockade from Nassau and Bermuda. "Pig-sticking, steeple-chasing, big game hunting, polo—I have done a little of each—all have their thrilling moments, but none can approach running a blockade."

Profits were fabulous, encouraging many a merchant sailor to discount the risk of capture. As the blockade tightened and the shortages worsened, a blockade-running captain's wages rose to as much as $5,000 in gold for each round trip. The runners used small, fast vessels and chose poor weather or moonless nights to make their dashes. Even when the runners got through, their cargoes were small and Confederate needs were large. The best estimate is that the Union blockade cut Southern trade to one-third of normal—and the war years, with their exaggerated demands for every sort of necessity, were not normal.

Brave, rough, cynical, and greedy, the runners took full advantage of Confederate needs. A favorite toast, usually made in champagne after a successful outward run, went: "Here's to the Confederates that produce the cotton; to the Yankees that maintain the blockade and keep up the price of cotton; and to the Britishers who buy the cotton

Well, yes!... it is certain that
cotton is more useful to me
than Wool!!—

JOHN BULL MAKES A DISCOVERY.

This satiric cartoon reflects Northern fears of English assistance to the
Confederacy by depicting John Bull saying that England is willing to abandon
its opposition to slavery because of its desire to import cotton from the
South. *(Library of Congress)*

and pay the high price for it. So three cheers to a long continuance of
the war, and success to the blockade runners!"

President Lincoln's proclamation of the blockade raised urgent diplomatic issues, especially with Great Britain, the world's leading maritime power and the South's chief trading partner. International law
states that a blockade is legal only when a nation has the naval power
to enforce it broadly. Mere proclamation of blockade, backed up by an
occasional seizure, is not sufficient. Confederate diplomats argued that
the Federals had imposed a paper blockade—one they were powerless
to enforce.

"You have heard, no doubt, Old Abe has blockaded our port," a
Charleston, South Carolina, man wrote a merchant friend in England.
"A nice blockade indeed! On the second day, a British ship . . . ran the
gantlet with a snug freight of $30,000. Don't you wish a hundred ships
for one voyage?"

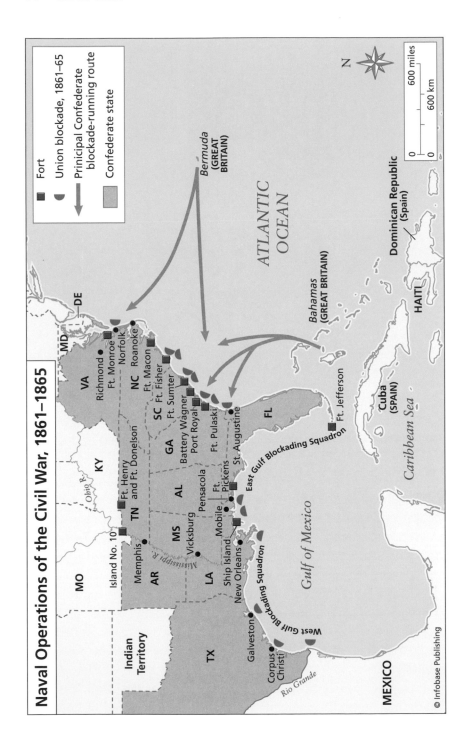

Naval Operations of the Civil War, 1861–1865

Legend:
- Fort
- Union blockade, 1861–65
- Prinicipal Confederate blockade-running route
- Confederate state

MO

Indian Territory

TX

Galveston
Corpus Christi
Rio Grande

MEXICO

AR

Memphis

Island No. 10

MS

Vicksburg

LA

Ship Island
New Orleans

West Gulf Blockading Squadron

Gulf of Mexico

KY

Ft. Henry and Ft. Donelson

TN

AL

Mobile
Pensacola

Ft. Pickens

East Gulf Blockading Squadron

VA

Richmond
Ft. Monroe
Norfolk
Roanoke

MD

DE

NC

Ft. Macon

SC

Ft. Fisher
Ft. Sumter

GA

Battery Wagner
Port Royal
Ft. Pulaski
St. Augustine

FL

Ft. Jefferson

Ohio R.

Mississippi R.

ATLANTIC OCEAN

Bermuda (GREAT BRITAIN)

Bahamas (GREAT BRITAIN)

Cuba (SPAIN)

Caribbean Sea

Dominican Republic (Spain)

HAITI

N

0   600 miles
0   600 km

© Infobase Publishing

Still, the blockade was effective enough by autumn 1861 to interrupt the journey to Europe of two Confederate emissaries. James Mason and John Slidell were bound for Great Britain and France, where they were to seek diplomatic recognition for the Confederacy. Evading Union patrols outside Charleston, they reached Havana, Cuba, and transferred to the British steamer *Trent*. On November 8, Capt. Charles Wilkes, commander of the sloop USS *San Jacinto*, stopped the *Trent* on the high seas and forcibly removed Mason and Slidell.

Wilkes allowed the *Trent* to continue on its way, but the arrests raised a storm of protest abroad. The British, enraged, demanded an apology and the immediate release of Mason and Slidell. They sent troops to Canada, alerted the Royal Navy's North Atlantic Squadron, and halted shipments of vital war supplies to the North. "One war at a time," President Lincoln advised, and William Seward, the secretary of state, searched prudently for a compromise. Saying Wilkes had acted without instructions, which was true, Seward freed Mason and Slidell and allowed them to resume their trip.

As it happened, Mason and Slidell failed to find allies in Europe, and the British never challenged the blockade. Union naval and land forces cooperated in 1861–62 to tighten the hold by seizing control of the North Carolina sounds, Port Royal Sound in South Carolina, the mouth of the Savannah River in Georgia, and other strategic points along the Confederate seaboard.

On August 28 and 29, 1861, Stringham's warships bombarded two forts guarding Hatteras Inlet, North Carolina. This enabled troops that had landed from the sea to gain control of the strong points without firing a shot. The capture of the Outer Banks—the long, narrow strip of sand that shelters the inland waterways of Pamlico and Albemarle Sounds—allowed the Federals to begin clearing out the "pirates' nest" of privateers and blockade runners operating there.

Two months later, the Federals moved again, this time to seize Port Royal Sound, a large anchorage midway between the important ports of Charleston and Savannah. Flag Officer Samuel DuPont assembled 75 vessels, including 25 transports carrying 17,000 troops, and the Port Royal expedition sailed from Hampton Roads, Virginia, on October 29, 1861. On November 7, DuPont's heavy warships, carrying 155 guns, opened fire on the two forts that guarded the approach to the sound.

DuPont sent his ships on a circular course past the forts. Firing broadsides as they glided by, the ships' motion made them a difficult target for the Confederate gunners, who were further handicapped by a light breeze that carried smoke from their own discharges back into their faces. After several hours of bombardment, the forts were abandoned. The 7th Connecticut Infantry Regiment came ashore and entered Fort Walker that afternoon. Other Union troops occupied Fort Beauregard later that night.

The capture of the Hatteras Inlet forts had not, however, entirely wiped out the pirates' nest, nor had it stopped all trade along the North Carolina coast. For that, the Federals needed Roanoke Island, which controlled the passage between Albemarle and Pamlico Sounds. On February 7, 1862, 13,000 Union troops under Gen. Ambrose E. Burnside landed on Roanoke. By midafternoon of the next day they had routed the defenders, taking 2,675 prisoners and 32 guns. Over the next several weeks, Union forces captured all the ports on the North Carolina sounds.

The Federal presence threatened nearby Norfolk, too, where Confederate shipbuilders were furiously at work on a not-so-secret weapon.

On March 8, 1862, the CSS *Virginia*—the former USS *Merrimack* converted into an ironclad—rammed and sank the USS *Cumberland*. *(Library of Congress)*

On March 9, 1862, the *Monitor* and the *Merrimack* engaged in the first battle between two ironclad ships. It ended in a draw, and neither ship ever fought in another battle. *(Library of Congress)*

Panicky Federals had abandoned the Norfolk Navy Yard, the country's most important naval base, in April 1861, setting fires, spiking cannon, and scuttling several ships, including the steam frigate USS *Merrimack.* By July, the Confederates had raised the ship, hosed the muck from her engines, and begun sheathing the superstructure with iron plating. When rebuilt, the *Merrimack,* though clumsy and overweight, carried 10 heavy guns, and its armor made it all but invincible.

Spies passed on the news of the reborn warship, and the Federals were soon at work on their own ironclad. Iron casing four and one-half inches thick protected the USS *Monitor,* which carried two big guns in a unique revolving turret. Naval traditionalists doubted that this strange ship would be able to stay afloat, even in harbor. And supporters conceded that the *Monitor* looked like nothing else on the sea— some of them said it resembled "a cheesebox on a raft."

On March 8, 1862, as General McClellan was planning his move to the Virginia Peninsula, the *Merrimack,* renamed the CSS *Virginia,* steamed out of Norfolk on its shakedown cruise. Watching from shore, an Indiana soldier thought the ship looked like "a house submerged to the eaves, borne onward by the flood." The strange vessel moved ponderously out into the broad estuary of Hampton Roads, heading toward five Union warships of the blockading squadron lying at anchor there.

The *Merrimack*'s captain, Franklin Buchanan, decided he might as well test the ship's guns along with its engines, so he steered for the Union warships. Men rushed to the guns of these stately wooden vessels, soon to be as obsolete as Greek galleys. "As she came plowing through the water toward our port bow, she looked like a huge half-submerged crocodile," said A. B. Smith, pilot of the sailing sloop USS *Cumberland*. Moving at a top speed of five knots, the *Merrimack* rammed the *Cumberland*, tearing a huge hole in the Federal ship's oaken side. The *Cumberland* continued firing bravely as it settled into the harbor mud, but the shots made no impression on the *Merrimack*'s iron skin. Buchanan turned next to the old frigate USS *Congress*, and the *Merrimack*'s broadsides soon set that ship ablaze. The *Congress* burned fiercely for several hours. After midnight, when the fire finally reached the *Congress*'s powder store, the vessel burst into a million wooden fragments.

After disposing of the *Congress*, the *Merrimack* broke off the battle and returned to Norfolk, expecting to complete the destruction of the Union fleet the next day. It reckoned without the weird little *Monitor*, however. The Union ironclad had arrived from Brooklyn during the night, and it eased into Hampton Roads alongside the USS *Minnesota* early on March 9. There it lay waiting, steam up, for the *Merrimack*'s return. "We thought at first it was a raft on which one of the *Minnesota*'s boilers was being taken to shore for repairs," a *Merrimack* midshipman recalled of his ship's first sighting of the *Monitor*, "and when suddenly a shot was fired from her turret we imagined an accidental explosion of some kind had taken place on the raft."

The *Monitor* soon began circling the *Merrimack* "like a fierce dog." But neither ship could do much damage to the other. After four hours of mutual pounding, the *Merrimack* scored a direct hit on the *Monitor*'s pilot house, temporarily blinding the captain, John L. Worden. "Sheer off," the dazed and sightless Worden ordered, and the Union ironclad retreated into the shallows. The *Merrimack*, ready enough to call it a day, turned and headed back to Norfolk, not responding when the *Monitor*, recovered now, issued a challenge to resume the battle.

"CHEESEBOX ON A RAFT"

Sensing the U.S. Navy's reluctance to experiment, Congress in August 1861 passed legislation for the construction of three prototype ironclad warships. The first two were conventional vessels covered with iron sheathing. The third, *Monitor,* effected a revolution in naval architecture.

John Ericsson, the builder, designed a flat-decked ship, 172 feet long, protected by armor plating four and one-half inches thick with a revolving turret housing two 11-inch naval guns. In theory, the *Monitor* would be fast, with a top speed of eight knots, maneuverable, and virtually indestructible. Ericsson himself suggested the name. "The impregnable and aggressive character of this structure will admonish the leaders of the Southern Rebellion," he wrote the Navy Department. "The iron-clad intruder will thus prove a severe monitor to those leaders."

Skeptics dubbed the ship "Ericsson's Folly" and doubted it would float. Ericsson launched the $275,000 vessel at his New York City shipyard on January 30, 1862. Five weeks later, fully equipped though untested, it sailed south for a date with the Confederate ironclad *Virginia,* the former Union ship *Merrimack.*

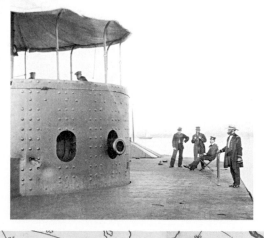

The deck of the *Monitor,* dented by the steel-pointed shot from the guns of the *Merrimack* during their fight in 1862 *(National Archives)*

The encounter made all the world's navies suddenly obsolete. No wooden ship could stand up to an ironclad. Interestingly, neither vessel ever fought again. Stranded by McClellan's advance up the peninsula, the *Merrimack*'s crew blew their ship up in May 1862. The *Monitor* went down in a storm off Cape Hatteras the following December.

David G. Farragut was chosen to command the Union naval assault on New Orleans because of his willingness to take great risks to obtain great results. *(National Archives)*

The Confederates could put up a good fight in a single engagement, but they were finding it impossible to concentrate adequate forces at every threatened point. Troops assigned to defend the Gulf Coast and New Orleans were required elsewhere, particularly to assist the hard-pressed Albert Sidney Johnston in Tennessee. By early April 1862, as the beaten Confederates were retreating from the Shiloh battlefield, 3,000 militiamen, a few gunboats, and two forts were New Orleans's sole protection against a Union invasion. Against this makeshift force, Federal flag officer David G. Farragut assembled a fleet of eight steam sloops, a sailing sloop, 14 gunboats, and 19 mortar schooners. By April 18, Farragut had his saltwater ships over the sandbars and in the Mississippi River just downstream of the forts, only 75 miles from New Orleans.

Sixty years old in 1862, Farragut had joined the navy as a midshipman at age nine. Because he was born in Tennessee and married to a

Virginian, his loyalty was suspect at first. But when Welles needed an energetic officer to command the New Orleans expedition he chose Farragut, because, Welles said, he would "more willingly take great risks to obtain great results than any officer in either army or navy."

The mortar schooners blasted away at Forts Jackson and St. Philip for six days, making a terrible noise and shifting rubble around but doing little serious damage. At 2 A.M. on April 24, Farragut ordered the fleet to weigh anchor and dash past the forts and through the chain barrier the Confederates had stretched across the river. He had prepared his vessels well. Chains hung overside protected the engines and powder stores. Tubs of brown river water were available at various points on the deck to douse fires. Sand and ashes had been strewn near the guns so the crews would not slip in the blood of the wounded as they worked.

Gunboats cut a gap in the chain wide enough for the ships to pass in a single file, and the first vessels got through untouched. Soon, though, the forts were delivering a heavy and accurate cannonade. "My signal quartermaster and my boy aide were both swept away from my side," an officer of the sloop USS *Pensacola* wrote afterward. "At daylight I found the right leg of my pantaloons and drawers cut away by the knees, and the skirt of my coat cut in a strip; yet my body was untouched."

Farragut's flagship, the USS *Hartford,* took several hits, caught fire, and temporarily ran aground. But Farragut pressed coolly on. By dawn, the fleet had completed the run past the forts, though at a cost of 37 dead and 149 wounded. The battered *Hartford* glided up to the quayside in New Orleans at 1 P.M. on April 25, and Farragut sent two officers through the streets to City Hall to demand a surrender. On April 30, the first of 18,000 Union troops arrived to occupy the South's largest city and most important port.

The Northern newspapers rejoiced. Union forces had taken New Orleans with ease, and it seemed the war must end soon. Sea power alone could not defeat Robert E. Lee on the battlefield, though the blockade would do much to weaken the Confederate armies, keeping them ill-clad, often barefoot, and frequently hungry. After the battle between the *Monitor* and *Merrimack,* Civil War naval engagements were nearly always one-sided. Union vessels could strike at rebel interests anywhere, from Hatteras to the English Channel to the coast of Mexico. Stringham and Farragut proved that naval forces in concert

On April 24, 1862, as Com. David Farragut led his fleet through the Confederate forts and ships on the Mississippi, the USS *Mississippi* destroyed the Confederate ram CSS *Manassas*. *(Library of Congress)*

with troops could assault and capture coastal forts protecting strategic harbors. They could steam hundreds of miles up the Mississippi and help cut the Confederate nation in half.

Meanwhile, far from the tedium of the blockade, McClellan's Virginia offensive was about to fail, and Lee soon would deliver a blow that would stagger the Union and extinguish all hope for an early end to the fighting. The land war ground on—but the long, slow, almost unnoticed application of sea power quietly pushed the Confederacy toward defeat.

AMERICA'S
BLOODIEST DAY

By midsummer 1862, President Lincoln badly needed a victory. The Union war effort had begun to falter, and the springtime successes in Kentucky and Tennessee and along the Mississippi River had not been sustained. By the end of June, General McClellan's Army of the Potomac had been defeated in the Battles of the Seven Days, the drive on Richmond abandoned. In early July, President Lincoln issued a call for another 300,000 volunteer soldiers. Earlier enthusiasm had faded, though, and even the offer of a $25 advance on the $100 bounty paid at discharge failed to spur enlistments.

At the same time, political attitudes toward the war were hardening in the North. After the Seven Days battles, many came to doubt whether a limited war could be fought. "When I say that this rebellion has its source and life in slavery, I only repeat a simple truism," said abolitionist congressman George W. Julian of Indiana. Lincoln, pressured by the Radical Republicans in Congress, gradually came to agree. The North would fight not just to restore the Union, he decided, but to end slavery too.

Some cautious steps had already been taken. In March 1862, army officers were forbidden to return fugitive slaves to their masters, whether or not they were loyal to the Union. The following month, Congress approved a measure offering compensation to owners who voluntarily freed their slaves. Finally, in July, in an action that sent waves of anger through the Confederacy, Congress empowered the president to enlist blacks in the military services.

For the time being, Lincoln resisted pressures from radicals to move faster. Leading generals, including McClellan, opposed mixing up the issues of slavery and disunion, suggesting that their troops would refuse to fight to free Southern blacks. The president had to balance their views against those of the abolitionists, who pressed for immediate freedom for slaves everywhere. "My paramount object is to save the Union," Lincoln said in a letter to *New York Tribune* editor Horace Greeley. "If I could save the Union without freeing any slave I would do it, and if I could save the Union by freeing some and leaving others alone I would also do that. What I do about slavery . . . I do because I believe it helps save the Union."

Even as Lincoln wrote that letter, a preliminary emancipation proclamation lay in his desk. By authority of the president's war powers, the proclamation would free slaves in the rebel states. But battlefield setbacks caused him to delay issuing it. For now, Washington itself seemed secure, protected by a newly formed army under the aggressive Gen. John Pope. In the West, however, the Union drive to reopen the Mississippi River had stalled in front of the fortress of Vicksburg. Confederate armies had moved into eastern Tennessee and were preparing an invasion of Kentucky that would threaten Federal control of the Ohio River valley. In northern Virginia, Robert E. Lee's army was rested and on the move again. In these conditions, issuing an unenforceable proclamation freeing the slaves would be taken as a sign of weakness—of, in the words of Secretary of State Seward, "a cry for help, our last shriek, on the retreat."

Lee decided to attack Pope before McClellan's army could return from the Virginia Peninsula to reinforce him. For 10 days in mid-August, the two armies maneuvered along the Rappahannock River in northern Virginia. Lee had already shown dazzling military skills. He had shown, too, a willingness to take risks, to stake everything on a bold move. Now, tiring of inconclusive march and countermarch, he gambled. Lee divided his army, hoping to destroy Pope, then turn on McClellan when he arrived.

Lee sent 24,000 men under Stonewall Jackson on a long flanking march to the north, with the aim of cutting the railroad line supplying Pope. On August 26, Jackson's hungry "foot cavalry" fell upon the Federal supply base in Manassas near the old Bull Run battlefield of 1861. The rebels took whatever they could carry, set the rest ablaze, wrecked the railroad, and vanished.

As Pope turned to meet this threat 25 miles in his rear, Lee marched north from the Rappahannock to rejoin Jackson, who had gone to ground on a wooded ridge two miles west of the site of the First Battle of Bull Run. For two days, a bewildered Pope wandered in search of his enemy. Jackson finally came out to meet him at Groveton on August 28. A fierce battle there left many dead and wounded on both sides, but settled nothing.

The Second Battle of Bull Run began on August 29 with a series of Federal assaults on strong rebel defenses. Lee's vanguard arrived during the day to reinforce Jackson, and the fighting ended in a draw. The Confederates pulled back slightly to stronger defensive positions, an adjustment Pope mistook for a retreat. That evening, he telegraphed a victory message to Washington.

The next morning the Federals encountered ferocious resistance when they renewed the attack. Lee allowed Pope's assault to develop fully, then hurled Gen. James Longstreet's corps into the Federal left flank. The disoriented Yankees broke under the pressure and retreated raggedly toward Washington. Pope recovered sufficiently to fight a successful rearguard action at Chantilly on September 1, then withdrew into the Washington defense lines.

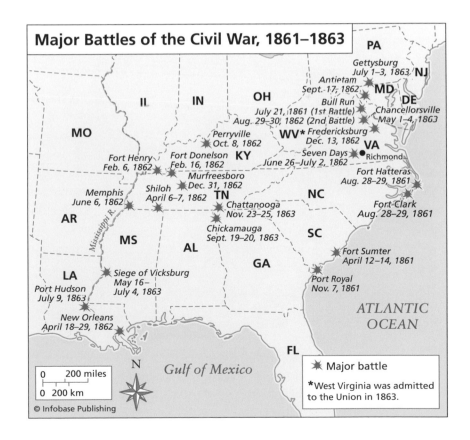

Major Battles of the Civil War, 1861–1863

The battle spread alarm through the North, just as the first Bull Run battle had done the year before. Once again, there were fears for the safety of the capital; once again, government clerks formed militia companies for the city's defense. Lincoln acted decisively. He merged Pope's army with McClellan's and banished Pope himself to the Minnesota frontier to fight Indians. Overall command went to McClellan. "We must use what tools we have," the president told his secretary, John Hay, apologetically. "There is no man in the Army who can lick these troops of ours into shape half so well as he. . . . If he can't fight himself, he excels in making others ready to fight."

Lee, however, allowed McClellan little time to repair the army. He meant to keep the initiative. Lee knew his forces were not strong enough to attack the Federals in their Washington defenses. He could lure McClellan out into the old northern Virginia battlefields, but a year's campaigning had left the region war-damaged and stripped of food and other supplies. North of the Potomac, though, lay the rich state of Maryland, untouched by war. Maryland's farmers were about

At the second battle at Bull Run, or Manassas, on August 29–30, 1862, Confederate troops under Gen. Robert E. Lee effectively defeated the Union troops. (*Library of Congress*)

to take in the year's harvest; Maryland's shops and warehouses were full of shoes, clothes, and other necessities. An invasion could have political consequences, too—after all, Maryland was a slave state. Perhaps citizens there might rally to the Confederacy. A new state joining the rebellion might even lead the British to offer diplomatic recognition. If nothing else, Lee could embarrass the Union military and political leadership and give Northerners a dose of war's bitter realities.

"The Lord bless your dirty ragged souls," an old woman called out to the Confederates as they passed through Leesburg, Virginia, on the way to the Potomac fords. Lee's army began crossing the half-mile-wide Potomac at White's Ford, about 30 miles north of Washington, during the night of September 4. As the troops waded into the warm, waist-deep water, the regimental bands played "Maryland, My Maryland."

Lee approached the Potomac with 55,000 men, but straggling soon began to cut into his strength. Some soldiers, especially those from western North Carolina and Tennessee, refused to go north, saying they had enlisted to protect their homeland, not to take part in an invasion. Others, tired, hungry, and footsore, simply could not keep up. They melted away in ones and twos.

Most of the troops were confident, though, and they marched jauntily in their tattered clothes and bare feet. They were dirty too—unshaven and crawling with lice. Hunger had left them thin and drawn. "Our menu consists of apples and corn," wrote Alexander Hunter, a private in the 17th Virginia. "We toasted, we burned, we stewed, we boiled, we roasted these two together, and singly, until there was not a man whose form had not caved in, and who had not a bad attack of diarrhea."

"They were the dirtiest men I ever saw," a citizen of Frederick, Maryland, recalled of the Confederates' arrival there on September 6, "a most ragged, lean and hungry set of wolves. Yet there was a dash about them that the northern men lacked."

For three days, Lee's army fed and rested in Frederick. The rebels had lost at least 10,000 men to straggling and sickness. What remained, though, were the army's toughest, most battleworthy veterans. "None but heroes are left," one soldier wrote home.

McClellan left Washington in cautious pursuit of Lee on September 7, the army marching slowly northwestward toward Frederick. Lee, meanwhile, decided to gamble yet again. Although he had planned to live off the land, he needed one safe supply route. To open a supply line from Virginia's Shenandoah Valley, Lee had to capture the 13,000-man-strong Federal garrison at Harpers Ferry.

He sent two-thirds of his strength under Stonewall Jackson to Harpers Ferry, then took the remaining forces west across the long ridge of South Mountain to Boonsboro and Hagerstown. Here Lee would wait for Jackson. When he returned, the reunited army would strike north into Pennsylvania. The first objective would be the railroad bridge over the Susquehanna River near Harrisburg, a key link in the North's east-west transportation system.

With his army safely behind South Mountain's 50-mile-long spine, Lee counted on McClellan's timidity to give him time to carry out the Harpers Ferry operation. "He is an able general but a very cautious one," rebel general John G. Walker quoted Lee as saying of McClellan. "His army is in a very demoralized and chaotic condition, and will not be prepared for offensive operations—or he will not think it so—for three or four weeks. Before that time I hope to be on the Susquehanna."

As McClellan plodded toward South Mountain, he had little idea of Lee's objectives, or even of his whereabouts. Confederate cavalry under J. E. B. Stuart dropped an impenetrable veil over Lee's movements, chasing off the Federal squadrons before they could come within miles of the rebel columns. McClellan and his superiors in Washington were in a constant state of uncertainty. Lee, they believed, could be headed for Washington, Baltimore, or even Philadelphia. Then fortune presented McClellan with a full account of Lee's plans. In a meadow near Frederick on September 13, two soldiers of the 27th Indiana found a copy of Lee's Special Orders 191, which detailed the division of the army for the Harpers Ferry attack. "Here is a paper with which if I cannot whip Bobbie Lee, I will be willing to go home," McClellan gleefully told one of his generals.

Lee's daring had given McClellan the opportunity to destroy the Army of Northern Virginia piece by piece. He could overwhelm Lee's small force around Boonsboro, then turn south and maul Jackson at Harpers Ferry. But McClellan delayed. The army did not move until the morning of September 14, some 18 hours after McClellan had been put in possession of Lee's plans—and after Lee himself had learned of the security lapse that threatened his destruction. A pro-rebel Marylander had seen McClellan's excited reaction to Special Orders 191 and had alerted Lee. He at once sent forces to defend the passes through

New York infantry at Maryland Heights, Harpers Ferry. General Lee sent Stonewall Jackson with troops to capture Harpers Ferry and open a supply line between the Shenandoah Valley in Virginia and Lee's Confederate army. *(National Archives)*

South Mountain and ordered the army to concentrate in the little town of Sharpsburg on Antietam Creek.

In sharp battles at Turner's and Crampton's gaps in South Mountain on September 14, outnumbered Confederate forces held off Union attacks long enough to cover Lee's withdrawal to Sharpsburg. At Harpers Ferry, 17 miles to the south, Jackson responded with characteristic energy, forcing the Federal garrison's surrender on September 15. Leaving A. P. Hill's division behind to collect the spoils, he turned and headed for Sharpsburg.

Advance elements of McClellan's army arrived at Antietam Creek on September 15, though too late in the day, in the general's judgment, to initiate a battle. McClellan remained idle on September 16 too, when Jackson's divisions began taking their places in the Confederate battle line. Even with the addition of Jackson's troops, McClellan had nearly twice Lee's numbers, although he did not know this. Faulty intelligence and his own caution had led him to wildly overestimate his opponent's strength. McClellan believed Lee faced him with 100,000 men. In actuality, at nightfall on September 16, 70,000 Federals were opposite only 40,000 rebels.

Lee had chosen his ground well. The army was deployed on a long ridge overlooking the valley of Antietam Creek. Here the terrain provided good natural cover. Troops could fire from behind split-rail fences and outcroppings of rock. There were small stands of trees and, along one section of the line, a half-mile length of country lane worn several feet below ground level by the passage of generations of farm wagons. The army would fight with the Potomac at its back, however, less than a mile away and with only a single ford for crossing. Even so, Lee confidently awaited McClellan's attack.

At dawn on Wednesday, September 17, the Federals opened the action to begin what would be America's bloodiest single day of fighting. As the day advanced, the Battle of Antietam resolved itself into three separate engagements, each clash flaring up around a landmark: in the north, a church; in the center, the sunken road; in the south, a bridge. The 12-hour ordeal of flame, smoke, thunder, and shrieking agony left 23,000 men killed or wounded, most of them in the course of attacking or defending these three landmarks.

McClellan aimed the first blow from the north, at the Confederate left flank. Gen. Joseph Hooker's 8,700-man I Corps went forward out of a thick ground fog at 5:30 A.M. Advancing on a half-mile-wide front astride the Hagerstown Turnpike, the Yankees crossed a cornfield, with woods on either side, en route to their first objective, the plain, white-washed brick church of the German Baptist Brethren—the Dunker church. As the Federals came on, the cannonade roared overhead. Soon the leading brigades were furiously engaged, exchanging volley after volley with the rebel defenders.

"They stood and shot one another till the lines melted away like wax," wrote Isaac Hall of the 97th New York. Hall and the others fought and died in what was at the time an anonymous landscape. Later, these woodlots and farmlands would be given proper names: East Woods, West Woods, the Cornfield—once-peaceful places forever transformed by a morning's violence.

Hall was recalling the fight in the East Woods, where attackers and defenders were locked in a stalemate. Two hundred yards to the west, however, the Federals made progress for a time. By 6:30 A.M., the Iron Brigade, comprised of Indiana and Wisconsin regiments, had

At the Battle of Antietam in Maryland, on September 17, 1862, Union troops known as the "Iron Brigade" charged the Confederate forces near the Dunker church. Like the entire day's engagements, this one ended in a costly stalemate. *(Library of Congress)*

pressed to within 300 yards of the Dunker church. "The hostile battle lines opened a tremendous fire," wrote Maj. Rufus Dawes of the 6th Wisconsin. "Men were knocked out of the ranks by the dozens. But we jumped over the fence, and pushed on, loading, firing and shouting as we advanced." The Confederate line sagged, but before the Iron Brigade could break it the 1st Texas under John B. Hood launched a furious counterattack, yipping the rebel yell as they closed on the Yankees.

Hooker's men gained no further ground. Hood had broken the I Corps advance. By 7:30 A.M., Hooker's corps had taken 2,600 casualties and was through for the day. The Texans had suffered 186 killed and wounded out of 226 engaged—the heaviest loss in any regiment during the entire war.

"Where is your division?" someone asked Hood later.

"Dead on the field," he replied.

As Hooker withdrew, the fresh XII Corps under Joseph Mansfield appeared, trying roughly the same line of attack with the same objectives. The XII Corps had a roughly similar experience. For two bloody hours, the fighting surged back and forth over the Cornfield and the

THE ANTIETAM KILLING GROUND

Two days after the Battle of Antietam, the colonel commanding the 14th Indiana infantry took up pen and paper to prepare his official report. The result, published with thousands of like documents in the *Official Record of the War of the Rebellion* in the 1880s, is a model specimen of bureaucratic prose, flat, undistinguished, colorless. Even so, the horror of William Barlow's morning on the battlefield of September 17, 1862, echoes in every passage.

"We passed through an orchard, emerging into a plowed field, receiving during the execution of this movement a rapid fire from the enemy; this about 8 o'clock A.M.," Barlow wrote. "The contest continued here for near four hours, during which time the enemy poured upon us a terrific and murderous fire."

The troops used up every one of their 60 rounds of ammunition, replenishing their stocks from dead and wounded comrades. The Confederates in the 14th Indiana's front withdrew at noon, but the regiment's agonies had not yet ended. The men lay flat upon their arms until nightfall under a "hot fire" from the rebel artillery. Two days later, Barlow reported losses of 181 killed and wounded out of a total of 320 engaged—a casualty rate of 57 percent.

"General, our record is a proud one," Barlow concluded, "but one which can never be thought of save with feelings of the most intense sorrow for the brave dead and wounded."

West Woods. This time, a Federal charge came within 200 yards of the Dunker church. Again the rebels counterattacked, and again the Yankees fell back.

By midmorning, the fighting on the Confederate left had died out, and the action shifted to the center of the line. Here, rebels under D. H. Hill were in good defensive positions along a half-mile stretch of country road so eroded that it formed a natural trench. Soon, it would be called Bloody Lane. McClellan ordered the Federal II Corps to advance in the center, and from 10 A.M. on, Hill's regiments repulsed successive waves of Yankees.

"My rifles flamed and roared in the Federals' faces like a blinding blaze of lightning accompanied by a quick and deadly thunderbolt," Col. John B. Gordon of the 6th Alabama recalled. "The effect was appalling. The entire front line, with few exceptions, went down in the consuming blast. Before [the Yankees'] rear lines could recover, my exultant men were on their feet, devouring them with successive volleys."

Still, II Corps kept up the pressure. Eventually two New York regiments managed to creep around the flank of Bloody Lane and begin pouring a murderous fire into the rebels crouching the length of it. At about the same time, a Confederate officer misunderstood an order to wheel to meet this flanking fire and instead pulled his regiment out of the line. Federal troops streamed through the gap and pushed the rebels back toward Sharpsburg.

For a moment, a decisive victory seemed within McClellan's reach. "We were already badly whipped, and were only holding our ground by sheer force of desperation," Confederate general James Longstreet wrote afterward. But McClellan, fearing a Confederate counterattack, refused to commit his 20,000-man reserve, giving Lee time to shift forces to meet the threat in the center. Soon Longstreet

The signal tower at Elk Mountain, overlooking the battlefield at Antietam, September 1862 *(National Archives)*

had formed a makeshift defensive line, and McClellan's moment had passed.

Fighting sputtered out in the center at about 2 P.M. By then, the third battle in the series had been under way for some time. McClellan ordered Gen. Ambrose E. Burnside's IX Corps to cross Antietam Creek by a 125-foot-long, 12-foot-wide stone bridge and attack the Confederate right flank. Burnside took his instructions literally, even though the creek was only 50 feet wide and nowhere more than four or five feet deep. Burnside funneled two heavy assaults onto the narrow bridge. Rebels on the high ground opposite the bridge broke up both attacks with ease.

Finally, under prodding from McClellan, Burnside launched a third effort, this time with support from a division sent belatedly to cross a ford

The Battle of Antietam (also known as the Battle of Sharpsburg) left the Union forces in place and the Confederates forced to withdraw, but only after what is known as "America's bloodiest day," owing to an estimated 6,000 dead or dying on the battlefield. *(Library of Congress)*

Major Allan Pinkerton, President Lincoln, and General John A. McClernand at Antietam, Maryland, in October 1862 *(National Archives)*

downstream. The 51st New York and the 51st Pennsylvania swept across the bridge and established positions on the far bank. Burnside paused to bring up ammunition for his assault brigades. From their positions on the heights, the rebels watched uneasily, awaiting the Federal onrush.

Finally the attack came. In the words of Private Hunter of the 17th Virginia, "The first thing we saw appear was the gilt eagle that surmounted the flagpole, then the top of the flag, next the flutter of the Stars and Stripes; then their hats came in sight; still rising, the faces emerged; next a range of curious eyes appeared, then such a hurrah as only the Yankee troops could give broke the stillness, and they surged towards us."

On the other side, Pvt. David Thompson of the 9th New York described the strange mental state that seems to come over soldiers at the moment of battle. "Between the physical fear of going forward and the moral fear of turning back, there is a predicament of exceptional awkwardness," he wrote. Then the New Yorkers advanced. Thompson, resolving the dilemma, advanced with them. "In a second the air was full of the hiss of bullets and the hurtle of grapeshot. The mental strain was so great that I saw at that moment [a] singular effect . . . the whole landscape for an instant turned slightly red."

Hunter and his comrades broke under the charge of the maddened Yankees, and the Federal surge carried to the outskirts of Sharpsburg. Again McClellan seemed on the verge of a complete victory. Again, though, Lee's gambler's luck held. Lee had summoned A. P. Hill from Harpers Ferry, and after quick-marching 17 miles in eight hours Hill and his 3,000-man division arrived just in time to stop the Federal advance. Again McClellan refused to follow up his initial success by committing his reserves. The spent IX Corps withdrew to the old rebel defensive positions above Antietam Creek.

Said Longstreet: "We were so badly crushed that at the close of the day ten thousand fresh troops could have come in and taken Lee's army and everything in it."

The Battle of Antietam—the Dunker church and the dead *(Library of Congress)*

But McClellan hesitated, and at sunset the sounds of battle died away. Next day the armies rested. Parties fanned out to tend to as many of the 17,000 wounded as lay within reach. For the 6,000 dead, equally divided between rebels and Yankees, there was no succor. But at least the killing had ended for now. Lee remained in line with 30,000 exhausted men through September 18, as though taunting McClellan to come at him again. The Federal commander declined the challenge. That night, Lee ordered a retreat across the Potomac. By dawn on September 19, the Army of Northern Virginia had gone.

McClellan failed to seize his chance to destroy Lee, but he had won a strategic victory, chasing the rebels off Northern soil. The result caused the British once again to draw back from offering diplomatic recognition and material aid to the Confederacy. And it gave President Lincoln the success he needed to carry the war deep into the enemy's country. On September 23, 1862, six days after the Battle of Antietam, he issued the preliminary Emancipation Proclamation—the order that would turn the limited war for reunion into a crusade against slavery.

The crusade would take time to build. The president concluded he had no power to interfere with slavery in the loyal states, and consequently the proclamation applied only to those in rebellion. It gave the rebel states until January 1, 1863, to rejoin the Union. If they failed to return by the deadline, advancing Federal armies would liberate the slaves, who would be "then, thenceforward and forever free."

THE WAR AT HOME

Behind the battle lines there were conflicts too. At home in the North and the South, dissident politicians attacked the conduct of the war and challenged basic war aims. Some Northern Democrats called for a negotiated peace with the Confederacy and for the preservation of slavery. Throughout the North and South, widespread and sometimes violent resistance to military conscription laws developed. The Confederacy tolerated dissent to a surprising degree, and tended to be lenient even with army deserters. In the North, however, authorities dealt with dissent by closing opposition newspapers and imprisoning the government's harshest critics without trial.

A booming Northern economy supplied the materials of war in abundance to the Federal armies, but it also enriched speculators and profiteers, created social tensions, and widened the gap between the rich and the poor. In the South, the economic system all but collapsed under the stress of war. The Union blockade cut off essential supplies of all kinds. Food shortages touched off riots in many Southern towns. Hunger behind the lines depleted the armies in the field. Thousands of civilians evaded military service, and thousands of soldiers deserted in order to return home and support their families.

After all the great battles, the hospital trains steamed slowly homeward with their freights of the mutilated and the dead, evidence for everyone to see of the war's awful price. No one had expected it to last so long, and weariness gradually set in. But in the early years, there remained, North and South, a powerful will to go on. Although the pace slowed, men continued to volunteer for the army. Women took their places in the factories and fields. Women who stayed at home did their share as well, knitting woolen caps, mufflers, and mittens for the troops, making bandages, aiding the widows and orphans of soldiers. Still the war ground on, and the casualty lists grew longer.

In both the North and the South, women knitted, wove, and sewed clothes for the men in the family, while they also ran farms and businesses, made bandages, and helped to care for the widows and orphans of soldiers. This 1864 etching by Adalbert Volck is of Confederate women. *(Library of Congress)*

From mid-1862 onward, President Lincoln fought what he called "the fire in the rear"—Democratic opposition to the war and to Republican war aims. Northern Democrats made Lincoln's call for the emancipation of slaves their chief issue in the autumn 1862 election campaign. Their arguments were frankly racist. They claimed the Republicans would allow "two or three million savages [to] overrun the North and enter into competition with the white laboring masses." Further, they argued, the freed slaves would force themselves socially on whites, in schools, churches, neighborhoods, and public places. One prominent Democrat, Ohio congressman Samuel S. Cox, warned that troops from his state would refuse to fight if a mass movement of blacks northward were the likely result. Echoing anti-Republican sentiment, Archbishop John Hughes proclaimed, "We Catholics, and a vast majority of our brave troops in the field, have not the slightest idea of carrying on a war that costs so much blood and treasure just to gratify a clique of abolitionists."

The Democrats cut into Republican strength in the 1862 election, taking the governorships of New York and New Jersey and winning 34 new congressional seats. The Republicans remained firmly in control, however, and their political losses were balanced by diplomatic gains. Before the election, Confederate leaders had still entertained faint hopes of British intervention. The election results, coming on the heels of the Emancipation Proclamation, seemed to end all chance of that. At first, the British were skeptical of Lincoln's proclamation. But as soon as it became apparent that the administration meant to enforce it, British antislavery opinion rallied strongly in support of the Union.

Still, a strong faction of Peace Democrats known as the Copperheads emerged in the North, and their call for reunion through negotiation rather than military conquest continued to irritate the Republicans. The Copperheads' leader, 42-year-old Clement L. Vallandigham of Ohio, lost his congressional reelection bid after the state's Republican legislature gerrymandered his district to assure a Republican majority, but the loss hardly silenced him. "It is the desire of my heart," Vallandigham had said after the fall of Fort Sumter, "to restore the Union, the Federal Union as it was 40 years ago." Now, he said, 18 months of fighting proved the South could not be conquered. War brought only "defeat, debt, taxation, sepulchers."

It brought, too, unprecedented breaches of civil liberties. On September 24, 1862, responding to opposition to a state-by-state draft for militia service, Lincoln suspended the writ of habeas corpus. This meant that now anyone suspected of disloyalty could be arrested and held without trial for an indefinite period. Almost at once, several hundred draft resisters—among them newspaper editors, judges, and elected officials—were imprisoned. Over a two-year period, federal agents made 13,000 such arrests. Some pretexts were absurd. In one case, authorities jailed a man for "hurrahing for Jeff Davis." In another, agents charged a New Jersey newspaper editor with obstructing the war effort. "Those who wish to be butchered please step forward," the editor had written. "All others will please stay at home and defy Old Abe and his minions to drag them from their families." For this, the editor was convicted and fined.

Vallandigham became the best-known victim of the federal government's war on dissent. He spoke so persistently against the war that General Burnside, commander of the military Department of the Ohio, ordered his arrest for disloyalty. Federal soldiers broke down the door

Clement L. Vallandigham of Ohio led a strong faction of Peace Democrats from the North, known as the Copperheads. *(National Archives)*

of Vallandigham's Dayton house on the night of May 1, 1863, and carried him off to jail. On May 6, a military commission convicted him of having uttered "disloyal sentiments and opinions." The commissioners ordered him imprisoned for the duration of the war. Lincoln commuted the sentence to banishment, however, and on May 25, Union cavalry escorted Vallandigham through the Confederate lines at Murfreesboro, Tennessee.

Lincoln vigorously defended this attempt to silence Vallandigham for his political beliefs. "Must I shoot a simple-minded soldier boy who deserts," the president asked, "while I must not touch a hair of a wily agitator who induces him to desert? I think that in such a case to silence the agitator and save the boy is not only constitutional, but withal a great mercy." Many Northerners evidently agreed. Vallandigham managed to make his way to Canada, where he carried on a campaign for the Ohio governorship from the border town of Windsor, Ontario. Lincoln took no chances that autumn. He granted furloughs to Ohio troops and leaves for federal clerks from the state so they could go home and vote for the administration candidate. As it turned out,

A print based on David Gilmour Blythe's fanciful painting of President
Lincoln writing the Emancipation Proclamation. In a cluttered study, Lincoln
sits in shirtsleeves and a single slipper, at work on the document near an
open window. His left hand is placed on a Bible that rests on a copy of the
Constitution in his lap. A bust of former president James Buchanan, who was
widely viewed as ineffectual against secessionism, hangs by a rope around
its neck from a bookcase behind Lincoln. The scales of justice appear in
the left corner, and a railsplitter's maul lies on the floor at Lincoln's feet.
Emboldened by the withdrawal of the Confederate forces after the Battle
of Antietam, Lincoln issued the preliminary Emancipation Proclamation on
September 23, 1862, not to go into effect until January 1, 1863. *(Library of
Congress)*

arrest and exile had not made a martyr of Vallandigham. He lost in a
landslide. "The people have voted in favor of the war," a discouraged
Copperhead wrote.

Even so, substantial opposition to the war remained, especially in
such midwestern states as Ohio, Indiana, and Illinois, with their large
Southern-born populations. Citing Lincoln's "wicked and unholy"

Emancipation Proclamation, the Democratic-controlled lower houses of the Indiana and Illinois legislatures passed resolutions calling for an armistice and a peace conference. Those states' Republican governors ignored the resolutions, but such calls had their effect, especially on recruiting efforts.

As the war continued on its bloody course, serious resistance developed to federal military conscription laws. To encourage enlistments, the authorities used recruiting posters, mass revival-style meetings, and appeals such as the famous "Father Abraham" poem, later set to music, by New York newspaper editor John Gibbons. "We are coming, Father Abraham, 300,000 more . . . From Mississippi's winding stream and England's shore. . . ." Combined with enlistment bonuses, or bounties, which could amount to several hundred dollars, the 1862 efforts produced 509,000 recruits.

By early 1863, however, battlefield losses had made it clear that many thousands more would be needed. In March, Congress enacted a conscription law calling for 300,000 new troops for three years. There were many loopholes. A draftee could volunteer before he was

Rioters in New York City destroy the draft office at Third Avenue and 46th Street, July 13, 1863. (*Library of Congress*)

mustered into service, thereby collecting the enlistment bounty and, in many cases, choosing the regiment in which he would serve. The law permitted a draftee to avoid service altogether by hiring a substitute, usually at a cost of several hundred dollars. It allowed liberally for medical exemptions, too. A Litchfield, Connecticut, physician named Beckwith became famous for selling bargain-rate $35 certificates declaring a draftee unfit for service.

Those who could not find a loophole resisted the draft by other means, some of them violent. In 1863, an estimated 20,000 men fled the state of Ohio to avoid service—they "skedaddled," in the word of the day. In Rush County, Indiana, two federal enrollment officers were ambushed and murdered. In some large cities, draft dodgers directed their hostilities toward blacks, who were increasingly competing with whites, especially Irish immigrants, for jobs. Blacks soon would "fill the shops, yards and other places of labor [and] compel us to compete with them for the support of our families," one working-class Democratic newspaper complained.

Draft officials in New York City began drawing names on Saturday, July 11, 1863, and the first 1,236 conscripts were listed in the next day's newspapers along with the casualties from the Battle of Gettysburg. On Monday, July 13, mobs formed in the streets, determined to interrupt the draft. They sacked and burned the draft office at Third Avenue and 46th Street, touching off three days of arson and murder in the wildest and most destructive rioting in American history.

By Monday evening the mob, largely Irish, had grown to 5,000 strong. Rioters stormed an armory at 21st Street and Second Avenue and seized weapons there. Another group attacked an orphanage for black children at Fifth Avenue and 43rd Street. "Burn the niggers' nest!" the mob screamed. The 237 children, all younger than 12, managed to escape through a back entrance before the rioters burst in and set the building afire. Roving gangs assaulted blacks at random. In one terrible incident, they hanged an African American named William Jones from a tree, then set fire to his corpse; in addition, dozens of blacks were beaten.

Militia reinforcements arrived Monday night, but street fighting continued through Tuesday. The 7th New York Infantry Regiment arrived on Wednesday. By Thursday, 4,000 troops were in the city, and calm had been largely restored. The rioting left 119 dead and 306 injured. When the authorities resumed the draft a month later, more

A federal recruiting poster in New York's City Hall Park in 1864 (*National Archives*)

than 40 regiments were stationed in and around the city to maintain order.

However widely detested, the conscription law did spur enlistments. After exemptions, commutations, and evasions, the 1863 draft yielded only 36,000 men. But several states, including Ohio, Indiana, and Illinois, provided so many volunteers that quotas were met and drafting turned out to be unnecessary. In 1864 and 1865, more than 1 million Northerners volunteered for service.

In the South, the quarrelsome Confederate Congress had taken a break from its disputes in April 1862 to pass North America's first conscription act. Like the Union law, it contained many loopholes, including a broadly unpopular one that exempted from service planters or overseers on plantations with more than 20 slaves. The exemption had two purposes: It provided security against slave insurrection, and it promoted greater efficiency in growing food for the armies and for city dwellers. But it also gave rise to a common Southern grievance: "It's a rich man's war and a poor man's fight." As in the North, thousands resisted the draft. Estimates are that fully half the conscripts never reported for duty.

Even more than the draft, Southerners on the home front hated impressment—the army's seizure of food, livestock, and farm equipment in return for near-worthless Confederate IOUs. The impressment gangs, especially the cavalry, swarmed over the countryside and stripped it bare. "We often hear persons say, 'The Yankees cannot do us any more harm than our own soldiers have done,'" the *Richmond Examiner* reported.

Still, the Southern troops were hardly better off than civilians at home, especially those in the cities. From the start, the Confederate government promoted the planting of food crops over cotton, but increased production failed to make up for the loss of imported beef, pork, corn, and flour from the North. Besides, the Confederacy's inefficient administration, interstate rivalries, and an inadequate transportation system made distribution of goods difficult. Food rotted in warehouses while many in the cities were near starvation. Some sections of the interior had abundant supplies while the armies went hungry.

"I saw a ham sell today for $350," Richmond diarist John B. Jones wrote wistfully. That may have been extreme, but prices for all goods rose, doubling, then doubling again and again. By 1863, the average family food bill had increased tenfold, to nearly $70 a week.

War-weary Southerners responded to shortages and inflated prices with violence. After a food riot in Salisbury, North Carolina, in March 1863, Mary C. Moore wrote to Governor Zebulon Vance to complain about prices—meat at one dollar per pound, flour at $50 per barrel. "There are few of us who can make over a dollar a day," she wrote, "and we have on average from three to five helpless children to support. . . . Now Sir how in the name of God are we to live?"

On April 2, rioting broke out in the Confederate capital. "We are starving," a hollow-eyed 18-year-old Richmond girl explained. "We are going to the bakeries and each of us will take a loaf of bread. That is little enough for the government to give us after it has taken all our men." The rioters, 100,000 strong, ransacked shops and warehouses, dispersing only after a column of troops—with President Davis at its head—threatened to fire into them.

In increasing numbers, Confederate soldiers at the front responded to the crisis behind the lines by deserting, usually in reaction to

"I HAVE SEEN MY HOME AGAIN"

Twenty-year-old Sarah Morgan returned to her home in Baton Rouge in late August 1862, three weeks after Union and Confederate forces fought a sharp battle on the outskirts. Federal troops had occupied the Louisiana capital in May and repulsed a Confederate counterattack in early August. Morgan described the aftermath of the battle and occupation in her diary.

"Just back of our house was all that remained of a nice brick cottage—namely, four crumbling walls," she wrote. "The offense was that the husband was fighting for the Confederacy, so the wife was made to suffer."

Morgan pushed on through the neighbor's ruin, left the buggy in the back lot, skipped down the alley, and entered the house through the front door. She paused in the parlor, looking around in "silent amazement," and could only laugh when her companion asked, "Well?" Union troops had visited her house too.

She took inventory of the room's missing contents. "I could hardly believe that Abraham Lincoln's officers had really come so low down as to steal in such a wholesale manner," she marveled. Her papier-mâché workbox, crochet work, knitting needles, and wool: All were gone. In the library, only a solitary copy of Tennyson's *Idylls of the King* remained.

Then she moved on to the dining room. The cut glass celery and preserve dishes and champagne glasses had disappeared. "There was plenty of split up furniture though." She stood before a shattered armoire in her mother's room. "I could hardly believe [it] the same that I had smoothed my hair before, as I left home three weeks previously." In her own room, visiting Yankees had shattered the tall mirror into a thousand fragments.

"I am satisfied," Sarah Morgan wrote. "I have seen my home again."

despairing news from home. "I can't manage a farm well enough to make a supporte," a Georgia woman wrote, asking the authorities to discharge her husband. M. M. Fortinberry explained the ordinary soldier's point of view to Mississippi governor Pettus: "To stay in the army at eleven dollars per month and if we live to get home pay sixty dollars for a sack of salt if we can get it at that and corn at two Dollars

Recruiting poster for the Confederate navy *(National Archives)*

per bushel . . . We are poor men and are willing to defend our country but our families come first."

Desertion became so common that Confederate commanders often tried to overlook it in hopes the men would eventually return. In August 1863, Davis declared an amnesty for deserters who came back within 20 days. A Virginia general, finding that most of his command "had all gone to their homes without leave," granted the men a 30-day furlough.

Many, however, had made a separate peace. Armed bands of deserters controlled entire Southern counties, keeping the military police at bay. A Confederate officer assigned to hunt deserters in hilly, sparsely settled western South Carolina suggested how difficult his task could be. "Almost every pass and valley [is] occupied by a deserter's cabin, who on the approach of a stranger flies to the rocks and ravines where, taking his perch, he sees and observes all that is going on, safe from the eyes of his pursuers," the officer wrote. By the end of 1863, of the Confederate army's 465,000 men, about 187,000—40 percent of the total—were absent, most of them at home with their families or, like the South Carolinians, hiding away from the authorities.

As desertion and want weakened the Confederate cause, the Federal forces grew steadily stronger. Union soldiers were adequately fed and well equipped beneficiaries of an unprecedented economic expansion set off by vast wartime demand. At home, goods of all kinds were in abundance, though prices were rising faster than wages for many working people. At first, the crisis of secession and war had sent Northern business into a slump. Northern merchants had to write off $300 million in Southern debts after Fort Sumter, causing a financial panic and a series of business failures. Some 6,000 businesses went under in 1861. The New England textile industry starved for lack of cotton. Midwestern farmers were hurt too, by the closing of the Mississippi and the loss of Southern markets.

But the Northern economy soon recovered under the stimulus of war. The federal government fueled the boom with capital as well as with war orders. Beginning in February 1862, Congress approved a series of legal tender acts authorizing the printing of $450 million in paper money—"greenbacks." The money, said *Harper's Magazine,* "circulated like the fertilizing dew," permitting businesses to expand and trade to flourish. As orders for arms, munitions, uniforms, and other military equipment came pouring in, Yankee ingenuity soon found substitutes for scarce materials and contrived mechanical means to counter the labor shortage that resulted when workers left the shops and factories for the army. Cotton mill owners converted to wool processing and soon were competing for contracts to make woolen cloth for army uniforms. Foundries in Pennsylvania and New York cast cannon. Shipyards in New England and along the midwestern rivers built warships and transports.

War accelerated the sometimes painful transition from handwork to mass production. In 1860, the shoe industry employed 123,000 men and women, and they did much of their work by hand. Two New Englanders, Lyman R. Blake and Gordon McKay, changed all that. They invented and marketed a machine that stitched the uppers of shoes to the soles. Blake and McKay demonstrated their new device on army shoes at first, providing boots for the Massachusetts Light Artillery and other Bay State regiments. By late 1863, many factories had installed Blake-McKay machines, enabling them to produce more shoes with fewer workers. "Buildings for shoe factories are going up in every direction; the hum of machinery is heard on every hand," the Lynn, Massachusetts, *Reporter* wrote.

Machinery came to the farm, too. More reapers and mowers were manufactured than ever before, and now their operators were often women. From 1861 to 1864, 197,000 men from Illinois, 70,000 Iowans, and 75,000 Wisconsin men joined the army; altogether, a full third of Northern farmers went off to war. Some enlistees used their bounties to buy labor-saving machinery for the wives they left behind: a reaper cost between $155 and $255, a seed drill cost $80, a cultivator cost about $30. As a popular song had it:

> Just take your gun and go,
> For Ruth can drive the oxen, John,
> and I can use the hoe.

"I met more women driving teams on the road and saw more at work in the fields than men," a traveler in Iowa wrote in 1862. "Our hired man left to enlist just as the corn planting commenced, so I shouldered the hoe," said an Iowa farm woman, as though to confirm the song. "I guess my services are as good as his." Despite the labor shortage, the Union states produced more wheat in 1862 and 1863 than the entire country had produced in 1859, a record year. Northern farms fed the nation and the army, and at the same time managed to double their exports to Europe.

Inevitably, corruption and speculation fed on wartime opportunities. A new class of profiteers grew rich by inflicting inferior goods on the troops—shoes with wooden soles, which were so uncomfortable that marching in them was nearly impossible; spoiled food; shirts and trousers that came apart in the first rain. Partly out of necessity, partly out of greed, textile manufacturers recycled woolen garments into a material for army uniforms called "shoddy." Disgusted soldiers soon applied the word to all kinds of defective products: not only clothes that unraveled, but shoes, blankets, and weapons too. "The world has seen its iron age, its silver age, its golden age and its brazen age," the New York *Herald* griped. "This is the age of shoddy."

Fortunes were to be made even out of so humble a product as salt, an essential dietary item for people and livestock and a necessity for preserving meat. The Onondaga Salt Company of New York had on its board of directors a speaker of the New York State Assembly and a powerful member of the tax-writing committee of the U.S. House of Representatives. Hard lobbying in the New York legislature gave the company a monopoly on the huge salt deposits near Syracuse. Working on the company's behalf in Washington, the congressman convinced his committee colleagues to approve three successive increases in the tariff on imported salt, effectively blocking foreign competition. The Onondaga Salt Company soon doubled the price of its product. The company eventually distributed $6 million in profits on an initial investment of only $160,000.

Speculators Arthur Eastman and Simon Stevens got rich even faster. Eastman bought a large stock of old rifles from the government for $3.50 each, then sold them to Stevens for $12.50. Stevens sold the entire stock back to the government, suddenly short of rifles, for $22 each.

At least Eastman and Stevens dealt with their own side. Some Northern dealers traded medicines, clothing, and even weapons to the South in exchange for precious cotton. "Every colonel, captain or quartermaster is in secret partnership with some operator in cotton," a federal investigator reported from Union-occupied Memphis. "Every soldier dreams of adding a bale of cotton to his monthly pay." The profits, and therefore the temptations, were enormous. Cotton could be bought for 20 cents a pound in Memphis, then sold in Boston for $1.90 a pound, a gain of nearly 1,000 percent. "I wish to fill my pockets," Mississippi planter James Alcorn said, explaining why he sold cotton to both sides throughout the war. Some army officers looked with envy on the fortunes being made behind the lines. "If I could now be at home, I would rake down largely!" Union general Cadwallader Washburn wrote his brother.

For every home-front grafter, though, there were many more farmers who collected firewood for women whose husbands were at the front and parsons' wives who knitted caps and socks for the soldiers. Children joined "Alert Clubs" and canvassed their neighborhoods for donations of crackers, jellies, and liquor to send to the Union troops. Schools sponsored collections of onions and potatoes—vegetables known to prevent scurvy—to supplement the soldiers' diet of hard bread and bacon. One Illinois town collected and shipped 500 bushels of potatoes.

Southern communities were equally resourceful. "Ladies who never worked before are hard at work making uniforms and tents," Catherine

A JUST WAR?

Thinkers on international law since St. Augustine (354–430) and St. Thomas Aquinas (1225–74) have developed seven principles or considerations to determine whether a war is "just" or legitimate. Although few Americans now debate the justice of Lincoln's decision to fight rather than allow the nation to fracture, the question is whether the Confederate cause could be considered just in terms of the principles articulated below.

1. A just war must be authorized by a legitimate authority.

   Proponents: The seceded states had a constitutional right to break away from the Union and to agree to establish their own independent system of confederated government.

   Opponents: As Daniel Webster argued, the Union is perpetual. And Lincoln observed that it was illogical to suggest that any governing system would contain a mechanism for its own destruction.

2. A just war can only be fought if it is started with right intentions, such as to redress a wrong.

   Proponents: Southerners fought for their rights, for their way of life, and for the protection of their (human) property. Fundamentally, they fought to preserve the political principles of the American Revolution.

   Opponents: The Union had done the South no wrong. As a candidate and as president-elect, Lincoln had offered ironclad assurances he would not interfere with slavery where it existed.

3. A war cannot be justified if its chances of success are low and it appears that it will drag on for an extended period.

   Proponents: The South could win by not losing. There was every prospect of a Confederate victory, because the North could only win by invading and occupying the Southern states.

   Opponents: The North's preponderance of manpower, matériel and industrial potential meant the Confederacy stood little chance of prevailing.

4. The damage of the war must be proportional to the injury suffered.

   Proponents: No sacrifice could be too great to assure that Southerners would live in freedom.

Opponents: Given the slight nature of the injury (that is, restrictions on the expansion of slavery), losses on both sides were catastrophic, though heavier proportionally for the Confederacy: One in every four Southern white men of military age was killed in battle or died of wounds or disease. Additionally, the war devastated the Southern economy, leaving it the poorest of U.S. regions for generations.

5. A just war should be waged only as a last resort.

Proponents: The rise to power of the "Black Republicans" and Lincoln's decision to assert federal authority over military outposts in Confederate territory left no room for compromise.

Opponents: Lincoln showed himself willing right up to the end to strike a political deal with the seceded states; his First Inaugural Address, delivered a month before the Confederates fired on Fort Sumter, famously offered the South an olive branch.

6. The real reason for the war should show right intent and should be the stated reason.

Proponents: Southern purposes and motives were plain: The associated states left the Union to preserve their freedom and the Southern way of life.

Opponents: The Southern states left the Union to protect their "Peculiar Institution"—they fought to preserve slavery. And, in any case, the Confederate government's demands of total war made a mockery of states' rights, one of the South's most cherished political principles.

7. The goal of a just war should be to reestablish peace. The peace established after the war should be better than the peace that would exist if the war were not fought.

Proponents: The South fought only to be independent and would have agreed to an armistice at any point in exchange for autonomous existence.

Opponents: Peace established a perpetual Union and left the South a ruin. For African Americans, the postwar Southern social and economic system—peonage and rigid racial separation, both fundamentally intact for nearly a century after Appomattox—represented but a slight improvement over slavery.

Wives and other women often accompanied the troops, performing such tasks as cooking or doing laundry. The woman shown here with three children in a camp of a Pennsylvania unit may have been the wife of the soldier standing beside her. *(Library of Congress)*

Edmonston, a North Carolina plantation mistress, wrote in her diary. In one month, the 20-member Society of Center Ridge, Alabama, sent off 422 shirts, 551 pairs of drawers, 80 pairs of socks, and six boxes of hospital stores to the battlefront. These relief activities left little time for popular pastimes such as croquet and lawn parties. In any case, those who indulged in them risked the disapproval of the most ardent patriots. "In all this death and destruction," a Virginian wrote icily, "the same chatter, patter, clatter."

But he was wrong. Life could never be the same. By 1863, the fighting had swept over huge areas of the South. Yankee invasions put thousands of refugees in motion, and those who stayed behind had to face the rapacious second-line troops and camp followers who trailed the fighting columns. "Yesterday we had another visit from the Lancers," wrote Virginian Judith McGuire. "Four officers went over every part of the house, even the drawers and trunks. . . . While I write, I have six wagons in view at my brother's barn, taking off his corn, and the choice

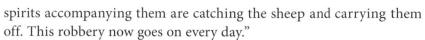

spirits accompanying them are catching the sheep and carrying them off. This robbery now goes on every day."

On the roads leading away from the Federal army advances, the hardships could be greater still. A Louisiana woman described the Yankees' arrival in Baton Rouge in May 1862: "Women searching for their babies along the road . . . others sitting in the dust crying and wringing their hands. All the talk of burning homes, houses knocked to pieces . . . famine, murder, desolation."

"Bitter cold this morning," South Carolina refugee Joseph LeConte recorded. "Water poured into the basin for face-washing freezes instantly. Ladies suffered extremely in the open wagons today. Made about 20 miles and stopped at the house of a very poor woman. She could give us shelter, but neither food nor bedding."

In the North, there were no plundering cavalry, no dazed and dull-eyed refugees, no destruction of battle. Still, if home front Northerners needed any reminders, there were the returned wounded, leaning on their crutches in front of the courthouse, and the absent dead. And from thousands of Northern homes came an outpouring of prayers, and of tangibles such as food, clothing, medicines, and money. "Inside the parlor windows the atmosphere has been very fluffy, with lint-making and the tearing of endless lengths of flannel and cotton bandages," New Yorker Jane Stuart Woolsey wrote a friend. "It seems as if we never were alive till now; never had a country till now."

JUBILEE

The guests began arriving at the camp of the 1st South Carolina Volunteers at midmorning of New Year's Day, 1863. The regiment, the first unit of freed slaves to be mustered into the Union army, had invited some 5,000 people for a formal reading of the Emancipation Proclamation. Many of the African Americans in and around Beaufort, South Carolina, had been nominally free since Federal forces had occupied the Sea Islands region two years before. Still, the proclamation became law this first day of January, and so the holiday and the regimental ceremonial carried a solemn significance.

As Thomas Wentworth Higginson, the regimental commander, recalled later, something of the buttoned-up formality of a Sunday pervaded the camp. There were the soldiers in their new blue uniforms, and women from the neighboring plantations wearing their best bright scarves. People milled about under the enormous branches of the live oaks, and beyond the officers on horseback watching from the edge of the grove glimmered the blue strip of Port Royal Sound. Sides of beef had been roasting all night over the fire pits. Molasses-and-water, spiced with ginger, had been mixed and allocated, one barrel for each of the regiment's 10 companies. Now the band of the 8th Marine Regiment tuned up on the flag-decked platform, and the dignitaries silently rehearsed their speeches. Moving around the camp, Colonel Higginson detected a thoughtfulness in the soldiers and their visitors, a quiet conviction, as though each had reached his own private conclusion about the day's meaning.

"I tink myself happy this New Year's Day, for salute my own Cunnel," one of the soldiers told Higginson. "Dis day las' year I was servant to a Cunnel ob Secesh; but now I hab de privilege to salute my own Cunnel."

The privilege had been slowly won, and still there were no assurances it would be permanent. There had been intense opposition in

This watercolor depicting an African American reading a newspaper with the headline "Presidential Proclamation, Slavery" conveys the feeling that swept the land in January 1863. *(Library of Congress)*

the North to arming freed slaves, and even those who supported the raising of black troops saw them as destined only for labor service and garrison duty, dull assignments that would free white regiments for the real business of war.

Higginson, a Harvard graduate and former Unitarian clergyman, had been one of the Secret Six conspirators who helped John Brown prepare the Harpers Ferry raid, and his commitment to the cause of black soldiery ran deep. He had arrived to take command of the 1st South Carolina in late November, and in the weeks since, he and his officers—all white—had worked hard to prepare the regiment for active service. The skeptics, he knew, were watching closely, and many were expecting failure.

"A single mutiny, such as happened in the infancy of a hundred regiments, a single miniature Bull Run, a stampede of desertions, and it would have been all over with us," Higginson wrote after the war. "The party of distrust would have got the upper hand, and there might not have been, during the whole contest, another effort to arm the negro."

So far, the experiment had been a success, and the New Year's celebration in Beaufort would celebrate the fact. At 11:30 A.M., the regimental chaplain read out President Lincoln's Emancipation Proclamation. Then, as Higginson stood to deliver the opening speech, two or three voices were raised, soon joined by others in the crowd:

> My country 'tis of thee
> Sweet land of liberty
> Of thee I sing!

Higginson motioned those on the platform to keep silent, and listened with something approaching reverence. "I never saw anything so electric," he wrote later. "It made all the other words cheap; it seemed the choked voice of a race at last unloosed. . . . When they stopped, there was nothing to do for it but to speak, and I went on; but the life of the whole day was in those people's song."

Union authorities had recruited the 1,000-man 1st South Carolina from the former slaves of the Sea Islands. When their masters fled with the arrival of Federal forces in November 1861, some 10,000 slaves were declared "contrabands of war." They continued to work the islands' cotton plantations, though now their overseers were Treasury Department agents, and they were paid wages of 25 cents a day.

For most of the South's 4 million slaves, the proclamation meant little until the liberating Union armies could come. Even then, blacks could be in great peril. "One night there'd be a gang of Secesh, and the next one, there'd come along a gang of Yankees," an Arkansas slave recounted. "Pa was 'fraid of both of them. Secesh said they'd kill him if he left his white folks. Yankees said they'd kill him if he didn't leave 'em."

Recalled a North Carolina freedman, "I guess we must have celebrated emancipation about 12 times. Every time a bunch of Northern soldiers would come through they would tell us we was free and we'd begin celebratin'. Before we would get through somebody else would tell us to go back to work and we would go."

At first, the Southern blacks who came under Union army control were collected in camps, where disease soon took a heavy toll. There were many cases, too, of maltreatment by the forces of liberation. The fighting troops often found the slaves to be in the way, and their attitudes toward them were hostile. "Many, very many of the soldiers and not a few of the officers have habitually treated the negroes with the coarsest and most brutal insolence and inhumanity," a New York war correspondent wrote, "never speaking to them but to curse and revile them."

Northern charitable organizations soon followed in the wake of the armies, however, bringing food, medicine, and clothing. Groups such as the American Missionary Association and the National Freedmen's Aid Society sent volunteers south to set up hospitals and schools. Along the South Carolina coast, some 9,000 former slaves were enrolled in 30 schools. The new black soldiers learned too. "Their love of the spellingbook is perfectly inexhaustible," Higginson wrote. "The chaplain is getting up a schoolhouse, where he will soon teach them as regularly as he can."

The South Carolina freedmen may have been more fortunate than most. For many blacks, especially those who continued to work on plantations, there seemed little difference between freedom and slavery. Southern planters often were allowed to take the oath of loyalty to the Union and continue to use blacks as farm labor for low wages. In Louisiana, Union military regulations required blacks to sign one-year

Frederick Douglass, ca. 1876 (*National Archives*)

labor contracts with planters, and barred them from leaving their plantations without a pass. "Any white man subjected to such restrictive and humiliating prohibitions would certainly call himself a slave," a black New Orleans newspaper argued.

New Orleans had a large free black community, and the first black Union regiments were raised there in the summer of 1862. Until then, the army had refused to accept black enlistees, whether freedmen or former slaves, even though the navy had accepted blacks from the outset. Although black sailors were most often firemen and stewards, a crew of six blacks served a gun aboard the USS *Minnesota* at Hatteras Inlet in August 1861, marking the first time blacks entered combat during the war.

African-American leaders pressed hard for the army to accept black recruits, viewing war service as a means to full acceptance. "Once let the black man get upon his person the letters U.S.; let him get an eagle on his button, and a musket on his shoulder and bullets in his pocket, and there is no power on earth which can deny he has earned the right to citizenship," said the former slave and abolition leader Frederick Douglass.

Douglass and other leaders made no special claims for black soldiers. "Give them a chance," Douglass asked. "I don't say they will fight better than other men. All I say is, Give them a chance!"

Still, many prominent Northerners argued strongly against recruiting blacks. Some claimed blacks were incapable of standing up to the strain of combat; others that they were intellectually incapable of learning the soldier's art. But increasing casualties and lagging enlistments finally persuaded the government to override these objections. In August 1862, the War Department announced it would recruit freed slaves. Gen. Benjamin Butler, the commander of the Union occupation forces in New Orleans, mustered in the first regiment of free blacks, the 1st Louisiana Native Guards, on September 27. In November, Higginson's 1st South Carolina became the first regiment of former slaves to be sworn into Federal service. The 1st Kansas became the first black regiment to see combat, losing 10 killed in a skirmish with Confederate guerrillas at Island Mounds, Missouri, in late October.

By autumn, Federal recruiters were seeking black enlistees in several Northern states, and more regiments of former slaves were being formed. When freedmen arrived to enlist, they were stripped and bathed; their old clothes were burned; and they were dressed in army blue. These simple actions effected a transformation. "This was the biggest thing that ever happened in my life. I felt like a man with a uniform on and a gun in my hand," a former slave recalled. "I felt freedom in my bones," another said.

Many black troops encountered Northern racism long before they were exposed to Confederate fire. They were segregated. They were officered by whites. They were paid less than whites—$10 a month, compared to $13 a month for white enlistees. And they were sometimes

EQUAL HAZARD, EQUAL PAY

The Union Army enlisted African-American volunteers reluctantly at first, then with increasing enthusiasm as casualties mounted. Black troops were dealt with unfairly in many ways, not least of which was pay. The War Department offered black privates $10 a month, three dollars less than whites, and deducted another three dollars for clothing.

In protest, the black 54th Massachusetts for 16 months in 1863 and 1864 refused to accept any pay at all, and some of the men even spoke openly of stacking arms and refusing duty. The regiment, assigned to the forces investing Charleston, South Carolina, had seen some combat duty along with the fatigue and monotony of siege duty on sandy, wind-swept Folly Island.

"I am not willing to fight for anything less than the white man fights for," wrote Cpl. John Payne, an Ohioan. "If a white man cannot support his family on seven dollars a month I cannot support mine on the same amount."

In July 1864, 74 soldiers petitioned President Lincoln for equal pay or discharge. "If immediate steps are not taken to Relieve us we will resort to more stringent measures," they wrote. Rumors spread of a possible mutiny. The Massachusetts legislature offered to make up the difference in pay, but the rank and file of the 54th rejected the compromise on principle.

"The men all say they will not take anything but full pay from the government while they are in the field," Sgt. William Logan wrote. "They say it would not be right for the state to pay what the government owes them unless she chooses to draw us home and pay us the whole amount."

The War Department relented finally, sending an army paymaster to Folly Island to distribute the full $13 a month to the men of the 54th Massachusetts. The regiment took part in the battle of Honey Hill a few weeks later, suffering heavy casualties—some 100 men killed or wounded.

subjected to insult and injury from white troops. "Jack what do you think about them dam niger Regiments," an untutored member of the 90th Pennsylvania wrote a soldier friend. "They better not send any of them out hear for if they do our own Soldiers hate a niger more than they do a Reb."

Firsthand experience of slavery softened the attitudes of some Federals. "This cursed slavery that gives one man power over another to whip or do as he pleases with him . . . I would just like to see a man whipping a negro. I would try the virtue of my sword if he did not stop it," a New York soldier wrote. And many white officers—they were all volunteers, and many had experience as noncommissioned officers in white regiments—were deeply impressed by the black troops they led. "A great many have the idea that the entire negro race are vastly their inferiors," a captain in a black regiment wrote his wife. "A few weeks of calm unprejudiced life [in camp] would disabuse them. . . . I know that many are vastly the superiors of those who would condemn them to a life of brutal degradation."

The new regiments of free blacks and former slaves soon had answers for those who claimed blacks could not fight. By the spring

Company E, 4th U.S. Colored Troops *(National Archives)*

of 1863, the new units were seeing their first heavy combat. At Port Hudson, Louisiana, in late May, two regiments proved that black troops could throw themselves at the enemy with the same reckless courage as white ones.

The Louisianans were part of a Union force that moved on Port Hudson in conjunction with Grant's campaign to take the Mississippi River stronghold of Vicksburg. The Federals found 6,000 Confederates entrenched outside the town, protected by high ground and wetland. They decided to attack anyway. On the morning of May 27, the 1st and 3rd Louisiana Native Guards went in with the first assault wave.

The Louisianans struggled through swampland, dense undergrowth, and fallen trees while the rebels poured down volley after volley from bluffs overlooking their line of attack. The two regiments charged at least three times into the Port Hudson defenses, and were thrown back each time. Despite heavy losses, they fought with courage and skill. Some continued to fight on despite serious wounds. One soldier, his leg nearly severed, "sat with his leg in a swing and bleeding and fired thirty rounds of Ammunition," one survivor reported. Another wounded man refused to go to the rear for treatment, saying "I guess I can gib 'em some more yet."

In this first general engagement for black troops, the Louisianans lost more than 20 percent of their regiment as casualties before Union commanders called off the assault. Though their attack failed, it convinced many doubters of the fighting abilities of blacks. "The man who says the negro will not fight is a coward," Union general Benjamin Butler wrote. "His soul is blacker than the dead faces of these dead negroes, upturned to heaven in solemn protest against him and his prejudices."

Ten days later, at Milliken's Bend on the Mississippi north of Vicksburg, blacks proved equally adept on the defensive. There a brigade of Confederates attacked two regiments of poorly armed and ill-trained black soldiers. The defenders stood, however, and drove off a series of rebel assaults. In the aftermath, the attackers murdered several black prisoners, and others were later sold as slaves. "A very large number of negroes were killed and wounded," reported Confederate general Richard Taylor, who favored dealing with captured blacks immediately on the battlefield, "and, unfortunately, some 50, with two of their white officers, captured."

Confederate troops reacted furiously in combat encounters with blacks. Senior Confederate officials urged military commanders to turn over captured blacks and their white officers to the states, where they could be tried for inciting slave insurrection. The penalty for this was, of course, death. As at Milliken's Bend, rebels sometimes executed wounded or captured blacks. Black troops were occasionally "shot while trying to escape." After one skirmish, a North Carolina soldier wrote, "Several [blacks were] taken prisoner & afterwards either bayoneted or burnt. The men were perfectly exasperated at the idea of negroes opposed to them & rushed at them like so many devils."

Word of such atrocities soon spread, and African Americans went into battle knowing they risked torture and execution as well as the accepted hazards of combat. Most were unintimidated, however. They had much at stake, free blacks and former slaves alike. "We are fighting for liberty and right," a black sergeant declared, "and we intend to follow the old flag while there is a man left to hold it up to the breeze of heaven. Slavery must and shall pass away."

Northern recruiters tapped the antislavery impulse to raise black troops and white officers to lead them. The most famous black regiment, the 54th Massachusetts, contained as many recruits from midwestern states as from Massachusetts. Some of the 54th's officers, including the regimental commander, Robert Gould Shaw, were the sons of prominent abolitionists, and two of Frederick Douglass's sons served in the ranks.

On May 28, 1863, the 54th Massachusetts paraded through the streets of Boston, the regimental band playing "John Brown's Body." Governor John Andrew and other dignitaries reviewed the troops and sent them south with a flourish of speeches. This regiment from abolitionist Massachusetts would be part of a renewed Union effort to take Charleston, South Carolina, the birthplace of secession. As a preliminary measure, Federal forces were to seize Fort Wagner on Morris Island, which commanded Charleston Harbor and from which fire could be directed into the city itself.

Fort Wagner's 1,700 Confederate defenders had driven off a daylight assault with heavy casualties on July 10. For the encore, scheduled for July 18, Union general Quincy A. Gillmore planned an assault at dusk, preceded by a daylong bombardment. Colonel Shaw, with the backing of his brigade commander, Gen. George C. Strong, pressed for a leading role for the newly arrived 54th. Shaw got his wish—the right result, as far as he was concerned, for the wrong reasons.

"I guess we will let Strong lead and put those d——d niggers from Massachusetts in the advance," Gen. Truman Seymour, the division commander, confided to Gillmore. "We may as well get rid of them one time as another."

To reach Fort Wagner, the attackers would have to advance over a 25-foot-wide strip of sand bordered by marsh on one side and the Atlantic on the other. The 54th led out at sunset, moving slowly at first through the deep sand. The Confederates sent a heavy fire into the troops funneling down the narrow sandspit. "Not a man flinched," recalled Sgt. Lewis Douglass. "A shell would explode and clear a space of 20 feet, and our men would close up again."

With Shaw out in front, the regiment quickened the pace and reached the three-foot-wide ditch in front of the fort at a dead run. Soon men were swarming up the embankment. Shaw, wounded several times by now, reached the parapet, then fell dead, shot through the heart. Some troops actually fought their way into the fort and struggled among the cannon with the rebel defenders. The few who survived this

This print shows the African-American Massachusetts regiment's assault on Fort Wagner, near Charleston, South Carolina. Although the assault failed, it was symbolically important because it proved to many the bravery and loyalty of African-American troops. *(Library of Congress)*

melee were sent reeling back down the slope, where they retreated with the remains of the 54th.

In its brief exposure to combat, the regiment lost 40 percent of its strength in killed and wounded. But the failed assault took on great symbolic significance in the North. "Through the cannon smoke of that dark night, the manhood of the colored race shines before many eyes that would not see," the *Atlantic Monthly* wrote in the aftermath. A week before the Fort Wagner attack, rioters in New York City had hunted down blacks and lynched them in the streets. By autumn, black New York regiments were parading through the city past cheering crowds. There may have been an element of cynicism in the response, however. Charles G. Halpine created the fictitious Pvt. Miles O'Reilly, a New Yorker, and wrote this doggerel, sung to an Irish tune:

> Some tell us 'tis a burning shame
> To make the naygers fight;
> An' that the thrade of bein' kilt
> Belongs but to the white;
> But as for me, upon my soul!
> So liberal are we here,
> I'll let Sambo be murthered instead of myself
> On every day of the year.

For whatever motive, the performance of black troops in the spring of 1863 quieted Northern doubts. By war's end, 300,000 African Americans were serving in the Union army, nearly 180,000 of these in combat roles. Although Douglass's dream of full citizenship would be long deferred, there were some who recognized how much blacks had given, and how little they received in return.

"We called upon them in the hour of our trial, when volunteering had ceased, when the draft was a partial failure, and the bounty system a senseless extravagance," Col. Norwood P. Hallowell, a white officer in the black 54th Massachusetts, wrote after the war. "They were ineligible for promotion, they were not to be treated as prisoners of war, nothing was definite except they could be shot and hanged as soldiers."

BATTLES LOST
AND WON

Poor generalship handicapped the Union forces from the start, especially in the Virginia theater. McClellan succeeded brilliantly in organizing and training the Army of the Potomac, but faltered when the time came for fighting. In McClellan's own valuation, Antietam had been a great victory, a military masterpiece. In Lincoln's view, only a vigorous chase and the destruction of Lee's army could complete what McClellan had begun along Antietam Creek on September 17, 1862. But he delayed, offering what by now had become familiar excuses: The army had to be reorganized, reinforcements were needed, the horses were fatigued. "He has got the slows," the president said. McClellan did not begin crossing the Potomac in pursuit of Lee until October 26. By then, Lincoln had lost all patience. On November 7, he fired McClellan.

"He is an admirable engineer," Lincoln said of McClellan, "but he seems to have a special talent for a stationary engine."

The president had replaced McClellan once before, with the incompetent General Pope, whom Lee and Jackson befuddled at the Second Battle of Bull Run in August. Pope had gone, McClellan had returned and gone once again. Now it would be 38-year-old Gen. Ambrose E. Burnside's turn. Lincoln had approached Burnside about the command twice before; both times Burnside had turned him down, protesting that he was unqualified for the job.

A graduate of West Point, the Indiana-born Burnside was sent to the U.S.-Mexican War too late to take part in the action, and served through the mid-1850s in various frontier posts. With time on his hands, he invented a breech-loading rifle; he eventually left the army to settle in Rhode Island and manufacture the new weapon. By 1855, the business had failed and Burnside was broke. McClellan, an old friend, gave him a job on the Illinois Central Railroad, where he had become

Brig. Gen. Ambrose Burnside, after a somewhat uneven record in battles, replaced Gen. George McClellan as commander of the Army of the Potomac in early November 1862. (*Library of Congress*)

a senior official by the time of the attack on Fort Sumter. Burnside returned east after the Confederate attack, and led a Rhode Island brigade at the First Battle of Bull Run.

He later commanded the successful Union amphibious operations along the North Carolina coast, then led a corps at Antietam, where he missed an opportunity to deal a decisive blow to the Confederate right wing. In spite of that failure, Burnside retained his reputation. Nobody could deny that he at least looked the part of a great commander. Tall, broad-chested, handsome, he wore a set of dark whiskers that swept down his jawline, then curved upwards to meet in a full mustache. His last name, with the two halves reversed, became the general term for this fashion in facial hair—sideburns.

Burnside's impressive presence masked his lack of other qualities. "You would think he had a great deal more intelligence than he

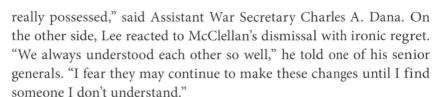

really possessed," said Assistant War Secretary Charles A. Dana. On the other side, Lee reacted to McClellan's dismissal with ironic regret. "We always understood each other so well," he told one of his senior generals. "I fear they may continue to make these changes until I find someone I don't understand."

Lee would learn soon enough about Burnside. The new Union commander started fast. By November 17, only 10 days after he had taken charge, Burnside had moved the 110,000-man Army of the Potomac from Manassas southeast to Falmouth, Virginia, not far from Fredericksburg on the Rappahannock River. Burnside proposed to cross there, take the town, and drive on to Richmond. But delay now set in. The pontoons Burnside needed to bridge the 400-yard-wide Rappahannock arrived more than a week late. While Burnside waited McClellan-like, Lee rushed the Army of Northern Virginia to the Fredericksburg area. By the end of November, his 78,000 troops were digging in along the ridgelines behind the town.

Whatever advantage surprise might have brought had long since been lost. From the heights, the Confederates could see every detail of Burnside's preparations. He originally planned a crossing downstream from the town, and a sweeping movement around Lee's right. He now decided instead to make his main crossing opposite the rebel center at Fredericksburg. Burnside hoped, evidently, that a frontal assault into strong positions would seem so foolhardy a move that Lee would dismiss the possibility, and the Federals could thus achieve surprise after all.

Union combat engineers began laying five pontoon bridges on the night of December 11. Over the next two days, Burnside sent most of the army, now grouped into grand divisions of two corps each, across the Rappahannock. Two corps under Gen. Edwin Sumner entered Fredericksburg, the town now battered and burning after a long Federal bombardment. Gen. William B. Franklin's two corps crossed a mile downstream and deployed opposite Stonewall Jackson's well-placed Confederates on Prospect Heights. Burnside kept the third grand division, under Gen. Joseph Hooker, in reserve on the east bank.

Franklin's assault divisions went forward under cover of thick fog at 8:30 A.M. on December 13, forming a line of battle along the Old Richmond Road at the base of Prospect Heights. The rebels could see nothing, though they could hear the clang of metal on metal, the creak of the gun caissons, and other unmistakable sounds of an army in

On December 13, 1862, Federal troops crossed the Rappahannock River to commence the assault on the Confederate forces at Fredericksburg. The ensuing battle proved to be a disaster for the Federals. *(Library of Congress)*

motion. The fog lifted suddenly at about 10 A.M., and bright sun lit the plain below.

"I could see almost every soldier Franklin had," recalled General Longstreet, observing from Marye's Heights behind the town, "and a splendid array it was."

Jackson, commanding on Prospect Heights, could see, too, but he had become too busy to be impressed. He directed his artillery to rake the advancing divisions of Gen. George G. Meade and Gen. John Gibbon, and rebel shot ripped wide gashes in the long blue battle line. On the left, Meade's Pennsylvanians pushed ahead into the welcome cover of a triangle of woods. They emerged on the far side into a gap in Jackson's defenses, and the surprised rebels, hit in the flank, were sent reeling. Regrouping quickly, the Confederates slowed, then stopped Meade's advance. Down on the plain, Franklin refused to send in fresh troops to exploit the opening, and a counterattack pushed Meade back into the woods. Gibbon's attack sputtered as well. Both divisions were driven gradually off the slopes, and by lunchtime the Federals were back at their start lines.

Franklin, shaken by the loss of 4,800 killed, wounded, and missing in two hours of fighting, ignored Burnside's order to renew the assault that afternoon. Burnside did not insist, his attention by now taken up by an even bloodier confrontation at the base of Marye's Heights. There Longstreet's corps carried out an unprecedented slaughter.

The Confederates waited in their advance positions at the base of Marye's Heights, all but invulnerable to frontal assault. Standing in a sunken lane bordered by a four-foot-high stone wall, Longstreet's Georgia and North Carolina regiments could calmly aim volley after volley into a Union charge. From the heights, rebel cannon could contribute their share to the shredding of the Union regiments, as E. Porter Alexander, the Confederate artillery commander, had promised. "A chicken could not live on that field when we open on it," Alexander told Longstreet before the attack began.

Gen. William French's division opened the assault. The lead brigade, New Yorkers and Pennsylvanians under Gen. Nathan Kimball, advanced at 11 A.M., moving slowly toward three narrow bridges that spanned a deep ditch on the outskirts of the town. Kimball's men sprinted across under heavy cannon fire and deployed for the attack on the ridge. "The clink, clink, clink of cold steel made one's blood run cold," one veteran recalled. The barrage rained down, and soon blood was running everywhere. The brigade came within 125 yards of the stone wall before the rebels opened fire. Within seconds, scores of Federals were dead or wounded. Next in line, Col. John Andrews's brigade came on over the dead from Kimball's regiments, some of the men slipping in grass now wet with blood. Rebel volleys took half the brigade down. When French's third brigade came forward, it, too, was shot to rags. Hundreds of blue-clad bodies lay piled up in front of the stone wall.

Still, the senior Federal commanders barely paused. They ordered Gen. Winfield Scott Hancock's division forward over the human wreckage of French's regiments. Three more Union brigades were expended against the stone wall.

Gen. Darius Couch, the II Corps commander, observed the assaults from the steeple of the Fredericksburg courthouse. "As they charged," he reported, "the artillery fire would break their formation and they would get mixed; then they would close up, go forward, receive the withering infantry fire, and those who were able would run to the houses and fight as best they could; and then the next brigade coming up in succession would do its duty and melt like snow coming down on warm ground."

Couch looked on as Hancock's division lost more than 2,000 men—42 percent of the complement, the heaviest divisional loss of the war. Burnside, stubbornly insistent, sent still more brigades up for the attack. "It's only murder now," Couch said.

A last charge failed, and the firing died away with the early December twilight. Hooker, sent across the river with his reserve divisions, refused finally to prolong the Union sacrifice. "Finding that I had lost as many men as my orders required me to lose," he wrote acidly in his official report, "I suspended the attack."

The Federals left 7,000 dead and wounded at the base of Marye's Heights, against only 1,200 rebel casualties. Burnside had a near breakdown after the battle. One of his generals found him in agony in his tent. "Oh, oh those men," Burnside lamented. "Those men over there! I am thinking of them all the time." He cried, an aide recalled, when the time came to order the Army of the Potomac back across the Rappahannock.

"They went as they came—in the night," Lee wrote his wife. "They suffered heavily as far as the battle went, but it did not go far enough to satisfy me."

The casualties had been terrible, but half the Army of the Potomac never saw action at Fredericksburg. The dead and wounded could be replaced, as Lee well knew, and the army would fight again. Still, the result had a disastrous effect on Northern morale, including the president's. "If there is a worse place than hell, I am in it," Lincoln told his secretary.

The problem of generalship seemed more perplexing than ever. After the Fredericksburg disaster, four of the Army of the Potomac's corps commanders went directly to Lincoln to complain about Burnside's management of the battle. McClellan's friends argued for his restoration. Hooker schemed on his own behalf. The soldiers were miserable. Desertions reached as many as 100 a day. Sick lists grew. Fresh vegetables and bread failed to reach the camps; the men subsisted on hardtack, salt pork, and coffee.

Burnside made a last effort to save himself. An unusually dry first half of January led him to plan a new crossing of the Rappahannock. This time the army would go over north of Fredericksburg and outflank Lee, forcing him out of his defensive positions. The army began

THE BATTLE HYMN

A Virginian wrote the pounding, pulsing music for an evangelical camp meeting in 1852. Not long after the outbreak of the Civil War, a quartet of singers in the 12th Massachusetts popularized it as an Army of the Potomac marching song. When Julia Ward Howe, a Northerner, added stirring lyrics after a visit to Union troops encamped near Washington, D.C., late in 1861, words and music together became an instant patriotic hit as "The Battle Hymn of the Republic."

> Mine eyes have seen the glory of the coming of the Lord:
> He is trampling out the vintage where the grapes of wrath are stored;
> He hath loosed the fateful lighting of his terrible swift sword:
>   His truth is marching on.

◆ ◆ ◆

> In the beauty of the lilies Christ was born across the sea,
> With a glory in his bosom that transfigures you and me;
> As he died to make men holy let us die to make men free,
>   While God is marching on.

The 12th Massachusetts quartet initially sang the camp meeting tune with their own informal stanzas that began, "John Brown's body lies a-moulderin' in the grave." Northern audiences assumed this was a memorial to the abolitionist martyr John Brown, hanged in the aftermath of the Harpers Ferry raid in 1859. In fact, it referred to a tenor member of the quartet, Sgt. John Brown, and it was widely popular in the Army of the Potomac, especially among New England troops, before Mrs. Howe's words were published in the *Atlantic Monthly* in February 1862.

Fletcher Webster commanded the 12th Massachusetts. He was killed in action at the Second Battle of Bull Run in August 1862, and the regiment suffered heavy casualties at Antietam in September.

to move on January 20, 1863. As though by some malign fate, clouds moved in and rain began to fall, and it came down continuously for three days. The countryside all around disappeared under the flood.

"Three times we started out, but the roads were so blocked up we made only 1½ miles," wrote Pvt. Alfred Davenport of the 5th New York. "Across the river the rebels set up a big sign board: 'Burnside's Army Stuck in the Mud,' and they were asking our pickets if they wanted any help laying pontoons, and so the rebels seem to know everything we are doing anyway and laugh at us."

Burnside called off the advance, now dubbed "the mud march," on January 22. In the aftermath, his generals' scheming intensified. He prepared an order dismissing several of them from the service, then drafted his own resignation, asking Lincoln to make the decision. Lincoln dismissed Burnside and, on January 26, put Hooker in his place.

Burnside and other senior officers detested Hooker, who could be scathing in public about the performance of rivals and who in private agitated tirelessly on his own behalf. The newspapers called him "Fighting Joe." In camp, Hooker's manners were relaxed, his companions seedy. His headquarters, according to Capt. Charles Francis Adams, Jr., "was a combination of barroom and brothel." No decent lady or gentleman would be seen there.

The troops responded, however. Hooker, 49 years old, proved to be a good administrator. He strictly enforced sanitary regulations in the great camp at Falmouth. He ordered the men to keep their hair cut short, to bathe twice a week, and to change their underwear at least once a week. He made sure onions, potatoes, and fresh bread were available. Scurvy, dysentery, and malnutrition had been endemic under Burnside. Within weeks, the sick list had been cut in half. "Under Hooker, we began to live," one of his soldiers wrote.

Hooker took his turn at reorganizing the army, breaking up Burnside's grand divisions and having the seven corps commanders report directly to him. He also formed the cavalry, heretofore assigned by detachment to the infantry divisions, into an independent corps of more than 10,000 horsemen. The reforms, and the troops' response, left Hooker supremely confident. "If the enemy does not run, God help them," he said. Later, he boasted that his plans for an offensive were perfect. "When I start to carry them out, may God have mercy on General Lee, for I will have none."

In early April, Lincoln came down to Falmouth to observe Hooker. His bluster greatly disturbed the president. "That is the most depressing thing about Hooker," he said. "It seems to me he is overconfident." Lincoln must have wondered about his military skills too. In an allusion to Fredericksburg, he offered Hooker this advice: "In your next fight, put in all your men."

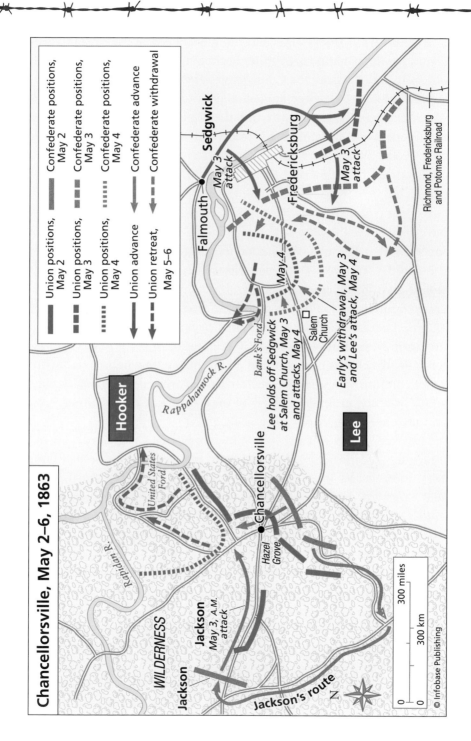

Chancellorsville, May 2–6, 1863

Union positions, May 2
Confederate positions, May 2
Union positions, May 3
Confederate positions, May 3
Union positions, May 4
Confederate positions, May 4
Union advance
Confederate advance
Union retreat, May 5–6
Confederate withdrawal

Hooker

Lee

Sedgwick

Falmouth

Fredericksburg

May 3 attack

May 3 attack

Richmond, Fredericksburg and Potomac Railroad

Bank's Ford

May 4

Salem Church

Lee holds off Sedgwick at Salem Church, May 3 and attacks, May 4

Early's withdrawal, May 3 and Lee's attack, May 4

Rappahannock R.

United States Ford

Rapidan R.

Chancellorsville

Hazel Grove

WILDERNESS

Jackson

Jackson May 3, A.M. attack

Jackson's route

N

300 miles

300 km

0

0

© Infobase Publishing

By mid-April Hooker was ready to move. He sent the cavalry corps across the Rappahannock 20 miles upstream from Fredericksburg with orders to get in behind the Confederates and shoot up their communications. Maj. Gen. George Stoneman led the cavalrymen out on April 13. Once again the rains came, and the Rappahannock rose so rapidly that Stoneman could not get his troops across. Rain fell ceaselessly for two weeks. When the skies finally cleared on April 25, Hooker had changed his plans. Stoneman would cross at the upstream fords as before, but now Hooker would follow with three infantry corps, leaving two corps commanded by Gen. John Sedgwick in front of Fredericksburg to pin Lee's defenses there. Following separate roads through a forest maze called the Wilderness, the flanking corps would meet at the country crossroads of Chancellorsville. If all went well, Hooker would have 70,000 men on Lee's left flank and rear before the Confederate commander could turn and shift forces to meet him.

The Federal V, XI, and XII Corps began crossing at Kelly's Ford on April 27. By sunset on April 30, they were in place near Chancellorsville, which was not a town at all but only a lone house, brick with white columns, in a small forest clearing. All around were the jack pine, scrub oak, and bramble thickets of the Wilderness, dark, mysterious, and now beginning to fill with rebels.

Lee had begun to catch on. When Sedgwick's two corps did not attack at Fredericksburg, Lee suspected a diversion. As he had done with such success in the past, Lee divided his army. On April 30, he sent Stonewall Jackson with 40,000 men north toward Chancellorsville. He left only a single division to watch Sedgwick's 40,000 Federals, calculating that the Federals would not react swiftly enough to cause him to lose his gamble.

Lee reacted decisively, but so far everything had gone largely Hooker's way. Fighting Joe had matched wits with the incomparable Lee and ended up on the Confederate flank with a numerical advantage of nearly two to one. At 11 A.M. on May 1, the advance got under way. Jackson responded immediately, throwing vicious little attacks at the Federal vanguard. Although these were parried, Hooker suddenly reconsidered. To the amazement of his generals, he stopped the advance and ordered the three corps to fall back into defensive positions around Chancellorsville.

"To hear from his own lips that the advantage gained by the successful marches of his lieutenants were to culminate in fighting a defensive battle in that nest of thickets was too much, and I retired from his presence with the belief that my commanding general was a whipped man," Couch, the II Corps commander, wrote afterward.

Some of his critics claimed later that Hooker had been drunk. In fact, he had sworn off liquor weeks before and had entered the battle absolutely clear-headed. Hooker could be blunt about himself as well as others, and his own explanation was that he simply lost his nerve. "For once," he said afterward, "I lost confidence in Joe Hooker."

So Lee regained the initiative. That night, he and Jackson met in the woods to discuss what could be done to harm "those people," as Lee referred to his adversaries. Lee decided to divide his forces yet again, leaving 14,000 men in Hooker's front and sending Jackson with 26,000 against the Federal right flank. The two generals rested for a few hours while aides scouted a route. By 8 A.M., Jackson's men were on the move.

On May 1–4, 1863, at Chancellorsville, Virginia, Union troops under command of Gen. Joseph Hooker suffered a decisive defeat by the Confederates under Generals Lee and Jackson. *(Library of Congress)*

The Federals had warnings—even Hooker glimpsed Jackson's column passing across his front—but misinterpreted or ignored them. By the late afternoon of May 2, Union general O. O. Howard's right-hand XI Corps had stacked their arms and begun preparing dinner, the day's work done. Shortly after 5 P.M., the men looked up to see deer, rabbits, and other wildlife racing out of the woods. They stood and pointed, laughing at the animals' strange antics. Then the first shots sounded. Moments later 26,000 rebels, screaming their awful yell, were upon them.

The 153rd Pennsylvania, facing west, checked the assault briefly, then disintegrated. The 41st and 45th New York, facing south, turned and ran without firing a shot. Within minutes, Charles Devens's division, holding the extreme right of the XI Corps line, had collapsed. The rebels came on hard, rolling up the right flank. By dusk Howard's corps had been pushed back two miles, nearly to Chancellorsville, where Hooker left his headquarters in the mansion to organize a makeshift defensive line.

The attack spent itself as night fell, despite Jackson's efforts to keep up the momentum. As the full moon began to rise he decided to order a night attack, and rode forward himself to scout Hooker's positions. As he returned to his own lines, jittery pickets in the 18th North Carolina opened fire, wounding him and several others. Later that night, a surgeon amputated Jackson's left arm two inches below the shoulder.

Lee had little time to lament his loss. The rebels were still divided and vulnerable to a strong counterattack. Hooker ordered up reinforcements overnight; however, he refused to leave his defensive positions. As a result, the Federal counterattack was not as strong as it might have been. Jackson's replacement, the cavalry commander J. E. B. Stuart, attacked all through the day on May 3, finally pushing the Federals out of Chancellorsville. Giving up all chance of beating Lee, Hooker ordered a withdrawal that night to a defensive perimeter guarding the river fords.

As a last hope, Hooker had earlier instructed the inert Sedgwick to attack at Fredericksburg, with the object of driving westward toward Lee's rear. On the morning of May 3, Sedgwick's assault brigades pushed the rebels off Marye's Heights, regrouped, and began moving glacially toward Chancellorsville. Late in the day, rebels in a hastily organized defensive line repulsed an attack near Salem Church.

Confederate caisson and eight horses are found destroyed by a 32-pound shell from a 2nd Massachusetts siege gun. Fredericksburg, Virginia, Marye's Heights, May 3, 1863 *(National Archives)*

The next day Lee gambled a third time, though now the risk seemed negligible. He left Stuart to watch Hooker and turned with 22,000 men to hit Sedgwick. As stubborn in defense as he had been sluggish on the attack, Sedgwick parried Lee's attacks the afternoon of May 4. That night, he withdrew his entire force across the Rappahannock to safety. The three corps with Hooker followed the next night, recrossing in a driving rain.

The four-day battle cost the Federals 17,000 casualties, and once again exposed the flaws in the leadership of the Army of the Potomac. Hooker had failed, as had McDowell, McClellan, Pope, and Burnside before him. At various times, Hooker tried to put the blame on others. But the soldiers knew better. Like Lincoln, they could not understand the generals' inability to make full use of their resources. "The wonder of the private soldiers was great," one of them wrote when he got back to the Falmouth camp. "How had one half of the army been defeated while the other half had not fought?"

As for Lee, historians would call his Chancellorsville campaign "the perfect battle." He had once again shown himself able to take the

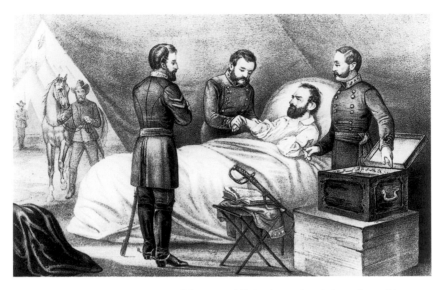

A Currier and Ives print shows "Stonewall" Jackson, Lee's irreplaceable chief lieutenant, who was wounded in the Chancellorsville campaign and died on May 10, 1863. *(Library of Congress)*

measure of, and then dominate, the opposing commander. But Lee bought his masterpiece at a high price. Among the rebels' 13,000 casualties was his irreplaceable chief lieutenant, without whom the victory would have been impossible.

At first, Jackson seemed to rally from his wound. Then pneumonia set in. On Sunday, May 10, he slipped into a delirium. At intervals through the bright spring day he would call out commands, always urging his aides to move things along, to go faster, faster. "Pass the infantry to the front," Jackson shouted once. Then, late in the afternoon, with a final quiet remark—"Let us cross the river and rest in the shade of the trees"—he died.

Lee mourned, then got on with the job. A month later, in the greatest of his gambles, he had the Army of Northern Virginia on the march toward the little Pennsylvania town of Gettysburg.

LONG REMEMBER

Gettysburg

Robert E. Lee led the victorious Confederate army north from Chancellorsville during the first week of June. Richmond seemed safe, the Yankees had been beaten again, but elsewhere there were severe pressures on the Confederacy, especially on the Mississippi River and in eastern Tennessee. Invasion and victory would relieve these pressures and encourage the Northern Copperheads to agitate for peace, Lee reasoned; the old dream of British recognition might be revived; and the underfed, poorly equipped rebels could replenish their supplies from Pennsylvania's farms and shops. Although his soldiers may have lacked for food and clothing, to Lee they seemed invincible. "There never were such men in an army before," he said. "They will go anywhere and do anything if properly led."

Under President Lincoln's prodding, Gen. Hooker followed Lee's army. At first the Union commander wanted to attack Lee's rear as the rebel columns headed for the Potomac. Then he proposed breaking off contact altogether and turning south to march on Richmond. Lincoln rejected both schemes. He told Hooker to advance in step with Lee, to stay between the rebels and Washington and to attack when opportunity offered. But Fighting Joe had seen enough of Lee. Sounding like McClellan the year before, he reported that the rebels outnumbered him and asked for reinforcements. When they were denied, he complained that Lincoln and the other Union leaders were failing to support him.

The president dismissed Hooker's claims, and even Hooker himself acknowledged his inability to see matters clearly. "I don't know whether I am standing on my head or my feet," he admitted. Lincoln decided not to risk another battle with Hooker in command. On June 28, with the Army of the Potomac in Frederick, Maryland, 40 miles south of Lee, he replaced Hooker with Maj. Gen. George Gordon Meade.

On June 28, 1863, President Lincoln appointed Maj. Gen. George Meade to replace General Hooker as commander of the Union forces that within four days would confront the Confederates at Gettysburg, Pennsylvania. *(Library of Congress)*

By then, Confederate forces were operating over a wide arc west of the Susquehanna River in Pennsylvania. As usual, Lee had divided the army. Longstreet's and A. P. Hill's corps were in Chambersburg. Elements of Richard S. Ewell's corps were off to the north and east in Carlisle and York—some more than 30 miles from Longstreet and Hill. Lee had lost touch with J. E. B. Stuart's cavalry, and had only a hazy idea of the enemy's whereabouts, so when he learned that the Federals had crossed the Potomac on June 27 and were heading his way, he sent out couriers to recall his scattered forces. He ordered a withdrawal southward, toward the prosperous crossroads town of Gettysburg.

Meade, meanwhile, had taken over an army without a plan. A 48-year-old Pennsylvanian, thin, gray, and balding, nervous and short-tempered, he had not sought Hooker's job, and had even tried to refuse it. However, Lincoln gave him no choice. Contemporaries judged Meade a commander of ordinary competence and a good handler of troops. He now brought these stolid qualities into play. By the afternoon of June 28, he had decided to move the army north toward the

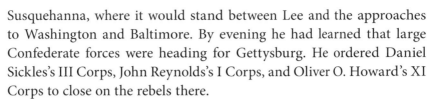

Susquehanna, where it would stand between Lee and the approaches to Washington and Baltimore. By evening he had learned that large Confederate forces were heading for Gettysburg. He ordered Daniel Sickles's III Corps, John Reynolds's I Corps, and Oliver O. Howard's XI Corps to close on the rebels there.

Federal outriders reached Gettysburg first. Two cavalry brigades under Brig. Gen. John Buford cantered in at midday on June 30, just ahead of a Confederate detachment foraging for shoes. Buford decided to defend the town, and he sent word to Reynolds to bring up the I Corps infantry. The rebels observed the arrival of the Yankee cavalry, then withdrew to the west and reported the enemy's presence to a higher authority—Gen. Henry Heth, commanding a division in Hill's corps. Scouts had said there were large supplies of shoes in Gettysburg, and Hill meant to have them. He told Heth to take the town the next morning.

At dawn on July 1, 1863, an 8th Illinois Cavalry advance guard fired the first shot in what would be the largest and deadliest battle ever fought in North America. Neither Lee nor Meade chose Gettysburg. Union engineers had prepared a defensive line along Pipe Creek in Maryland, and Meade hoped to entice the Confederates to attack him there. Lee, unsure of the enemy's movements, warned his subordinates not to bring on a general engagement until he could reunite the army. But thousands of men were converging on Gettysburg, and events were moving out of the generals' control.

Heth's skirmishers chased off the Federal cavalry advance unit, and the main body of the Confederate division reached the spine of Herr Ridge, the westernmost of four north-south ridgelines outside Gettysburg, at about 8 A.M. From there Heth could see Federals moving into position along a sluggish stream called Willoughby Run. Beyond the valley rose McPherson's Ridge, with a house known as McPherson's Farm and the 17-acre McPherson's Woods. Heth observed the terrain, thought about those shoes, and calculated that his 7,400 infantrymen could roll over Buford's 2,700 dismounted troopers and parade into town.

However, the Kentucky-born Buford was prepared for Heth. "By daylight of July 1 . . . my arrangements were made for entertaining him until General Reynolds could reach the scene," he wrote afterward. These "arrangements" included the new seven-shot Spencer carbine his men carried. With this weapon, which could fire at a rate five times faster than a muzzle loader, Buford's troopers held off Heth's assault for more than an hour, then fell back across Willoughby Run just as Reynolds's lead brigade came loping into McPherson's Woods.

Heth followed closely, pushing two brigades across the creek and up the slope; the right-hand brigade under James Archer double-timed into the trees. Suddenly a powerful volley cut into Archer's ranks. The rebels, expecting lightly armed cavalry, soon discovered the source of the hurricane of fire. "There are those damned black hat fellows again," one called out. Archer had run into the tough midwesterners of the Iron Brigade in their unmistakable slouch hats. Two Union regiments, the 19th Indiana and the 24th Michigan, charged into the stunned rebels and sent them back across the creek. Heth's second brigade got similar rough handling from New York and Wisconsin regiments newly arrived on the Iron Brigade's right. By 11 A.M., the rebel assault forces had withdrawn to their start lines on Herr Ridge.

By now, fresh forces were arriving on both sides of the line. A second Confederate division moved up from the west to support Heth. On the Union side, Abner Doubleday, who had taken command of I Corps when a rebel sharpshooter hit and killed Reynolds, fed more troops onto McPherson's Ridge. Howard's XI Corps divisions began taking up positions along the third ridgeline in the series, Seminary Ridge, and on the high ground north of Gettysburg. These Yankees were barely settled in before the lead divisions of Ewell's corps appeared opposite them. Howard's men had taken the first and hardest hit at Chancellorsville, and they had broken under the weight of it. Here the process repeated itself. A heavy Confederate attack shattered Howard's line.

Lee reached the battlefield in time to witness the Federal XI Corps retreating in disorder through the town. He ordered Heth's and William Dorsey Pender's divisions up McPherson's Ridge to complete the victory. Howard's collapse exposed the I Corps defenders, and this time the rebels came in overwhelming numbers. Still the Iron Brigade held on, fighting furiously amid the shattered trees of McPherson's Woods. "The two lines were pouring volleys into each other at a distance not greater than 20 paces," recalled Maj. J. T. Jones of the attacking 26th North Carolina. "I have taken part in many hotly contested fights," another rebel wrote, "but this I think was the deadliest of them all."

Gradually the attackers pushed the midwesterners back. The Iron Brigade lost 1,153 of the 1,829 men engaged. The 24th Michigan took 80 percent casualties; the attacking 26th North Carolina lost 75 percent of its strength. Afterward, rebel captain Louis G. Young rode among the wounded. Some were howling in pain. "It was so distressing," he wrote later, "that I approached several with the purpose of calming them if possible. I found them foaming at the mouth as if mad."

Heth's and Pender's brigades cleared the woods and pitched into the makeshift Union line on Seminary Ridge. Soon I Corps joined the XI Corps in retreat. The Federals were withdrawing toward good defensive ground, however, and a general with authority and presence had arrived to steady them. People invariably remarked on II Corps commander Winfield Scott Hancock's soldierly appearance and his always spotless white shirts. Beyond appearances, however, Hancock, a 39-year-old Pennsylvanian, had become one of the Army of the Potomac's best generals. "One felt safe near him," a subordinate recalled. Now he acted decisively, forming a new line anchored on a series of natural strong points east and south of the town.

Lee, meanwhile, asked Ewell to renew his assault from the north "if practicable." Ewell declined, believing the Federal positions too strong, and a day that had seemed to promise a Confederate victory ended

Maj. Gen. Winfield S. Hancock played a significant role in leading the Federal forces to victory in the battle at Gettysburg. (*Library of Congress*)

Dead on the battlefield of Gettysburg, July 1863 *(National Archives)*

in a draw. Four more Union corps arrived during the night. By dawn of July 2, the Federals were entrenched along a two-mile line curling in the shape of an inverted fishhook from Culp's Hill southeastward along Cemetery Ridge to a rocky hill called Little Round Top. There they awaited Lee's next move.

"The roll was called in low tones," wrote Union gunner Augustus Buell, posted on Cemetery Hill that morning. "In the dim light of daybreak we could see the infantry in front of us astir, and looking a little farther out into the gloom we could see the enemy's gray pickets. The stillness of everything was oppressive. We felt that a few flashes of musketry would be a relief.

"But the daylight came on, the sun rose and mounted up higher and higher, and yet the enemy, though in plain sight, gave no sign of hostility. Our men looked at each other and asked, 'What does it mean?'"

Like Augustus Buell, Lee waited anxiously for action all through the morning. He and Longstreet had disagreed about tactics. Lee wanted to strike hard there and then with an assault on the Union left in the direction of Little Round Top. Longstreet proposed a flank maneuver to pry the Federals out of their defenses. Longstreet could not know this, but Lee's 50,000 Confederates were already heavily outnumbered. By midday Meade had 80,000 men on the battlefield. He also had the advantage of shorter lines, and could shift troops swiftly from point to threatened point.

Longstreet could not persuade Lee to call off the offensive. "The enemy is there," Lee said pointing toward Cemetery Ridge, "and I am going to attack him there." He ordered a series of division-strength assaults down the Union line from right to left, one following the other. The first division, John Bell Hood's, would strike Union positions near Little Round Top. The next in line, Lafayette McLaws's, would hit exposed Federal positions in a salient that jutted out from the main line. The third division, Richard Anderson's, would strike the Union center on Cemetery Ridge.

Hood opened the assault at 4 P.M., his lead brigades moving toward a maze of huge boulders called the Devil's Den. He sent his right-hand brigade to occupy Little Round Top, which the Yankees, unaccountably, had left undefended. An alert Union staff officer moved to correct

On July 2, 1863, the 20th Maine Infantry, led by Col. Joshua Chamberlain, after holding off a series of attacks by Confederates, ordered a bold counterattack, as depicted here. *(National Guard)*

the oversight, however, and a Union brigade arrived minutes before the rebels. These troops, single Pennsylvania, New York, Michigan, and Maine regiments, deployed into a battle line just in time to receive the attack. The rebels charged up the hill five times successively and were repulsed each time. The end regiment in the line, the 308-man 20th Maine, held off the attacking 15th Alabama in a desperate little fight that may have been the most critical single encounter of the entire battle.

"This is the left of the Union line," the 20th's commander, Lt. Col. Joshua L. Chamberlain, had been told. "You understand. You are to hold this ground at all costs."

Chamberlain, 34 years old, had come to the army from Bowdoin College in Maine, where he taught rhetoric and modern languages. Nothing at Bowdoin had prepared him for this. But even a college professor could see that if the rebels took Little Round Top their guns would command the entire Union line. Sword drawn, Chamberlain steadied the men as the 15th Alabama charged. When the rebels got in close, he gave the order to fire.

"My line wavered like a man trying to walk against a strong wind," William C. Oates, the Alabama 15th's commander, recalled. "The air seemed to be alive with lead," wrote Pvt. Theodore Gerrish

Lt. Col. Joshua L. Chamberlain (*National Archives*)

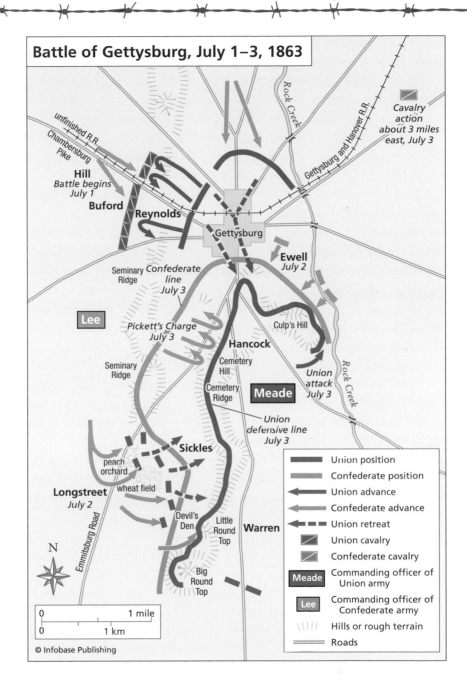

Battle of Gettysburg, July 1–3, 1863

Cavalry action about 3 miles east, July 3

Rock Creek

Gettysburg and Hanover R.R.

unfinished R.R.

Chambersburg Pike

Hill
Battle begins July 1

Buford

Reynolds

Gettysburg

Ewell
July 2

Seminary Ridge

Confederate line July 3

Lee

Pickett's Charge July 3

Culp's Hill

Hancock

Seminary Ridge

Cemetery Hill

Cemetery Ridge

Meade

Union attack July 3

Rock Creek

Union defensive line July 3

Sickles

peach orchard

wheat field

Longstreet
July 2

Emmitsburg Road

Devil's Den

Little Round Top

Warren

N

Big Round Top

▬▬▬	Union position
▬▬▬	Confederate position
◀▬▬	Union advance
◀▬▬	Confederate advance
◀---	Union retreat
▨	Union cavalry
▨	Confederate cavalry
Meade	Commanding officer of Union army
Lee	Commanding officer of Confederate army
||||	Hills or rough terrain
═══	Roads

0 ———————— 1 mile
0 ———————— 1 km

© Infobase Publishing

of the 20th Maine. "At times I saw around me more of the enemy than of my own men; gaps opening, swallowing, closing again with sharp convulsive energy," Chamberlain wrote. "All around a strange mingled roar."

The Alabamans kept coming until, in Oates's words, "the blood stood in puddles in some places on the rocks." Then the fire of the Twentieth Maine slackened. His men nearly out of ammunition, Chamberlain coolly ordered a bayonet charge. The 20th lurched down the hill, bayonets thrust forward clumsily. At the same time, a detachment of Federal sharpshooters began pouring fire into the rebel flank. "Some were struck simultaneously with two or three balls from different directions," Oates recalled. As he motioned the 15th to fall back, the men broke. "When the signal was given," he admitted afterward, "we ran like a herd of wild cattle."

As quiet returned to Little Round Top, Chamberlain's survivors could see the fighting spread erratically down the line. Hood's Confederate brigades were still mixing it up amid the fantastic rock formations of the Devil's Den. At 5:30, McLaws attacked the salient and in fierce fighting cleared the Yankees out of a wheat field and a peach orchard. Finally, at 6:30, in the third assault of the series, Anderson's division struck Hancock's II Corps positions on Cemetery Ridge, which had been thinned by the transfer of a division sent to help hold off McLaws.

Hancock rode up and down the line on his black charger, encouraging the defenders by his example. The shift of troops had opened a gap in the line, and he could now see one of Anderson's brigades charging straight for it. Hancock called for reinforcements, but it would be several minutes before fresh troops could arrive. In the meantime the rebels came on, yelling viciously. Looking about for the means to slow them, Hancock spotted an undersized regiment waiting in line behind a row of cannon.

"What regiment is this?" he called out.

"First Minnesota," the regimental commander, Col. William Colville, called back.

Hancock ordered Colville to charge into the oncoming rebels, and the 1st Minnesota obediently fixed bayonets and plunged forward. "The men were never made who will stand against leveled bayonets coming with such momentum and evident desperation," Lt. William Lochren wrote afterward. "The ferocity of our onset seemed to paralyze them for a time." The few moments' respite gave Hancock time to feed a full division into line to close the gap. Those moments had cost the 1st Minnesota all but 47 of its 262 officers and men.

Toward sunset the three-hour battle died down. To the north, at the far end of the Union line, Ewell launched evening attacks on Culp's Hill

The climax of the Battle of Gettysburg came on the afternoon of July 3, with the so-called Pickett's charge, when three Confederate divisions came charging across an open field only to be mowed down by the Union forces. *(Library of Congress)*

and Cemetery Hill, but these achieved only minor gains. The Union lines held. Meade and his subordinate commanders had made efficient use of their forces, putting in fresh troops where most needed as the rebel assaults developed. Longstreet's successive attacks on the Union left managed to gain only the peach orchard, and at a cost of 7,000 casualties. Ewell's attacks on the right cost several thousand more men.

The second day's fighting had shaken the Union commanders, however, and Meade called his senior generals into council late that night to consider what to do. After a short discussion, they voted to remain in line to await a renewed attack. As for Lee, he still believed he could achieve a decisive victory at Gettysburg. Concluding that the shift of troops to threatened positions on the right and left must have weakened the Union center, he decided to make his main effort there on the third day, using Gen. George Pickett's fresh divisions as a spearhead.

Pickett's 4,600 men, all Virginians, began forming up around 10 A.M. on July 3. Joining them were divisions under James J. Pettigrew and Isaac Trimble, giving Lee more than 11,000 troops for the assault. After a heavy preliminary bombardment, they planned to move out across nearly a mile of open ground toward a stand of umbrella-shaped trees in the center of the Cemetery Ridge line. There Hancock held a 1,000-yard front with three depleted divisions, about 5,700 men.

The Yankees waited through the morning, sweating in the hot sun, hungry and very thirsty. "We dozed in the heat, and lolled upon the ground, with half open eyes," a Federal officer remembered. "Our horses were hitched to the trees munching some oats. Time was heavy." For several hours the defenders could hear firing off to the north, where fighting again had broken out on Culp's Hill. By late morning the sounds of that battle had died away. "It became still as the sabbath day," a survivor wrote. Then a few minutes after 1 P.M., the Confederate bombardment began. Union gunners returned the fire in a roaring duel that could be heard as far away as Pittsburgh, 150 miles to the west.

The rebels aimed too high above the stone wall that protected the Union camp. As a result, the barrage caused more trouble in the rear, where it drove Meade from his farmhouse headquarters, than in the infantry lines. "All we had to do was flatten out a little thinner," recalled a veteran, "and our empty stomachs did not prevent that." The rebel miscalculation left the Union regiments largely undamaged.

On the far side of the valley, Lee's assault divisions awaited the order to advance. Finally, at about 3 P.M., the bombardment ended. The rebels moved out in tidy rows on a mile-wide front at a steady pace of 100 yards a minute. After a few minutes the Federal artillery opened up, tearing bloody gouges in the line. "We could not help hitting them at every shot," one of the gunners reported, almost apologetically. E. Porter Alexander, the Confederate artillery commander, observed the advance from his post on Seminary Ridge. "It seemed madness," he said.

From their high ground the entrenched Federals watched the guns do their terrible work. The easy, methodical killing reminded many of a futile charge of their own not so many months before. "Fredericks-burg!" some began to shout. "Come on, Johnny," they urged. "Keep on coming!" And on the rebels came, encouraging one another, telling one another it would be all over soon. "Home, boys, home," a rebel lieuten-ant called. "Remember, home is just beyond those hills."

For hundreds of Pickett's men, home would be a shallow grave. Some 300 of the Virginians managed briefly to pierce the Union line. However, they were soon rounded up. Union regiments swung out on the flanks and poured fire into what remained of the Confederate battle line. Those still on their feet turned and, as though in a daze, shuffled slowly back across the valley.

What became known as "Pickett's charge" cost more than 5,000 casualties—fully half the number engaged. In the five leading brigades, the casualty rate approached 70 percent. Pickett survived, but all three of his brigadiers were killed, along with eight of his 13 colonels. For the rest of his life Pickett would blame Lee for the destruction of his division. Lee accepted responsibility for all that had happened at Gettysburg. "It is all my fault," he said as he rode among the retreating troops. "It is I who have lost this fight."

Lee suffered severely in men, matériel, and—though this did not seem so clear at the time—political consequence. In the North, his aura of invincibility melted away. A Union commander had beaten the

CRAFTED WITH CARE

Lincoln had essentially completed the Gettysburg Address before he left Washington for the cemetery dedication. The notion that he dashed off the speech on an envelope as the train steamed northwest for Gettysburg or that he half-improvised it at the podium is an attractive myth.

The invitation came late—only three weeks before the dedication of the burying ground for thousands of dead from the battle of July 1–3, 1863. The dedication committee, it seemed, doubted Lincoln's "ability to speak upon such a grave and solemn occasion." The committee reluctantly invited him to follow the main speaker, Edward Everett of Massachusetts, with "a few appropriate remarks."

The president departed for Gettysburg around noon on November 18 with the speech largely intact, though he may have revised it slightly on the train ride. He certainly tinkered with it after he delivered it the next day, but the changes were minor and the final draft added only two words to the original.

It is misleading, too, to suggest that the speech fell entirely flat, even though Lincoln evidently believed it had. The Gettysburg Address, as it came to be called, was widely reprinted in the newspapers in the following weeks.

Gettysburg Battlefield, July 4, 1863 *(National Archives)*

seemingly indestructible Lee, and never again would he be strong and bold enough to invade the North. The victory quieted the Northern Copperheads too, muting their call for a negotiated settlement that would leave slavery intact. Finally, the threat of foreign intervention now disappeared entirely. "The disasters of the rebels are unredeemed by even any hope of success," wrote Henry Adams from London, where his father served as ambassador to the British.

Lee gave the order to return to Virginia on the night of July 3. Union forces did not pursue. "We have done well enough," an exhausted Meade said. Three days of fighting had cost Lee 3,903 killed, 18,735 wounded, and 5,425 missing—fully a third of his army. The Federals lost heavily too, with 23,000 killed, wounded, and missing—about a quarter of their total strength.

The next day, July 4, a hard rain fell, washing the blood from the grass. Thomas Marbaker, a sergeant in the 11th New Jersey, walked the battlefield, moving among the thousands of broken, bloated corpses. Marbaker wrote:

Upon the open fields, like sheaves bound by the reaper, in crevices of the rocks, behind fences, trees and buildings; in thickets, where they had crept in safety only to die in agony; by

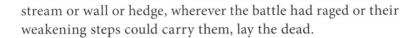

stream or wall or hedge, wherever the battle had raged or their weakening steps could carry them, lay the dead.

By November, many had been neatly buried under simple white crosses in the new Gettysburg National Cemetery. On November 19, 1863, President Lincoln came to help dedicate it. He had been assigned a small role in the ceremony. The chief orator, Edward Everett of Massachusetts, delivered a two-hour address. Then Lincoln rose and, with a single piece of paper in his hand, spoke for five minutes:

> Four score and seven years ago our fathers brought forth, on this continent, a new nation, conceived in liberty, and dedicated to the proposition that all men are created equal.
> Now we are engaged in a great civil war, testing whether that nation, or any nation, so conceived, and so dedicated, can long endure. We are met here on a great battlefield of that war. We have come to dedicate a portion of it as a final resting place for those who here gave their lives that that nation might live. It is altogether fitting and proper that we should do this.
> But in a larger sense we can not dedicate—we can not consecrate—we can not hallow—this ground. The brave men, living and dead, who struggled here, have consecrated it, far above our poor power to add or detract. The world will little note, nor long remember, what we say here, but it can never forget what they did here. It is for us, the living, rather to be dedicated here to the unfinished work which they have, thus far, so nobly carried on. It is rather for us to be here dedicated to the great task remaining before us—that from these honored dead we take increased devotion to that cause for which they here gave the last full measure of devotion—that we here highly resolve that these dead shall not have died in vain; that this nation shall have a new birth of freedom; and that this government of the people, by the people, for the people, shall not perish from the earth.

The crowd, wet, chilled, and perhaps stunned by the brevity of the president's remarks, applauded without enthusiasm.

SIEGE AT VICKSBURG

As Lee's army collected its wounded and prepared to retreat from Gettysburg, Confederate white flags were being raised a thousand miles to the southwest, over the forts, trenches, and caves of the Mississippi River fortress of Vicksburg. Ulysses S. Grant, commanding the Union forces outside, and John C. Pemberton, commanding the Confederates within, agreed to surrender terms early on July 4, 1863, ending a 48-day siege. By midday, Union troops were marching into the battered, starving city.

The surrender concluded a yearlong Union campaign to capture Vicksburg and reopen the entire length of the Mississippi. Together with Lee's defeat in Pennsylvania, the fall of Vicksburg marked the beginning of the end of the Confederacy. Both sides recognized the significance of Independence Day, 1863. "Events have succeeded one another with disastrous rapidity," Josiah Gorgas, a senior Confederate government official, wrote in his diary. "It seems incredible that human power could effect such a change in so brief a space. Yesterday we rode on the pinnacle of success—today absolute ruin seems to be our portion. The Confederacy totters to its destruction."

Grant's great victory at Vicksburg had been many frustrating months in the making. President Davis called Vicksburg "the vital point" of contact between the two halves of the Confederacy, and it had been a prime Union objective from the start. Established in 1810 on the ruins of a 17th-century Spanish fort, the city stood on a chain of hills overlooking a long horseshoe bend of the Mississippi. Before the war, it had been a prosperous trading center of 3,500 inhabitants. Now the fortress's guns commanded the river for miles in both directions. A frontal assault on such powerful defenses seemed bound to fail. To the north lay Mississippi's Yazoo Delta country, a 50-mile-wide, 200-mile-

The landing at Vicksburg, Mississippi *(Library of Congress)*

long stretch of drowned land cut by rivers and bayous and impassable to an army and its heavy train. An invader needed dry land and secure supply lines to approach the fortress with any prospect of success.

The first attempt at Vicksburg came in June 1862 when Admiral Farragut took his saltwater fleet north from New Orleans. A two-day bombardment from the Union warships failed to dislodge the defenders, and the 3,200 troops with the fleet were too few for an assault. Farragut put the soldiers to work digging a canal across the base of the peninsula formed by the horseshoe bend, with the idea of coaxing the Mississippi to change course and leave Vicksburg high and dry. The river refused to flow into the canal, the water level fell to dangerously low levels as the summer advanced, and Farragut, out of patience, called off the operation at the end of July. The fleet, moving slowly through the shallows, made its way back to New Orleans.

If the fortress could not be taken from the water, then the army would have to make the attempt by land. In early November 1862, Grant, with 40,000 men, moved south along the line of the Mississippi Central Railroad, which ran parallel to the great river about

60 miles inland to the east. At the same time, William T. Sherman took 32,000 men downriver from Memphis. By December, Grant had reached Oxford, Mississippi. Pemberton, facing him at Grenada with 20,000 men, ordered a series of large-scale cavalry raids in the Union rear. Rebel troopers burned supplies, tore up railroad tracks, and cut telegraph lines, forcing Grant to cancel the operation and retreat northward.

The raids left Grant temporarily out of touch with the river wing of his army, and Sherman failed to receive word that Grant had turned back. He landed his corps as planned at the mouth of the Yazoo River, north of Vicksburg, and moved on the strong point of Chickasaw Bluffs, which he meant to use as a dry-ground staging area for a drive on the fortress. The defenders easily repulsed the Union attacks on December 28 and 29, inflicting more than 1,700 casualties. "I reached Vicksburg at the time appointed," Sherman reported laconically to Grant, "landed, assaulted, and failed."

The overland campaign abandoned, Grant now shifted most of his forces westward to the river. By late January 1863, he had three corps, a total of 47,000 men, encamped along a 50-mile stretch of the west bank of the Mississippi opposite Vicksburg. Conditions were miserable. Rain fell constantly, and the troops slept, drilled, and worked in a gray, wet world of swamp, flood, and mud. As winter advanced, cases of the measles and typhus reached near-epidemic levels. "Go any day down to the levee and you could see a squad or two of soldiers burying a companion, until the levee was nearly full of graves and the hospitals still full of sick," an Ohio soldier wrote home.

With the army stalled, political pressures mounted. Northern newspapers revived all the old charges from earlier campaigns. One called Grant a drunk; another accused Sherman, his chief lieutenant, of being insane. Grant needed to press on, if only to quiet the critics at home, so during that sodden winter he launched four separate efforts to find a route through the low country to the dry ground east of the fortress.

Grant held out little hope that these "bayou experiments," as he called them, would open a way into Vicksburg. "I let the work go on," he wrote later, "believing employment was better than idleness for the men." The most promising experiment turned out to be the last of the four. Adm. David D. Porter, commanding the gunboat flotilla, had scouted a waterway called Steele's Bayou, the first in a 200-mile chain of creeks and rivers that he believed might carry the gunboats and troop transports around the Confederate northern flank. The expedition would end up only 20 miles from its starting point, but strong rebel defenses on the Yazoo at Haines Bluff would be bypassed, and the army would be in position for a final assault on the fortress.

The land all around was in full flood, and Porter persuaded Grant he could float an army through and onto Vicksburg's rear. He set out with 11 gunboats on the afternoon of March 16, Sherman following in transports with 10,000 foot soldiers. The flotilla steamed on through an eerie wilderness. At one point, the flagboat cruised along a wide corridor lined by trees on either side, coasting 20 feet above a main road that had carried wagons laden with cotton down to the Mississippi.

Soon, though, the waterway narrowed. One of the gunboats became wedged between two trees, and twists and turns in the channel slowed the flotilla to a speed of less than one mile an hour. "One minute an ironclad would apparently be leading ahead, and the next minute would as apparently be steering the other way," Porter wrote afterward. Overhanging branches knocked down smokestacks. Snakes, rodents, bobcats, and other creatures dropped from the trees onto the gunboats' decks, sending sailors armed with brooms hustling to sweep them overboard.

The flotilla crept on through the jungle. Finally, on March 20, near the entrance to the Sunflower River, the last in the chain of waterways, the boats glided into what proved to be an impenetrable thicket of willows. As the crews struggled to hack away an opening, rebel troops, supported by two batteries of artillery, appeared on high ground ahead and opened fire. By now Porter had had enough. "Dear Sherman," he wrote. "Hurry up for Heaven's sake. I never knew how helpless an ironclad could be steaming around through the woods without an army to back her."

Sherman's troops soon arrived, having marched through hip-deep swamp at times, to drive the rebels away. But the last of the bayou experiments had failed. "The game was up," Porter said, "and we bumped on homeward." Grant, however, was not discouraged. He had kept the troops busy and the enemy guessing. Now the time had come to take large risks. Against the advice of most of his staff, including an adamant Sherman, he decided to run the gunboats past the Vicksburg water batteries, put the army across the river south of the fortress, march overland, and attack from the southeast.

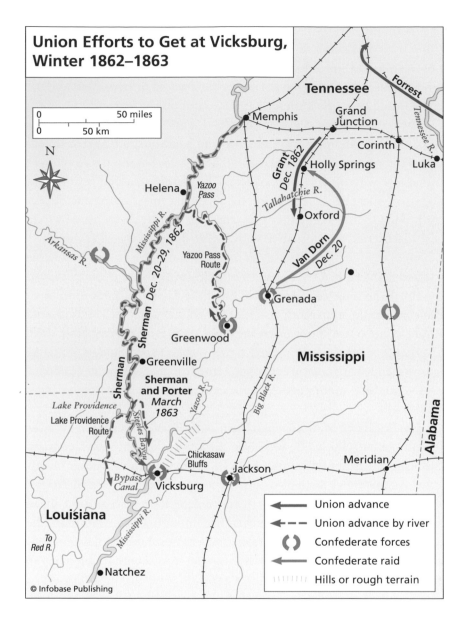

Union Efforts to Get at Vicksburg, Winter 1862–1863

0 — 50 miles
0 — 50 km

N

Tennessee

Forrest

Memphis

Grand Junction

Corinth

Luka

Tennessee R.

Grant Dec. 1862

Holly Springs

Helena

Yazoo Pass

Tallahatchie R.

Oxford

Mississippi R.

Arkansas R.

Yazoo Pass Route

Van Dorn Dec. 20

Sherman Dec. 20–29, 1862

Grenada

Greenwood

Mississippi

Greenville

Sherman

Sherman and Porter March 1863

Yazoo R.

Big Black R.

Lake Providence

Lake Providence Route

Steeles Bayou

Alabama

Chickasaw Bluffs

Jackson

Meridian

Bypass Canal

Vicksburg

Louisiana

To Red R.

Mississippi R.

Natchez

© Infobase Publishing

⟵	Union advance
⟵---	Union advance by river
( )	Confederate forces
⟵	Confederate raid
||||||	Hills or rough terrain

The Federals would be deep in enemy territory, cut off from their bases and operating without a secure supply line. No matter, said Grant, they could live off the land. "All we want now are men, ammunition and hard bread," he told Sherman, who would learn the lesson well. "We can subsist our horses on the country and obtain considerable supplies for our troops." Grant meant to travel light, move fast, and knock down any Confederates in his path.

The ironclad Union gunboat *Indianola* runs the blockade at Vicksburg, Mississippi, April 16, 1863. *(Library of Congress)*

Pemberton, however, could not know what Grant had in mind. Seeing failure all around, he believed Vicksburg to be safe. In front, Pemberton had actually sent troops out of the city in early April to reinforce the Confederate army in eastern Tennessee. The townspeople felt secure, too. "There is no immediate danger here," the *Vicksburg Whig* declared on April 16. That night, 12 Union vessels, transports lashed to the sides of the ironclads, headed downstream under the Vicksburg guns. The passage took two and a half thunderous hours, but the Federals lost only one transport and two barges. A week later, another five out of six vessels completed the run successfully.

Grant now ordered two diversions to confuse Pemberton and screen the landing of troops on the east bank. He sent Sherman with a small force toward Haines Bluff to give the impression he would make his main effort there. Then, on April 17, a Union cavalry brigade under Col. Benjamin H. Grierson set out from LaGrange, Tennessee, on what would be a 600-mile romp through the Confederate heartland.

Before the war, Grierson had taught music in Illinois. When he volunteered for the army, the mustering officers for some reason chose him for cavalry service. He pointed out that he had detested horses since he had been kicked by one as a child. His superiors were unmoved, however, and the horse-hating Grierson went on to pull off the most brilliant Union cavalry raid of the war. In 16 days, his troopers won several skirmishes, pulled up miles of railroad track, burned freight cars and depots, and destroyed hundreds of tons of Confederate supplies. By the time they rode, exhausted, into the Union lines at Baton Rouge, Louisiana, they had so confused Pemberton that Grant managed to ferry thousands of troops across the river without opposition.

By April 30, Grant had one of his three army corps on the east bank, and the other two would soon join him there. Now, after months of grasping, he could get a firm hold on Pemberton. "When [the crossing] was effected I felt a degree of relief scarcely equalled since," Grant wrote. "I was on dry ground on the same side of the river with the enemy."

Now Grant made another bold decision. He would first strike directly east toward Jackson, the Mississippi capital, and deal with Confederate forces concentrating there under Gen. Joseph E. Johnston, before moving on Vicksburg. Cutting loose from their supplies, the Federals advanced through rugged country thickly grown with timber and crossed by deep ravines filled with underbrush and canebrakes. By May 7, the army had taken the river strong points of Port Gibson and Grand Gulf. When Sherman arrived with the last of the three corps, Grant turned east with 40,000 men and swiftly covered the 40 miles to Jackson.

The capital fell to Grant on May 14. Leaving Sherman's corps behind to destroy the city's military installations, he set the balance of the army, John B. McPherson's XVII Corps and XIII Corps under John A. McClernand, on the road to Vicksburg. Pemberton, meanwhile, had sent a mobile force of 20,000 men into the field, leaving 10,000 troops behind in the fortress. On May 16, McClernand's leading division bumped into the rebels at Champion's Hill. In the key battle of the campaign, the attacking Yankees pushed the rebels off the hill after several hours' hard fighting. Next day, the leading Federals scattered Pemberton's rear guard at the Big Black River, the last water barrier before Vicksburg, and drove the disorganized rebels into the city's defenses.

"Until late in the night the streets and roads were jammed with wagons, cannons, horses, men, mules, stock, sheep," diarist Emma Balfour wrote. The Confederates were badly beaten. In a remarkable 17-day campaign, Grant's army had marched 180 miles, fought and won five major battles, and burned a Confederate capital. On May 18, Sherman's corps moved onto high ground near the Yazoo, north of Vicksburg. Here fresh troops and supplies could be landed. Grant had completed the circle, restoring his supply links and closing in for the final push.

On May 19, however, the string of Federal successes came to a bloody end. Sherman's corps failed to pierce the northern end of the heavily fortified rebel line at Vicksburg. "This is a death struggle," he wrote his wife that night, "and will be terrible." On May 22, Grant tried a second time to rush the rebel defenses. The Federals attacked all along the front, the men in the first waves dragging long ladders

After months of unsuccessful attempts to take Vicksburg, Mississippi, Union troops under General Grant, here *(lower right)* receiving a report of its progress, commenced a siege that began in late May and ended with the Confederate surrender on July 3, 1863. *(Library of Congress)*

needed to scale the fortress's steep ramparts. "For about two hours we had a severe and bloody battle," wrote Sherman, "but at every point we were repulsed." The effort cost 3,000 Union casualties and convinced Grant he could not carry Vicksburg by assault. That evening, the Federals pulled back and began constructing a trench system of their own a few hundred yards from the rebel works. "We'll have to dig our way in," Grant said.

So the siege began. Within a few days, the Yankees had fortified a 15-mile arc from the Yazoo north of Vicksburg around to the Mississippi bottomlands to the south. "Every man in the investing line became an army engineer day and night," one Federal wrote. "The soldiers got so they bored like gophers and beavers, with a spade in one hand and a gun in the other." Behind the lines, Federal artillery kept up a monotonous fire, the guns booming dully at all hours of the day and night. Sweating in their woolen uniforms in the heat and humidity of the Mississippi summer, the Federal troops settled into a routine of digging and firing, firing and digging.

As the siege wore on, they entertained themselves as best they could. "A favorite amusement of the soldiers was to place a cap on the end of a ramrod and raise it just above the head-logs, betting on the number of bullets which would pass through it in a given time," an officer recalled. Even Grant found time for amusement, reverting to his old habit of drinking hard when bored—or so went a long, detailed, and much debated account by a Northern journalist named Sylvanus Cadwallader.

On June 6, Grant set out on an inspection of Union positions up the Yazoo River. According to Cadwallader, the tour supplied the occasion for a two-day drinking spree. Cadwallader said Grant stayed drunk most of the time, alternating between periods of lethargy and wild bursts of activity, including a wild nighttime gallop on horseback through a Union encampment. Grant ended up being carried back to headquarters in an ambulance. Cadwallader left the only eyewitness account of the supposed binge, and some historians question it. But in any event, they all agreed that Grant's 48-hour absence had no effect on the progress of the Vicksburg campaign.

With or without the commanding general, the burrowing went on. The Federals dug saps—trenches leading out at right angles from the main line—toward the rebel outworks. Soon the armies were within grenade-tossing range. "Fighting with hand grenades was all that was possible at such close quarters," a rebel soldier recalled. "As the Federals had the hand grenades and we had none, we obtained our supply by using such of theirs as failed to explode, or by catching them as they came over the parapet and hurling them back."

Inside the Vicksburg fortress, the soldiers and civilians ran short of all kinds of supplies. By mid-June, the troops were down to one-third rations. They ate bread made of ground peas, cane shoots, and even weeds. Mule meat went for one dollar per pound. Citizen and soldier alike ate horse, dog, cat, even rat.

"I have never understood the full force of these questions—what shall we eat? What shall we drink? And wherewithal shall we be clothed?" wrote diarist Dora Miller, a Union sympathizer caught in the siege. Always, too, there were the bombardments, though these caused surprisingly few civilian deaths, probably fewer than a dozen. To protect themselves, Vicksburg residents dug into the yellow clay hillsides, scooping out so many caves that the watching Federals began referring to the place as "Prairie Dog Village."

"Where is Johnston?" the Vicksburg newspaper, now printed on the back of wallpaper, demanded. Gen. Joseph E. Johnston waited with 30,000 troops near Canton, Mississippi, off to the northeast, certain of the inevitability of Vicksburg's fall and of the futility of moving against Grant's 70,000 men. He advised Pemberton to try a breakout. But Pemberton's troops were too weak for such an effort. Morale in the fortress had begun to collapse. "If you can't feed us, you had better surrender," suggested a letter dated June 28 to Pemberton signed by "Many Soldiers."

Johnston belatedly began an advance toward Vicksburg on June 29, and by July 1 his leading elements had approached Sherman's rearward defensive line on the Big Black River. On July 3, he sent Pemberton a note, smuggled through the Union lines, telling him that he would attack on July 7. But he had sent it too late. By then Pemberton, under a flag of truce, had asked Grant for surrender terms.

The guns fell silent on the night of July 3, the troops observing an informal cease-fire while their generals negotiated. Rebel and Yankee mingled under the summer stars. "Several brothers met, and any quantity of cousins," a Federal private wrote. "It was a strange scene." After midnight, Grant sent a note offering parole to the rebels, meaning they would remain in the Confederacy in return for their promise not to take up arms until they were exchanged for Federal captives. Pemberton accepted, and the North celebrated a glorious Fourth of July.

Port Hudson was a Confederate fortress on the Mississippi River down from Vicksburg; it served to block the movement of Union ships up the river, but with the fall of Vicksburg it surrendered on July 9, 1863. *(Library of Congress)*

The next day, Johnston retreated northeastward under pressure from Sherman. On July 9 the downriver fortress of Port Hudson, Louisiana, doomed by Vicksburg's fall, surrendered to Federal forces. A week later, a merchant steamboat arrived in New Orleans after making an uninterrupted trip down the Mississippi River from St. Louis.

Although nearly two years of hard fighting lay ahead, the Confederacy would never recover from the double blow of Gettysburg and Vicksburg. Of the two, Vicksburg may have done the most damage to the Southern cause. Grant's brilliant campaign cut the rebel nation in two. It opened the Mississippi to trade, restoring the rich Midwest's main route to the outside world. And it freed a veteran army for operations in Middle Tennessee, one of the last Confederate strongholds.

President Lincoln's Indiana and Illinois background had taught him the overarching significance of the great river. Now, in Washington, he exulted over news of Grant's triumph. In Lincoln's words, "The father of waters again goes unvexed to the sea."

IN THE
CHARNEL HOUSE

When nurse Georgeanna Woolsey arrived in Gettysburg soon after the end of the great battle she nearly sickened from breathing in the odor of the rotting dead. They were beyond help, but among the 7,000 corpses bloating in the July heat lay several times as many wounded—nearly 15,000 Yankees and thousands of rebels left behind in Lee's retreat. Regimental burial units went to work hollowing out hundreds of shallow graves in the Pennsylvania countryside. Woolsey and a few other volunteers, holding cloths soaked in cologne over their faces, sought out the living and tried to do the best they could for them.

The numbers were overwhelming. Stuart's Confederate cavalry had cut the rail lines leading north from Gettysburg, so the hospital trains could not run. There were too few doctors, too few supplies. Field hospitals, set up in haste on low ground during the emergency, were flooded in the heavy rains of July 4. Some of the wounded, unable to move, actually drowned. The fortunate ones, those who could walk or drag themselves off the battlefield, eventually received rudimentary treatment—had their wounds cleaned and dressed, and were given deep drafts of whiskey or brandy to dull the pain. The others, thousands of them, had to wait their turn.

John Dooley, a Confederate soldier shot through both thighs in Pickett's charge on July 3, 1863, survived his wounds to recall, years later, the unearthly sounds of the aftermath: men groaning for water, the shrieks and howls of men in terrible pain, the death rattles of men for whom help would never come. Some wounded went so long without attention that vermin infested their torn flesh. For Dooley, aid finally came on July 9—six days after the battle ended.

Dorothea Dix *(Library of Congress)*

The aftermath of Gettysburg strained medical resources to the limit, but even a minor battle could overtax the armies' inadequate medical services. Still, care of the sick and wounded had improved considerably by 1863, especially in the North, largely due to the efforts of individual volunteers such as nurse Woolsey, a well-to-do young New Yorker and niece of the president of Yale University, and of organizations such as the U.S. Sanitary Commission.

By then, prejudices toward women on the battlefield had dissipated, even in the South, where initial resistance had been greatest. Many Southern men at first could not reconcile the sight of women swabbing the wounds and emptying the bedpans of butchered soldiers with their ideals of serene, uncontaminated womanhood. Soon, though, Southern women were forcing a reconsideration. "The foul air from this mass of human beings at first made me giddy and sick, but I soon got over it," Kate Cumming, a 27-year-old volunteer nurse, wrote from a Corinth, Mississippi, hospital after the battle of Shiloh in April 1862. "We have to walk, and when we give the men anything kneel, in blood and water, but we think nothing of it."

To many skeptical Northerners, nurses were no different from any of the other camp followers—laundresses, cooks, prostitutes—who trailed every army. The Sanitary Commission, a private organization with excellent political connections, soon changed that perception. The commission provided hundreds of volunteer nurses, raised millions of dollars for facilities and supplies, and pressed for reforms in the army medical corps. Among other innovations, the reformers forced the army to accept women nurses, organized in an experimental volunteer corps headed by Dorothea Dix.

A 59-year-old reformer noted for her work in prisons and insane asylums, the dour and strong-willed Dix established strict standards for her volunteers, some of which had little to do with aptitude for the job. She preferred homely women between the ages of 30 and 45, required certifications of health and character, and prohibited the wearing of hoopskirts.

"I am in possession of one of your circulars and will comply with all your requirements," a volunteer wrote Dix. "I am plain-looking enough to suit you, and old enough. I have no near relatives in the war, no lover there. I never had a husband, and am not looking for one—will you take me?"

Altogether, North and South, 2,000 women served as nurses. They rarely had any medical training, although in that respect they were not inferior to some army surgeons. In one volunteer regiment, the surgeon had been a barber in civilian life; he brought along his son as assistant. Neither had been examined by any medical board. In many regiments, the soldiers feared the doctor more than the disease. "I pray the regiment may improve," Capt. E. G. Abbott of the 2nd Massachusetts wrote in December 1862, "but with our present surgeon I see no prospect of good medical attendance. . . . He is a jackass—a fool—and an ignorant man."

The medical arts were primitive in the 1860s. Surgery could be barbaric—arms and legs were amputated even in cases of minor wounds, for amputation was the accepted treatment for gangrene. Soldiers invariably remarked on the ghastly refuse of the field hospital, which typically consisted of severed limbs piled high outside the operating tent. Many observers noted, too, how men hit in the upper body would pull open their coats and shirts, searching for the exact location of the wound. The men understood that stomach wounds were likely to be fatal—as in fact they were in more than 90 percent of cases, because doctors did not know how to prevent internal infection.

Whiskey, calomel and rhubarb, mustard, Epsom salts, turpentine, and "blue pill and quinine" were commonly prescribed for diarrhea

TWO EXEMPLARY WOMEN

Most of the approximately 2,000 women who served as nurses on both sides in the Civil War have been largely forgotten—except, perhaps, by their descendants and the communities from which they came— but two individuals have entered the pantheon of notable Americans. The better known is probably Clara Barton (1821–1912), who is recognized primarily as the founder of the Red Cross in the United States. She was, in fact, motivated to work toward this goal because of her experiences in the Civil War. Never actually having trained as a nurse, she was working in the U.S. Patent Office in Washington, D.C., when the war broke out, and she began her career simply by seeking and distributing provisions for the wounded after the First Battle of Bull Run (1861). From this, she proceeded to function as a sort of "freelance" nurse to the Union troops of the Army of the Potomac. In 1864, she accepted her first and only official appointment to serve as superintendent of the nurses on the Virginia peninsula south of Richmond. When the war ended, she formed an agency to locate missing dead soldiers and, when found, see them buried in marked graves. She left for Europe in 1869 and, after serving as a nurse in the Franco-Prussian War and seeing the role of the International Red Cross, she returned and worked to establish an American branch, which was formally achieved in 1881.

Less widely known is Mary Edwards Walker (1832–1919). She was one of the first women in the United States to graduate from medical school (Syracuse Medical College, in 1855). Not surprisingly, she was dedicated to advancing women's rights, including dress reform; in particular, she insisted on wearing the new "bloomers" (loose trousers gathered at the ankles). Following the First Battle of Bull Run, she began to serve as a surgeon for the Union army, and in 1864, she was captured by Confederate troops and held prisoner for four months until exchanged for a Confederate officer. In 1865, she was awarded the Congressional Medal of Honor, the first and only woman to be so honored. She went on to campaign for the women's right to vote.

These, then, are only two of the many women who tended to the wounded and dying troops in the Civil War. And both Clara Barton and Mary Edwards Walker have been honored with U.S. commemorative postage stamps.

Mary E. Walker, one of the first American women to graduate from a medical school, went on to serve as a surgeon in the Union army. *(Library of Congress)*

and other camp complaints. "The first day Dr. gave me a powder that came very near turning my stomach inside out and today he gave me 20 drops of Aromatic Sulforic Acid 3 times a day; that goes better," a Connecticut soldier wrote home. "I will inclose one of my powders. It will cure any ails that flesh is heir to, from a sore toe to brain fever."

Such remedies worked by accident when they worked at all. As a result, disease claimed four times as many Civil War soldiers as battle did. In the Union army, diarrhea and dysentery alone caused more soldier deaths—about 100,000—than shot and shell. Measles, smallpox, and malaria were epidemic. Men from the cities seemed hardened to some diseases, but those from country districts, especially in isolated areas of the Midwest, were susceptible to every malady. In newly raised regiments, two-thirds of the men might be on the sick list at any given time. Even in veteran regiments, sick rates often reached 20 to 25 percent.

"We knew absolutely nothing of 'germs,'" Federal surgeon W. W. Keen recalled 50 years after the war. "Sanitation was crude and unsatisfactory . . . research had not discovered any of the antitoxins nor the role of the insect world in spreading disease. . . . We used undisinfected instruments from undisinfected plush-lined cases, and still worse, used marine sponges which had been used in prior pus cases and had only been washed in tap water," Keen went on. "If a sponge or an instrument fell on the floor it was washed and squeezed in a basin of tap water and used as if it were clean. . . . If there was any difficulty in threading the needle we moistened [the silk] with bacteria-laden saliva, and rolled it between bacteria-laden fingers. We dressed the wounds with clean but undisinfected sheets, shirts, tablecloths, or other linens rescued from the family ragbag. . . . We knew nothing about antiseptics and therefore used none."

No wonder, then, that soldiers learned to dread the hospital. "If a man Lives he Lives and if he Dies he Dies. A dog is more thought of [at home] than A Solger [soldier] is hear," a Confederate wrote from a Richmond hospital. "I had rather risk a battle than the Hospitals," a Yankee wrote.

Florence Nightingale, legendary for her work among the British sick and wounded during the Crimean War in the 1850s, had a simple first rule of nursing: "Do the sick no harm." Many nurses, aware of their ignorance and inexperience, realized that small comforts were often the best they could provide. A nurse could clean a wound, bandage it, and keep the bandage moist. Beyond that, kind attentions were as effective as science. "Apothecary and medicine chest might be dispensed with," nurse Hannah Ropes said, "if an equal amount of genuine sympathy could be brought home to our stricken men." The poet Walt Whitman visited Washington hospitals daily, distributing sweets, cool drinks, and tobacco, reading to the men, and writing letters for them. "I can testify that friendship had literally cured a fever, and the medicine of daily affection, a bad wound," he wrote.

Whitman also toured hospitals near the Virginia battlefront, where the horrors were at their freshest. A Civil War rifle discharged a large bullet at a relatively slow velocity. The impact caused terrible mutilations, and the low velocity meant that a ball rarely passed through the body, greatly increasing the risk of infection. At first, shock dulled the pain, but gradually the shock wore off. A wounded man would lie where

Walt Whitman (1819–
1892) (*National
Archives*)

he had fallen, cold, hungry, thirsty, and in pain, until a stretcher bearer
could get to him. Then he had an excruciating ride in an ambulance,
often a springless farm wagon. In the field hospital, surgeons provided
such emergency treatment as seemed necessary, from a simple scouring
of the wound to amputation.

So close to the battle, hospitals were "merely tents—and sometimes very poor ones—the wounded lying on the ground, lucky if
their blankets are spread on layers of pine or hemlock twigs or small
leaves," Whitman reported from Fredericksburg in December 1862.
"It is pretty cold. The ground is frozen hard, and there is occasional
snow."

Whitman responded poetically to what he saw after the Battle of
Chancellorsville in 1863. In "A March in the Ranks Hard-Prest," it is
nighttime in a makeshift hospital in a church at a country crossroads:

Faces, varieties, postures beyond description, most in obscu-
rity some of them dead, / Surgeons operating, attendants holding lights, the smell of ether, the odor of blood / The crowd, O
the crowd of bloody forms, the yard outside also fill'd / Some
on the bare ground, some on planks or stretchers, some in the

One of the largest of the Union army medical centers was the Mt. Pleasant Hospital in a neighborhood of Washington, D.C. Hundreds of troops who could not be treated in field hospitals were brought here. *(Library of Congress)*

death-spasm sweating / An occasional scream or cry, the doctor's shouted orders or calls, the glisten of the little steel instruments catching the glint of the torches. . . .

Union colonel T. D. Kingsley, shot in the face at Port Hudson, Louisiana, on May 27, 1863, recovered sufficiently to write home with full details a month later.

It was dark & the building lighted partially with candles: all around on the ground lay the wounded men; some of them shrieking, some cursing & swearing & some praying; in the middle of the room [were] some 10 or 12 tables just large enough to lay a man on; these were used as dissecting tables & they were covered with blood; near & around the tables stood the surgeons with blood all over them & by the tables was a heap of feet, legs & arms.

The Port Hudson surgeons worked at a furious speed, for the failed Union attack had cost many casualties. Kingsley's turn came finally, perhaps sooner than it might have had he not been a senior officer. "On one of the tables I was laid & [the surgeon] felt of my mouth and then wanted to give me chloroform; this I refused to take & he took a pair of scissors & cut out the pieces of bone in my mouth: then he gave me a drink of whiskey and had me laid away."

The wounded were eventually sent on to general hospitals behind the lines, sometimes in hospital ships, which could be fairly comfortable. More often they were sent in trains in which the men might be stacked on flatcars like firewood. Washington held the largest concentration of the sick and wounded; by mid-1862, there were some 50 hospitals in the capital treating 70,000 soldiers. Hotels, boarding houses, and government buildings were converted into hospitals, although they were rarely suitable for the purpose.

Louisa May Alcott, working in the Union Hotel Hospital in late 1862, started her daily routine by throwing open every window in her ward. "The men grumble and shiver, but the air is bad enough to breed a pestilence," Alcott wrote in her memoir *Hospital Sketches*. "Poke up the fire, add blankets, joke, coax, and command; but continue to open

The wounded at Fredericksburg, Virginia *(Library of Congress)*

NURSE IN THE WILDERNESS

As a doctor's son, Edward Bartlett knew something of pain, and he had caught a brief glimpse of battle as a nine-month enlistee in the 44th Massachusetts. But nothing in his experience prepared this young man from Concord, Massachusetts, for his work as a Sanitary Commission nurse in Fredericksburg, Virginia, during the Battle of the Wilderness in May 1864.

The lightly wounded were the first to arrive. Bartlett distributed lemonade and crackers and listened attentively to their accounts of the opening phase of the fighting in the northern Virginia scrubwoods on May 5. In return, he offered a squeeze on the shoulder and a comforting word. But as the battle intensified, the more seriously wounded began to flood the makeshift hospitals of the war-battered town.

"I saw a man named Adams from Stow who knew father," Ned Bartlett wrote home to Concord. "He is in the Thirty-fourth Massachusetts and his left arm was shot off."

By mid-May the battle had moved on to Spotsylvania Courthouse. Long lines of ambulances slowly jolted their way from the field stations west along dusty roads to Fredericksburg. Now the wounded were streaming in, arriving in batches of hundreds at a time and overwhelming the primitive facilities of the rearward hospitals.

Bartlett forced himself to face their agonies, and he quickly learned the arts of swabbing stomach wounds, splinting shattered limbs, and bandaging lacerations. One of the army surgeons complimented him on his technique.

"I told him I inherited it," the doctor's son replied.

doors and windows as if life depended on it. Mine does, and doubtless many another, for a more perfect pestilence-box than this house I never saw—cold, damp, dirty, full of vile odors from wounds, kitchens, washrooms and stables."

New hospitals, such as Armory Square in Washington, were built on the pavilion plan—a series of long, low buildings, each equipped for 50 to 60 patients, with separate tents or sheds for cooking and other services. Here at least a patient could be clean, warm, and as comfortable as his injury would permit. But death was everywhere. Even if he survived the battlefield, the brigade hospital, and the jarring trip to a general hospital, a Civil War soldier remained in danger. Roughly one in every six wounded men died.

Grant's 1864 campaign ground on remorselessly. With the bloody Battle of Cold Harbor in early June, casualties in the Army of the Potomac reached the heartbreaking total of 60,000 killed and wounded. The surgeons and the nurses followed in the battle's wake, doing what little they could to ease the army's suffering.

This sketch by Arthur Lamley shows soldiers injured in battle being carried on stretchers back to Fredericksburg. *(Library of Congress)*

When death came, it often went unremarked. There was too much of it. Whitman, on his hospital rounds, observed the passing of a young Wisconsin officer wounded at Chancellorsville:

> The poor young man is struggling painfully for breath, his great dark eyes with a glaze already upon them and the choking faint but audible in his throat. An attendant sits by him and will not leave him till the last—yet little or nothing can be done. He will die in an hour or two, without the presence of kith or kin. Meantime the ordinary chat and business of the ward goes on indifferently. Some of the inmates are laughing and joking; others are playing checkers or cards; others are reading.

Fairgrounds Hospital, Petersburg, Virginia, 1865 *(National Archives)*

Whitman was writing in 1863, when tens of thousands of men, Yankee and rebel alike, were still to suffer, weakened by disease, lacerated by gunfire in a hundred more battles—from Chattanooga and Atlanta to the Wilderness, Spotsylvania, Cold Harbor, Petersburg and, finally, Appomattox.

THE BATTLE FOR CHATTANOOGA

By midsummer 1863 Union armies were everywhere victorious. In the east, Meade had turned back Lee's invasion at Gettysburg, and in the west, Grant had taken Vicksburg and reopened the Mississippi River. In the third great theater of the Civil War, Gen. William S. Rosecrans's Army of the Cumberland had driven the Confederates under General Braxton Bragg out of middle Tennessee. By mid-August Rosecrans had closed in on Chattanooga, Tennessee, a junction of important east-west railway lines. Its capture would sever Confederate communications at a vital point and open Atlanta and interior Georgia, the last rebel bastion, to Federal invasion.

Rosecrans and Bragg had met before, along the Stones River near Murfreesboro, Tennessee, on the last day of 1862. Bragg had finally stopped there at the end of his long retreat after the Battle of Perryville, Kentucky, in October. The fight at Stones River settled nothing, however. When Bragg claimed victory after a fierce confrontation, Rosecrans refused to leave the battlefield. Casualties had been terrible, amounting to nearly a third of the 75,000 men engaged, and both sides were too weak to renew the battle. On January 3, 1863, the Confederates moved off, retreating 30 miles southward into defensive positions along the Duck River. Despite pressure from President Lincoln and General-in-Chief Halleck in Washington, Rosecrans did not disturb Bragg there, and the Tennessee winter passed uneventfully into spring.

The methodical Rosecrans waited more than six months after the Stones River battle to resume the offensive. When he finally moved, he advanced with speed and guile. In less than two weeks Rosecrans, ahead of Bragg at every step, flanked the Confederates out of their Duck River lines and chased them some 80 miles southeastward into Chattanooga. After resting several weeks, Rosecrans put the army in

George H. Thomas (1816–
1870), "The Rock of
Chickamauga" *(National
Archives)*

motion southwest of Chattanooga in an effort to trap the Confederates in the town and cut off their retreat. Again outmaneuvered, Bragg
fell back into the north Georgia hills in early September. Union forces
entered Chattanooga on September 9.

Hardly pausing this time, Rosecrans sent large forces to pursue
the Confederates southward into the valley of West Chickamauga
Creek. Bragg, however, expected reinforcements, including Gen. James
Longstreet's 12,000-strong corps from Lee's army in Virginia, and as
these troops began to arrive he prepared a counterstroke. For several
days, the armies groped for one another in the heavily wooded hills
and vine-choked ravines near the Chickamauga. Patrols skirmished
clumsily on September 18. Then, at daybreak on September 19, Yankee
infantry opened fire on probing rebel cavalry near a bridge over the
Chickamauga.

"Our tremendous volley rang along the whole line," Private T. B.
Kellenberger of the 6th Indiana wrote later. "At first all was smoke,
then dust from the struggling steeds. A few riderless horses were running here and there, save which nothing was seen of that cavalry troop.
Thus began the Battle of Chickamauga."

The fighting soon became general. Bragg concentrated his attack
on the Union left, sending assault after assault into General George H.

The Battle of Chickamauga Creek, one of the bloodiest of the war, was fought on September 19–20, 1863, and ended with the Federal forces retreating to Chattanooga, Tennessee. *(Library of Congress)*

Thomas's XIV Corps lines. Rosecrans fed in reinforcements throughout the day, and Thomas held. The fighting ended inconclusively at dusk, although both sides kept up a brisk fire in the darkness. Thousands of wounded lay untended, and even the unharmed passed a miserable night. "Water could not be found; the rebels had possession of the Chickamauga, and we had to do without," a Yankee veteran wrote. "Few of us had blankets and the night was very cold. All looked with anxiety for the coming of the dawn; for although we had given the enemy a rough handling, he had certainly used us very hard." Late that night, Bragg decided to renew the pressure against the Union left in the morning.

For two hours that Sunday, September 20, 1863, the battle went much as it had gone the day before. Then mischance presented the Confederates with an opportunity to turn the stalemate into a victory.

In shifting forces to meet Bragg's attacks, Rosecrans unwittingly opened a quarter-mile gap in the Union center. By coincidence, Longstreet at the same time aimed a powerful attack at just that place in the line. At 11:15 A.M., 16,000 rebels surged forward and exploded straight through the gap, breaking up parts of five divisions and penetrating a mile deep into the Federal positions.

Charles A. Dana, a New York journalist and an agent of Secretary of War Edwin Stanton (he filed regular confidential reports to Stanton), had been dozing at Rosecrans's headquarters when Longstreet struck. Waking up, he saw Rosecrans, a Roman Catholic, making the sign of the cross. "Hello," Dana said to himself. "If the general is crossing himself, we are in a desperate situation."

Longstreet's rebels came on in force, scattering the panicky Federals before them. "All was confusion," wrote Lt. Col. Gates Thruston of Alexander McCook's XX Corps staff. "No order could be heard above the tempest of battle. With a wild yell the Confederates swept on far to their left. . . . Rosecrans was borne back in the retreat."

Only Thomas's corps, which with reinforcements now contained nearly half the army, remained intact. Thomas, a tall, heavily built loyalist Virginian, withdrew his divisions a few hundred yards to a new defensive line on a rise called Snodgrass Hill. Thomas held his ground throughout the afternoon, allowing the bulk of McCook's and Thomas L. Crittenden's broken corps to cover the eight miles back to Chattanooga in safety. By Longstreet's count, the rebels launched 25 separate assaults against Thomas. Gradually the pressure wore away the Yankee line. Thomas, soon to be known as the "Rock of Chickamauga" for his efforts that day, began to disengage in the failing light of late afternoon, detaching one division after another. "Like magic," Longstreet wrote afterward, "the Union army had melted away in our presence."

Sensing that Thomas had gone, the rebels let out a mighty cheer. "It was the ugliest sound any mortal ever heard," wrote Union lieutenant Ambrose Bierce, who later would make enduring fiction out of his Civil War experiences, "even a mortal exhausted and unnerved by two days of hard fighting, without sleep, without rest, without food, and without hope. There was, however, a space somewhere at the back of us across which that horrible yell did not prolong itself—and through that we finally retired in profound silence and dejection, unmolested."

Bragg did not follow the retreating Federals. Casualties had reduced his army by one-third, and so many horses had been killed that he could not move his artillery. In the end, Chickamauga would turn out to have been the bloodiest of the western battles, with 35,000 dead, wounded, and missing on both sides—in proportion to the number of troops involved, the equal of Gettysburg in carnage. Bragg did, however, succeed in moving his Confederate forces forward onto the heights outside Chattanooga, on Lookout Mountain looming over the Tennessee River and the long spine of Missionary Ridge. Within a few days the rebels had sealed off the town on three sides, leaving Rosecrans only a single tenuous supply line over a rough mountain road to the north. Bragg settled in for a siege in early October, reckoning on starving the Federals into surrender.

Rosecrans, meantime, hunkered down behind Chattanooga's fortifications. He reorganized his corps leadership, relieving McCook

After defeating the Federals at Chickamauga, Gen. Braxton Bragg led his forces to Lookout Mountain overlooking Chattanooga, where he kept the Federals under siege. *(Library of Congress)*

and Crittenden from command. For the time being, Rosecrans stayed, though his days seemed numbered. After all, Stanton remarked, McCook and Crittenden had "made pretty good time away from the fight, but Rosecrans beat them both." Stanton's taunt was unfair, as Rosecrans had proven his physical courage beyond doubt. Still, the defeat at Chickamauga left Rosecrans dazed and despondent. He could

RAILROADS AND WAR

The United States led the world in railroad development in the 1850s. Some 21,000 miles of track were laid during the decade before the Civil War, bringing total U.S. mileage to 30,000—more than all the rest of the world combined. Railroads replaced cotton as the leading factor of U.S. economic growth.

Development was uneven; the North had more track, more locomotives, more passenger and freight cars. Both sides, though, used the rails for military advantage from the start. The first Northern militia regiments reached Washington, D.C., by rail in April 1861, and in July, Confederate general Joseph E. Johnston made strategic use of Virginia railroads to move forces from the Harpers Ferry area to Manassas on the eve of the First Battle of Bull Run.

In the autumn of 1863, both sides shifted forces from the Virginia theater to Chattanooga by rail. Confederate general James Longstreet's 12,000-strong corps, completing a roundabout trip via the Carolinas, reached the Chickamauga battlefield in time to exert a decisive influence on the outcome. A few weeks later, Union commanders transported two corps of the Army of the Potomac—20,000 men with horses and artillery—west to Chattanooga. The 1,233-mile journey took 11 days—the fastest movement of a large body of troops before the 20th century.

As the war advanced, Union forces became ever more dependent on the rails. Dependency carried a price, though: The long, thin ribbons of track were vulnerable to Confederate hit-and-run raids. Blown bridges, burned water towers, and torn-up track could choke off supplies for days.

"Railroads are the weakest things in war," said Union general William T. Sherman, who would sever his advancing army's dependence on the railroad and live off the land during the Savannah and Carolinas campaigns. "A single man with a match can destroy and cut off communications."

not regain his confidence. "Our fate is in the hands of God," he wired Lincoln resignedly. To the president, he seemed "stunned and confused, like a duck hit on the head."

Lincoln and Stanton acted speedily to contain the Chickamauga disaster. In late September, they approved the transfer west of two corps from the Army of the Potomac. In the largest and swiftest railroad movement of the war, 23,000 men were transported 1,200 miles from Washington to the Federal base at Bridgeport, Tennessee, in six days. In October, Lincoln established a new command, the Division of the Mississippi, consisting of the entire region between the great river and the Appalachians. He put Ulysses S. Grant in charge.

Grant's new command incorporated his old Army of the Tennessee, now marching eastward toward Chattanooga from Mississippi under William T. Sherman; the Army of the Cumberland; and Ambrose E. Burnside's Army of the Ohio, which had advanced to Knoxville in northeastern Tennessee in late August. Grant took control at once. He replaced the demoralized Rosecrans with Thomas on October 19. Then he approved a daring plan to open the river and road routes west of besieged Chattanooga.

By late October, Union forces in the city were down to quarter rations of hard bread—or "crackers," as the men called it—and there were serious shortages of clothing and firewood. Some soldiers were so hungry they stole the horses' rations of three ears of corn a day. The siege, wrote Capt. C. C. Briant of the 6th Indiana, reduced his men to "skeletons—pale, thin-faced, sickly looking . . . so weak they would stagger as they walked."

The Union chief engineer, Brig. Gen. William F. Smith, proposed breaking the siege by taking the Tennessee River crossing at Brown's Ferry and the high ground that dominated the road leading to it. Some 1,500 men from Chattanooga were to float downstream by night to seize Brown's Ferry. Meanwhile, the two corps from the Army of the Potomac under Joseph Hooker were to cross the Tennessee at Bridgeport and march west to meet the riverborne detachment.

The operation went off without flaw. By midafternoon of October 27, Union engineers were building a pontoon bridge across the Tennessee at Brown's Ferry. Hooker's corps arrived the next day to link up with the bridgehead. Chattanooga's western approaches were now open, and soon wagon after wagon would carry food, forage, and ammunition along what the soldiers dubbed the Cracker Line.

"The question of supplies may now be regarded as settled," Grant wired Halleck. "If the rebels give us one week more time I think all danger . . . will have passed away, and preparations may commence for offensive operations."

Meantime, on the other side, Bragg's Army of Tennessee had begun to erode. The rebels on the heights suffered ceaselessly through that cold, rainy autumn. "Nothing to eat but we are well supplied with lice," Robert Watson of the 7th Florida wrote in his diary. "Many of the regiment are sick from drinking bad water and eating poorly cooked food. I think we will all be sick soon if they don't give us more food."

There were inner weaknesses too. Bragg, stubborn and irritable, frequently afflicted with migraine headaches, often an unnecessarily strict disciplinarian, had never been a popular commander. He had never inspired the full confidence of his senior generals, and after

As part of General Grant's strategy to break out of the siege of Chattanooga, on November 23, Union forces under Gen. Philip Sheridan attacked Confederate troops at Orchard Knob, an outpost below Missionary Ridge. *(Library of Congress)*

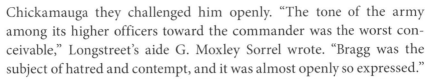

Chickamauga they challenged him openly. "The tone of the army among its higher officers toward the commander was the worst conceivable," Longstreet's aide G. Moxley Sorrel wrote. "Bragg was the subject of hatred and contempt, and it was almost openly so expressed."

On October 4, 12 of the Confederate army's leading generals petitioned President Davis to fire Bragg. Davis took the revolt seriously enough to travel west from Richmond to try to quell it. He arrived on October 9 and met with Bragg and the dissidents. Longstreet and others repeated the call for Bragg's removal. Davis, however, declined to act. Bragg eventually transferred, suspended, and demoted the most vocal of his critics. In early November, he sent Longstreet north to Knoxville with nearly a quarter of the army—apparently both to get a rival out of the way, and to threaten the Federal troops there under General Burnside.

Bragg probably hoped to lure Grant out of Chattanooga to go to Burnside's aid in Knoxville. However, Grant had no such intention. In fact, he resolved to attack the weakened Confederates as soon as possible. He sent orders to Sherman to hurry his army up to Chattanooga. Using these fresh troops, plus Hooker's two corps, Grant planned to strike the rebels on either flank. The center of the line, along dominant Missionary Ridge, he believed too strong to attack directly. While Thomas's Army of the Cumberland launched secondary assaults in the center, Sherman was to assail the northern end of Missionary Ridge and sweep southward along it, driving the rebels into Hooker's divisions advancing from the opposite direction.

However, the battle did not work out that way. The efficient Sherman successfully moved his army across the Tennessee on November 24 but made little progress against a strong defense directed by Irish-born rebel Gen. Patrick Cleburne. Operations went more smoothly on the right, where Hooker hoped to repair a reputation badly damaged at Chancellorsville earlier that year. Hooker sent three divisions up the north slope of Lookout Mountain and, encountering surprisingly light resistance in fog and light rain, advanced halfway to the crest by nightfall. Bragg pulled all the rebel forces off the mountain that night, permitting Yankee patrols to raise the Stars and Stripes over the bald face of Lookout early on November 25.

Away to the north, Sherman ordered assault after assault that morning against Cleburne's two divisions. These attacks cost heavily in casualties but gained no ground. Sherman watched impatiently as his

In a battle on November 24, Union troops drove the Confederates off Lookout Mountain. Because the Confederate forces were located at a height of some 1,100 feet, this became known as "The Battle Above the Clouds." *(Library of Congress)*

brigades charged and fell back. "The General was in an unhappy state of mind," one of his officers wrote, "his hopes of promptly overwhelming the enemy's right flank and thus striking the decisive blow of the battle having been dashed. It was a stinging disappointment. He gave vent to his feelings in language of astonishing vivacity."

By default, the key role would go to Thomas. Grant believed, mistakenly, that Bragg had heavily reinforced Cleburne during the day, and to relieve the pressure on Sherman he ordered Thomas to launch a limited attack on the first line of rebel positions at the base of Missionary Ridge. Late in the afternoon, 23,000 men of Thomas's Army of the Cumberland moved forward on a two-mile front, forcing the defenders out of their trenches and into the second line midway up the ridge. The attackers soon found themselves in an awkward position, however, for the rebels poured down a steady fire from above. "We can't live here," one regimental commander remarked. All at once, company and regimental and brigade officers up and down the line seemed to come to the same conclusion. From his command post on Orchard Knob, Grant watched with mounting anxiety as a mass of bluecoats swarmed up the slope.

"Thomas, who ordered those men up the ridge?"

"I don't know," Thomas answered. "I did not."

The battle had gone out of Grant's control, and for an agonizing 30 minutes, he could not be certain of the result. At first, the rebels resisted fiercely, and visions of the wreck of his army must have flashed through Grant's mind. Soon, though, the Confederates' second line began to waver. "The hill was dreadful steep and the enemy kept up a continual fire," wrote diarist Watson of the 7th Florida, describing the retreat to the third line on the crest. "I stopped several times and took a shot at the damned Yankees and at the same time it rested me." The last stretch to the top left him exhausted.

The Yankees kept coming on, surging up to the crest where, like Watson, many rebels were too dazed to regroup and defend themselves.

2nd Minnesota Regiment in the storming of Missionary Ridge, Chattanooga, Tennessee, November 26, 1863 *(Library of Congress)*

"Those defending the heights became more and more desperate as our men approached the top," an Illinois soldier remembered. "They shouted 'Chickamauga' as though the word itself were a weapon; they thrust cartridges into the guns by the handsful, they lighted the fuses of shells and rolled them down, they seized huge stones and threw them, but nothing could stop the force of the charge."

Suddenly the rebels broke. "Gray-clad men rushed wildly down the hill and into the woods," an 8th Kansas infantryman wrote, "tossing away knapsacks, muskets, and blankets as they ran. Batteries galloped back along the narrow, winding roads with reckless speed, and officers, frantic with rage, rushed from one panic-stricken group to another, shouting and cursing as they strove to check the headlong flight."

To many Federals, the success seemed miraculous—"as awful," Dana wrote, "as a visible interposition of God." In fact, there were rational explanations. Bragg had dangerously weakened his army by sending Longstreet off to Knoxville. His placement of his forces had been faulty too—many regiments were not well positioned to resist a charge. The advancing Federals often found themselves protected by folds in the ground from rebel defensive fire. Finally, hunger and dissension undermined the rebels' will to fight. In spite of it all, as Bragg noted afterward, the Missionary Ridge position ought to have been held. "No satisfactory excuse can possibly be given for the shameful conduct of our troops," he told Davis.

By sunset on that short late November day the Confederates were in full retreat. With Cleburne holding off pursuit with stubborn rearguard fighting, Bragg managed to form a new line near Dalton, Georgia, 30 miles to the south. If the loss of Vicksburg had cut the Confederacy in two, the retreat out of Tennessee made a third division. And Grant's victory put the Yankees on the road to Atlanta and beyond. From Richmond, Jefferson Davis ruled a dismembered nation, its surviving parts increasingly isolated.

After the Missionary Ridge rout, Sherman marched north to relieve the rebel pressure on Knoxville. Having failed in a direct assault on Burnside's lines, Longstreet prudently moved out of the advancing Sherman's path. Sherman, his sights fixed southward, resisted Grant's suggestion that he trail Longstreet into Virginia. "My troops are in excellent heart," he wrote Grant, "ready for Atlanta or anywhere." So Sherman turned his attention to the rich, so far untouched, Confederate heartland.

TECUMSEH
THE GREAT

In early March 1864, President Lincoln summoned Ulysses S. Grant east to Washington to become general-in-chief of the Union armies. The two met for the first time at a White House reception on the evening of March 8. The next day, Lincoln promoted Grant to the rank of lieutenant general and asked the victor of Fort Donelson, Shiloh, Vicksburg, and Chattanooga to deliver one final triumph—the defeat of the Confederates in Virginia. Moving off for his showdown with Robert E. Lee, Grant left the western theater in the charge of William Tecumseh Sherman, with orders "to move against [the rebel] army, to break it up, and to get into the interior of the enemy's country as far as you can." Sherman would carry out these instructions with a brilliance that would lead some historians to rate him the best Federal commander of the Civil War.

The Ohio-born Sherman, like Grant, had suffered through stretches of hard times. He commanded a brigade at the Bull Run disaster in the war's first summer. Later in 1861, General Halleck relieved him of command in Kentucky when newspapers circulated reports that he had gone insane. He had, in fact, shown symptoms of what today would be called a nervous breakdown. Halleck gave him three weeks' leave, then one or two easy jobs in Missouri. The respite seemed to restore Sherman's confidence. He succeeded Grant in command of the Cairo, Illinois, base in February 1862 and two months later led a division at the Battle of Shiloh. There, amid the near-disaster of the first day's fighting, he and Grant formed the great partnership of the war. Sherman led a corps in the Vicksburg campaign, then took over Grant's Army of the Tennessee when Lincoln gave Grant overall command in the East.

A fellow officer described the red-haired, red-bearded Sherman, 44 years old in 1864, as "the concentrated essence of Yankeedom . . . tall,

Major General Sherman *(front center, arms folded)*, with members of his
senior staff, ca. 1865 *(National Archives)*

spare and sinewy, a very homely man, with a regular nest of wrinkles
in his face." Brilliant, restless, expressive, he seemed always in motion.
"He walked, talked or laughed all over," a journalist wrote. "He per-
spired thought at every pore . . . pleasant and affable . . . engaging . . .
with a mood that shifted like a barometer in a tropic sea."

His soldiers called him Uncle Billy. These midwesterners—some
130 of Sherman's regiments were from Ohio, Indiana, and Illinois—
respected their commander for his boldness and liked him for his
casual approach to dress, drill, and discipline. He traveled light and
lived like an ordinary soldier, eating hardtack and bacon, wearing plain
faded clothes without symbols of rank, and low-cut shoes rather than a
general's burnished boots. Sherman would end the war with the most
ferocious of fighting reputations. Yet the troops appreciated the care he
took with their lives, and seemed to sense his ambivalence about war.
"Its glory is all moonshine," he said of battle, "even success the most
brilliant is over dead and mangled bodies, with the anguish and lam-
entation of distant families."

Nevertheless, Sherman had prepared himself for a hard war. He set
out from Chattanooga in early May of 1864 for Dalton, Georgia, where

62,000 Confederates under Joseph E. Johnston were dug in. Sherman distributed his 100,000 Union troops in three unequal wings: the Army of the Cumberland under George Thomas, the small Army of the Ohio commanded by James Schofield, and James McPherson's Army of the Tennessee. He planned to use Thomas's larger force to pin the rebels in their trenches, sending McPherson and Schofield out beyond Johnston's flanks. He meant to force the pace and to wait for nothing.

"I'm going to move on Joe Johnston the day Grant telegraphs me he is going to hit Bobby Lee," Sherman told his chief quartermaster officer. "If you don't have my army supplied and keep it supplied, we'll eat your mules up, sir—eat your mules up!"

By May 5, the Federals were opposite Johnston's lines on Rocky Face Ridge, a rugged mountain spine that dominated the pass through which the railroad ran to Atlanta nearly 100 miles to the southeast. Rather than try to enter by what he called this "terrible door of death," Sherman decided to go around. This would be the first in a series of

General Sherman marches his Union troops into Georgia. *(National Archives)*

flank marches that would force the rebels out of one stronghold after another and carry the battle to the outskirts of Atlanta.

For an opener, Sherman sent McPherson on a wide swing to the southwest toward Resaca, some 15 miles in Johnston's rear. The leading brigades met unexpected resistance there, however, and McPherson decided to pull up and await reinforcements. His failure to block the rebel line of retreat allowed Johnston, who now realized the situation had changed, to withdraw safely into new lines around Resaca the night of May 12–13. Sherman did not console the disappointed McPherson. "Well, Mac," he told him, "you missed the opportunity of a lifetime."

A second wide swing forced another rebel retreat, this time another 25 miles back to Cassville. Here, Johnston prepared an assault on Sherman, but the effort misfired and he pulled back yet again, retreating 10 miles to Allatoona Pass overlooking the Etowah River. Still another flank march soon levered Johnston out of this stronghold. By late May, the armies were in contact near the road junction of Dallas, Georgia, fighting intermittently in the woods and ravines there. Over the next few weeks, the opposing forces settled into fortified lines, moving in lockstep eastward as they built their earthworks until, by mid-June, they faced each other at Kennesaw Mountain.

In less than two months, Sherman had covered more than half the distance to Atlanta at a comparatively light cost in casualties—fewer than 10,000 killed, wounded, and missing. Now, though, he lost patience with this war of maneuver. He seemed to believe the marching and digging from Dallas to Kennesaw Mountain had dulled the army's aggressive instincts. "A fresh furrow in a plowed field will stop the whole column, and all begin to entrench," he complained. "We are on the offensive, and . . . must assail and not defend."

So, on June 27, in 100-degree heat, Sherman sent three of Thomas's divisions into the rebel entrenchments on the Kennesaw slopes. The assault failed at a cost, high for this campaign, of 2,500 casualties. Sherman took the check in stride. "Our loss is small compared with some of those in the east," he told Thomas. "It should not in the least discourage us. At times assaults are necessary and inevitable." And he gave McPherson a new set of marching orders for still another effort to move out to the southwest around the Confederate flank.

In response, Johnston continued to fall back toward Atlanta. From Richmond, President Davis urged him to hold the city, with its arms and munitions factories, at all costs. Atlanta's fall, he said, would "open

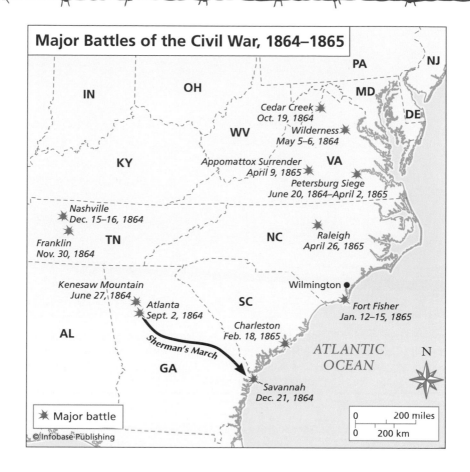

Major Battles of the Civil War, 1864–1865

the way for the Federal army to the Gulf on the one hand, and to Charleston on the other, and close up those rich granaries from which Lee's armies are supplied." In addition, it would sever Confederate communications. "It would give them control of our network of railways and thus paralyze our efforts," Davis said.

Johnston continued sliding backward, and by July 9, the Federals were across the Chattahoochee River and closing in on Atlanta from the north and east. Johnston finally stopped along Peach Tree Creek only four miles from the city. Davis, exasperated, fired his general on the evening of July 17, replacing him, against Lee's advice, with the aggressive John Bell Hood. ("All lion," said Lee of Hood, "none of the fox.") Union commanders hailed Davis's decision as the equivalent of a battlefield victory.

"Three months of sharp work had convinced us that a change from Johnston's methods to those which Hood was likely to employ was . . .

Union forces under General Sherman slowly advanced on Atlanta, Georgia, during summer 1864, and by late July, the city was effectively under siege. Sherman is here depicted observing the final days of the siege before Atlanta fell on September 2. *(Library of Congress)*

to have the enemy grasp the hot end of the poker," wrote Jacob D. Cox, one of Sherman's division commanders. "We were confident that a succession of attacks would soon destroy the Confederate army."

Hood, 32 years old, had lost the use of an arm at Gettysburg and had had a leg amputated almost at the hip after Chickamauga. Aides had to strap him into the saddle to keep him from falling off his horse. But he remained as aggressive—some would say reckless—as ever. He assaulted Thomas's army along Peach Tree Creek on July 20, losing 5,000 men to the Federals' 1,800. Two days later he tried again, striking the flank of McPherson's army at Decatur. This action cost him 10,000 killed, wounded, and missing to the Federals' 3,700. However, this time Sherman lost a key commander in McPherson, who was shot dead as he rode along his lines. Finally, on July 28, Hood attacked Oliver O. Howard, who had succeeded McPherson, at Ezra Church crossroads, taking 5,000 casualties to the Yankees' 600.

As Hood fell back into the Atlanta lines to refit his battered army, Sherman prepared for a siege. He soon lost patience with the operation. Halting the bombardment on August 26, he withdrew all but one corps from the Atlanta lines and drove the bulk of his forces south of the city, intent on cutting the rebels' surviving rail links. Hood completely misread the move, thinking Sherman had retreated northward to protect his own railroad from Confederate cavalry raids. By the time he guessed what had happened, the Federals were in the rebel rear and astride the last open supply line. Sherman had forced Hood to choose between losing his army or giving up Atlanta. Hood evacuated the city the evening of September 1, and Federal troops entered the next day.

"Atlanta is ours, and fairly won," Sherman telegraphed triumphantly to Washington.

The victory could hardly have come at a more critical moment, for in the late summer of 1864 Lincoln faced serious political challenges in his own party and from the resurgent Democrats. A summer of heavy casualties and military stalemate in Virginia left radical Republicans rebellious and encouraged peace Democrats to clamor for a negotiated end to the fighting. In late August, the Democrats nominated the former Union general George B. McClellan as their presidential candidate and adopted a platform calling for an armistice and peace talks. Then, in September, news of the fall of Atlanta stifled

Battery M, 5th U.S. Artillery, with General Sherman in the background, at a Union-occupied rebel fort near Atlanta *(National Archives)*

the Republican opposition and forced McClellan to distance himself from the Democrats' peace platform.

Meanwhile, Sherman worried about protecting his 300-mile-long supply line from Hood, who had moved off to the northwest after abandoning the city. Sherman detached large garrisons to guard key points on the railroad. To make Atlanta easier to defend, he ordered all civilians out of the city. Mayor James M. Calhoun and the City Council protested the eviction notice, saying Sherman had drawn innocents into the conflict. "You cannot qualify war in harsher terms than I will," Sherman replied. "War is cruelty and you cannot refine it. . . . The only way the people of Atlanta can hope once more to live in peace and quiet at home is to stop the war. . . . You might as well appeal against the thunderstorm as against these terrible hardships of war."

THE ELECTION OF 1864
The Soldier Vote

The war, its conduct, and how to end it: These were the overriding issues of the election of 1864. Republicans campaigned for peace through victory on the battlefield. Democrats called for an armistice and negotiations—a policy that most observers, North and South, assumed would result in a Confederate victory by default.

War-weary Confederate troops prayed for the success of the Democratic nominee, the former Union general George McClellan. Union troops overwhelmingly favored staying the course for an indisputable military decision.

"I had rather stay out here a lifetime (much as I dislike it) than consent to a division of our country," one Union veteran wrote.

By 1864, 19 states permitted soldiers to vote in the field. In 12 of these states, absentee soldier votes were counted separately. Lincoln won nearly 80 percent of this total—119,754 to 34,291 for McClellan. Lincoln polled 53 percent of the civilian vote in these states.

Overall, Lincoln rolled up a popular vote majority of 500,000 and carried all but three of the loyal states. And the Republicans gained three-fourths majorities in both houses of Congress. The political decision of 1864 forced Southerners to abandon their last hopes for a negotiated peace that would lead to Confederate independence.

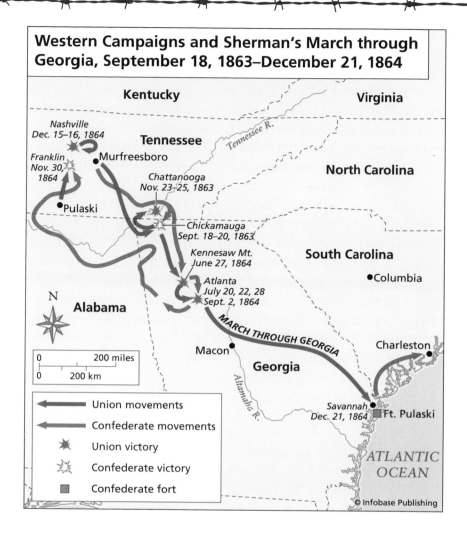

Western Campaigns and Sherman's March through Georgia, September 18, 1863–December 21, 1864

Kentucky

Virginia

Nashville
Dec. 15–16, 1864

Tennessee

Tennessee R.

Franklin
Nov. 30,
1864

Murfreesboro

North Carolina

Chattanooga
Nov. 23–25, 1863

Pulaski

Chickamauga
Sept. 18–20, 1863

South Carolina

Kennesaw Mt.
June 27, 1864

Columbia

N

Alabama

Atlanta
July 20, 22, 28
Sept. 2, 1864

MARCH THROUGH GEORGIA

Charleston

Macon

Georgia

0   200 miles

0   200 km

Altamaha R.

Savannah
Dec. 21, 1864   Ft. Pulaski

⟵ Union movements

⟵ Confederate movements

ATLANTIC
OCEAN

✳ Union victory

✳ Confederate victory

■ Confederate fort

© Infobase Publishing

Hood began hitting Federal communications north of Atlanta in mid-September, and for a time Sherman followed after him. Soon, however, the Union general began forming a plan that would bring unprecedented hardship to the civilians who made it possible for the rebel armies to fight. Resisting Grant's suggestion that he continue the chase and destroy Hood, Sherman proposed cutting loose entirely from the Atlanta base and the imperiled railroad and marching a stripped-down army eastward to the Atlantic.

"I could cut a swath through Georgia to the sea," he wired Grant in Virginia, "divide the Confederacy . . . and come up on the rear of Lee." Lincoln, Grant, and Halleck were all skeptical, and believed that Sherman should first smash Hood, who had begun dreaming of a campaign that would take him deep into Union-held territory. "Damn him, if he'll go to the Ohio River, I'll give him rations," Sherman volunteered. "Let him go north. My business is down south." Sherman, however, did offer to send the reliable Thomas with reinforcements to Nashville to block Hood. "If you can whip Lee and I can march to the Atlantic," he told Grant, "I think Uncle Abe will give us 20 days' leave of absence to see the young folks."

Grant remained doubtful. However, Sherman persisted. "I can make this march," he said, "and make Georgia howl!" Grant finally allowed himself to be persuaded. "Go on, then, as you propose," he wired on November 2. So, as Hood headed slowly toward Nashville, Sherman made final preparations to strike out in the opposite direction.

Sherman kept only what could be carried in 2,500 light wagons, sending back hundreds of tons of surplus stores to the Chattanooga base. To set an example, Sherman himself traveled with a single wagon for his gear and that of all his clerks. ("I think it's as low down as we can get," he said.) He also instructed regimental surgeons to examine every man in the army. "The sick were sent back to Chattanooga and Nashville," wrote Capt. Daniel Oakey of the 2nd Massachusetts. "The army was reduced to its fighting weight, no man being retained who was not capable of a long march."

On November 8, Lincoln won reelection with a comfortable 55 percent of the vote. The result determined the Confederacy's political fate—there would be no negotiated end to the war. On November 15, Sherman's army marched out of Atlanta on a campaign that would play a major role in settling the rebels' military fate.

Sherman's 60,000 men—four military corps and a cavalry division—were arranged in two wings that would follow parallel routes on a front from 25 to 60 miles wide. The wagons carried 200 rounds of ammunition per man, a 20 days' supply of salt pork, hardtack, coffee, salt, and sugar, and five days' rations of oats and corn for the animals. Georgia's plantations and farms would supply the balance of the army's needs.

As they moved out, Union rear guards set fire to railroad stations, factories, and other buildings of military value, burning some 200 acres in the heart of Atlanta. Sherman had hoped to contain the destruction, to keep it within military bounds. "An army is a terrible engine and hard to control," a staff officer, Maj. Henry Hitchcock, had noted. Already, that first night, troops pillaged houses and shops and burned private buildings without orders.

Close to 200 acres of land in the heart of Atlanta was destroyed as Sherman's Union troops set fire to the city when they departed in 1864. *(National Archives)*

For the Union troops, the operation, which came to be known as the March to the Sea, had the feel of a holiday. It aimed for Savannah, 285 miles away, but an advance on such a wide front confused the rebel resistance that lay ahead. The Confederate defenders could not be sure of Sherman's objective, for his two wings threatened Augusta to the north and Macon to the south. With little prospect of heavy fighting, the Federal troops were in high spirits. "This is probably the most gigantic pleasure excursion ever planned," an officer wrote early in the march. "It already beats everything I ever saw soldiering, and promises to prove much richer yet." Beyond Atlanta, whose environs had been stripped bare, the country supplied plenty of food and forage, and the Indian summer days were bright and mild.

"Skirmishers were in advance, flankers were out, and foraging parties were ahead gathering supplies from the rich plantations," remembered Oakey. "We were expected to make 15 miles a day; to corduroy the roads (build roads of logs) where necessary; to destroy such property as was designated by our corps commander; and to consume everything eatable by man or beast."

Sherman's orders were to "forage liberally off the country." Each regiment sent out one official foraging party a day. Sherman advised the troops to plunder rich and hostile civilians and to leave the poor and neutral ones alone, to keep out of private dwellings, and to leave sufficient supplies to sustain families. Usually, however, the "bummers," as they were called, interpreted Sherman's instructions in the broadest possible way.

"Like demons they rushed in," wrote Dolly Burge, a widowed plantation mistress. "My yards are full. To my smoke-house, my Dairy, Pantry, Kitchen and Cellar, like famished wolves they come, breaking locks and whatever is in their way. The thousand pounds of meat in my smoke-house is gone in a twinkling, my flour, my meat, my lard, butter, eggs, pickles both in vinegar and brine, wine, jars and jugs, are all gone. My 18 fat turkeys, my hens, chickens and fowl, my young pigs, are shot down in my yard and hunted as if they were rebels themselves."

Bummers were unmoved by such complaints, or by taunts that they were making war on women. "You urge young men to the battlefield where men are being killed by the thousands, while you stay home and sing 'The Bonnie Blue Flag,'" one Federal soldier told a defiant farm woman. "But you set up a howl when you see the Yankees down here getting your chickens."

A forager could easily become a looter. One stole a Revolutionary War uniform and wore it on the march. Others carried off pictures, mirrors, glass, and other valuables. Foraging parties would return with enormous quantities of plunder. Maj. Sam Merrill of the 70th Indiana provided a catalog of one foraging party's morning haul.

"At the head of the procession an ancient family carriage, drawn by a goat, a cow with a bell, and a jackass," Merrill wrote. "Tied behind . . . a sheep and a calf, the vehicle loaded down with pumpkins, chickens, cabbages, guinea fowls, carrots, turkeys, onions, squashes, a shoat, sorghum, a looking-glass, an Italian harp, sweetmeats, a peacock, a rocking chair, a gourd, a bass viol, sweet potatoes, a cradle, dried peaches, honey, a baby carriage, peach brandy and every other imaginable thing a lot of soldiers could take it in their heads to bring away."

Unofficial foragers—Yankees separated from their regiments, civilian criminals, and even rebel deserters—caused much of the damage. There were cases of rape, and an occasional murder. Sherman claimed that such acts were "exceptional and incidental." But some of his staff believed he could have done more to control the bummers' robbery

Andersonville, Georgia, was a Confederate prison camp where more than 33,000 Union prisoners of war were confined under increasingly deteriorating conditions. *(Library of Congress)*

and violence. "I am bound to say I think Sherman lacking in enforcing discipline," Hitchcock wrote in his journal. "Brilliant and daring, fertile, rapid and terrible, he does not seem to me to carry out things in this respect."

Sherman may have allowed the bummers a great deal of latitude intentionally, because their crimes served a purpose. He justified what some later called a "policy of terror" by claiming it would shorten the war by sapping the enemy's will to resist. "This may seem a hard species of warfare," he said, "but it brings the sad realities of war home to those who have been directly or indirectly instrumental in involving us in its attendant calamities."

So the army swept over the countryside like a pestilence, wrecking scores of miles of railroad track and burning cotton gins, factories, and warehouses. The two wings converged at Milledgeville, the state capital, on November 22. By December 1, leading brigades were in Millen, where the troops stopped to examine the remains of a prison camp for captured Federals. Soldiers there had lived in holes they dug in the ground. A sign above a freshly filled-in trench read, "650 buried here." The camp angered and sickened Sherman's men. "Everyone who visited this place came away with a feeling of hatred toward the Southern Confederacy we had never felt before," one officer wrote.

There were far worse places than Millen, as federal forces soon would learn. At Andersonville, in southwest Georgia, a Confederate prison built for 10,000 men actually held 33,000 by August 1864. Disease, exposure, and starvation had claimed 100 lives a day that summer. After the war, occupying Federals counted more than 13,000 Yankee graves at Andersonville, and the prison commandant, Henry Wirz, became the only participant in the Civil War to be tried and executed for war crimes.

Thousands of liberated slaves, perhaps as many as 25,000, trailed after the army. Sherman, noting that he could not feed, clothe, and shelter them, urged the freedmen to remain on their plantations until occupation forces arrived. Many, though, could not resist freedom's lure, even if that meant hunger. "It was very touching to see the vast numbers of colored women . . . following after us with babies in their arms, and little ones like our Anna clinging to their tattered skirts," an Indiana officer wrote his wife. "One poor creature . . . hid two boys, five years old, in a wagon, intending that they should see the land of freedom if she couldn't."

By December 12, the Union army had drawn up amid swamps, cypress, and live oaks outside Savannah. Behind them lay nearly 300 miles of ruin. "The destruction could hardly have been worse," one soldier wrote, "if Atlanta had been a volcano in eruption and the molten lava had flowed in a stream 60 miles wide and five times as long." Now, for the first time during the march, the Federals encountered formidable defenses, and Sherman began readying the army to overcome them. Instead, Savannah fell without a fight. Sherman made contact with the Union navy in Ossabaw Sound on December 13, and soon vessels were landing rations, ammunition, and tons of accumulated mail. Within a few days Sherman had received news of Thomas, who had smashed Hood's wandering army near Nashville on December 15 and 16. The last of the 10,000 rebel troops in Savannah slipped out quietly on the foggy night of December 20.

The Yankees occupied the city on December 21, and Sherman arrived the next day. He seemed bemused at first by his achievement. "Like a man who has walked a narrow plank, I look back and wonder if I really did it," he wrote his wife. He soon collected himself, however, and sent an exuberant telegram to President Lincoln. "I beg to present you as a Christmas gift the city of Savannah, with 150 heavy guns and plenty of ammunition, also about 25,000 bales of cotton."

The president welcomed the gift, as well as positive word from Sherman's army. The country had not heard from Sherman for more than a month and had been worried. "They called us the Lost Army," Theodore Upson of the 100th Indiana wrote in his diary. "And some thought we would never show up again. I don't think they know what kind of army this is that Uncle Billy has. Why, if Grant can keep Lee and his troops busy we can tramp all over this Confederacy."

Sherman had become a hero. In 1861, the newspapers had called him insane and nearly driven him out of the army. Now, they were calling him Tecumseh the Great. He had taken 60,000 men through hostile territory hundreds of miles from his base. He had destroyed the South's war-making potential in Georgia. And he had placed his army in position to march north and cooperate with Grant against Lee in what would be the concluding campaign of the war.

"I'm going to march to Richmond," Sherman said as 1864 ended. "I expect to turn north when the sun does—and when I go through South Carolina it will be one of the most horrible things in the history of the world."

WEAPONS
AND TACTICS

The Civil War has been called the first modern war. Armies were transported hundreds of miles by railroad; orders were sent to the field by telegraph; aerial observers telegraphed the results of artillery fire to troops on the ground; all of the infantry had rifles, some of them breech-loaders and some even repeaters. Some of the artillery was rifled—that is, interiors of barrels were grooved, giving the guns range and accuracy unheard of in previous wars. Infantry used and faced a variety of hand-operated machine guns, one of which—the Gatling— was used for the rest of the century, revived a 100 years later, and is still in use. At sea, ironclads fought ironclads—and there were far more ironclads in the United States than in the rest of the world combined. Both sides used submarines, and for the first time in history, a submarine sank a surface ship.

Progress in weaponry, powered by the Industrial Revolution, which was now in full force in the United States, greatly outpaced progress in tactics. That is a major reason why the Civil War was the bloodiest conflict in U.S. history. Another reason, of course, was that medical science lagged far behind mechanical design in the 1860s.

A widely promoted view of the Civil War holds that the Confederacy was greatly handicapped because of the greater population and industry of the Northern states. This version fails to acknowledge, however, that the populations being considered are the *white* populations. Much of the work that kept the civilian economy of the Confederacy alive was done by slaves. A much larger percentage of white men of military age in the Confederacy than in the Union were able to go to war. In the battles of the war, the Confederacy was seldom outnumbered by the mythical three-to-one ratio often referred to by some students of the war. In some battles, the Confederates outnum-

These African Americans, former slaves, are working for the Union army
by using levers to loosen the rails of Confederate train lines. Disrupting the
Confederate rail capacity was an important goal of the Federal forces.
(Library of Congress)

bered the Union troops. In most battles, like Gettysburg, the numbers were approximately even.

The extent to which the Confederacy depended on slave labor is
little understood today. As the sidebar on Robert Smalls illustrates,
slaves held some of the most sensitive jobs. This was not because masters thought they were loved by their chattels (although some masters
probably did think so), but because the Confederacy would collapse if
slaves did not do the vital jobs. The slave owners had to accept the risk.

Early in the war, the Confederate army included black soldiers.
Whether they were slaves or freemen is unknown, but Fredrick Law
Olmsted, the great park designer, saw them marching through Maryland after the Second Battle of Bull Run in 1862. The Confederate
army Olmsted watched consisted of some 64,000 men, 3,000 of them
black. They were probably teamsters, laborers, and other troops whose
primary duty was other than combat. They were armed, however. They
carried rifles, muskets, sabers and Bowie knives, and they wore bits
of captured Union uniforms, Confederate uniforms, and state militia

uniforms. They were shabby, but so were the whites. They carried knapsacks, haversacks, and canteens and, Olmstead reported, were obviously part of the Confederate army. He found that interesting, because Confederate leaders later complained bitterly when the Union began to enlist black soldiers.

In Louisiana, the Confederates organized a regiment of 1,400 black freemen. But when the Federals were about to take New Orleans in 1862, the Confederate government evacuated the white militiamen but left the blacks behind. When the Federal forces entered New Orleans, the black militia enlisted en masse in the U.S. Army.

With regard to industry, the South was certainly behind the North. Southerners did, however, start a surprising number of foundries and factories after the war began, and the South had acquired plenty of the products of Northern industry before the war began. These products

Located at City Point, Virginia, during the siege of Petersburg, these trains belong to the Federal Military Railroad. The Civil War was the first war in which the railroads played a major role in supporting combat operations. (*Library of Congress*)

ROBERT SMALLS—SEAGOING MOSES

Thousands of slaves found freedom on the side of the Union lines during the Civil War, but none did it as spectacularly—or as comfortably—as Robert Smalls.

Smalls was part of the crew of the *Planter,* a cotton boat that had been converted to an armed naval auxiliary steamer based in Charleston. *Planter* was the flagship for the commander of the forts guarding Charleston. The crew of the *Planter* were all slaves, except the captain and the first and second mates.

The officers and crew of the steamer all slept ashore, and there were no guards on the ship. The authorities saw no need for guards. The Yankees were all safely on the other side of Charleston's many forts.

Smalls considered the situation and talked to his fellow slaves. They finally agreed to join him and bring their families along in an escape attempt. The escapees would include Smalls; his wife and three children; his brother, John, chief engineer of the vessel; John's wife; and nine more slaves.

They all boarded the *Planter* at 3 A.M., May 12, 1862. The women and children hid below, and Smalls stood on the bridge with his arms folded, the way the captain usually did. Like the captain, he wore a huge straw hat that obscured his face. Smalls gave the appropriate signal as *Planter* approached Fort Sumter.

"The *Planter,* flagship for General Ripley, giving the prescribed signal," a sentry called out. A second later, he yelled, "Pass the *Planter,* flagship for General Ripley." Then he added, "Blow the damned Yankees to Hell and bring one of them in!"

"Aye, aye!" Smalls yelled back.

As soon as he got out of range of the Confederate guns, Smalls hauled down the Confederate and South Carolina flags and ran up a white bed sheet. The U.S. Navy took possession of the *Planter* and its six guns. Smalls got half the value of the ship, and the rest of the crew got the other half. The navy also got the benefit of Smalls's knowledge of Charleston Harbor, where he had been sailing for 10 years. That information, according to the secretary of the navy, made possible the seizure of Stono Inlet and River "and was virtually a turning of the forces in Charleston Harbor."

Smalls became the captain of his own ship, and after the war, he was elected to the South Carolina legislature and then to the U.S. Congress.

did not all vanish in 1861. When Gen. Braxton Bragg was preparing for the Battle of Chickamauga, he asked Robert E. Lee for help. Lee sent him Gen. Daniel H. Hill's whole corps from the Army of Northern Virginia by railroad, a movement of several hundred miles accomplished in three days. No comparable troop movement had ever been made in Europe. Helmut von Moltke, chief of the Prussian general staff, earned a reputation for being a master of railroad transportation because of his lightning mobilizations. But Moltke had years to plan his moves. Lee moved on the spur of the moment.

The most notable result of all the industrialization in the United States was the enormously increased firepower of both armies. In the Mexican War of 1846–48, the minié rifle, using a hollow-based bullet that could be loaded as quickly as a round ball in a smoothbore, was the latest thing in weaponry. Its bullet was smaller than the bore, but the hollow base expanded into the rifling when the gun was fired. By the Civil War, minié rifles were old-fashioned, and none of them was a flintlock, as many were 15 years earlier. In the Civil War, no one had a smoothbore, and no one had a flintlock.

The rifle was, as generations of fighting men knew, far more accurate than a smoothbore. Civil War snipers used rifles with extra-heavy barrels to dampen vibrations caused by the explosion of the powder charge. These rifles were often equipped with telescope sights. One of the most accurate standard rifles was a breech-loader invented by Christian Sharps. The shooter opened the breech by pulling down a lever that formed the trigger guard. He then inserted a paper cartridge containing the bullet and a powder charge and returned the trigger guard to its former position. The sharp edge of the breech block sheared off the end of the paper cartridge, exposing the powder to the explosion of the percussion cap.

The Sharps could be fired rapidly as well as with deadly accuracy. Union colonel Hiram Berdan organized a select body of marksmen and armed them with Sharps rifles. Berdan's Sharpshooters gave their name to a military specialty—snipers who usually but not necessarily use Sharps rifles. The Sharps was later modified to use metallic cartridges, a new type of ammunition that made the old paper cartridges obsolete and made possible repeating rifles.

The Sharps could be fired rapidly, but not as rapidly as repeating rifles, two of which were in fairly widespread use. One of these was the Spencer—named after its inventor, Christopher Spencer—which car-

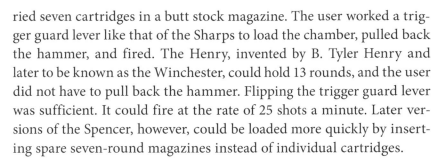

ried seven cartridges in a butt stock magazine. The user worked a trigger guard lever like that of the Sharps to load the chamber, pulled back the hammer, and fired. The Henry, invented by B. Tyler Henry and later to be known as the Winchester, could hold 13 rounds, and the user did not have to pull back the hammer. Flipping the trigger guard lever was sufficient. It could fire at the rate of 25 shots a minute. Later versions of the Spencer, however, could be loaded more quickly by inserting spare seven-round magazines instead of individual cartridges.

A wealthy Union officer, Colonel John Wilder, bought Spencers for all members of his brigade. He also bought horses for them and changed the unit from infantry to mounted infantry—that is, the brigade rode to the scene of the battle, dismounted, and fought on foot. (In the unconventional circumstances of the Civil War, such a thing was possible.) At one point during the Battle of Chickamauga, "Wilder's Lightning Brigade" was holding a bridge against General Nathan Bedford Forrest's cavalry and two Confederate infantry divisions. Forrest's men first charged on horseback, and the Spencers mowed them down. A man on horseback makes a good target, and he cannot hide behind a tree or a hole in the ground. The Confederate cavalrymen dismounted and charged again. The Lightning Brigade's fire sounded like a drumroll. The rebel troops rushed forward in a column, but according to witnesses, when they reached a certain point, they seemed to sink into the ground. Eventually flanked, the Lightning Brigade had to withdraw. But one brigade armed with repeating rifles had held off two infantry divisions—each containing at least two brigades—and Nathan B. Forrest's famous cavalry for most of a day.

The repeaters were deadly at short range, but at this stage of their development, they could not handle ammunition as powerful as that used in the single-shot rifles. The single-shots could just about outrange the smoothbore artillery. That forced a major change in artillery tactics. In the era of the smoothbore musket, artillery was often placed in the front line, among the infantry. When the enemy infantry had rifles, that was almost suicidal. Daring artillerymen still fought at close range, but they gradually realized that they would be more effective behind the infantry, a position the artillery still holds.

The artillery had to fire at long-range targets, over the heads of the infantry. Smoothbore cannons were not accurate at long range, and hard cast-iron cannon balls would destroy the rifling in a cannon, if not the gun itself. That prompted the development of rifled artillery

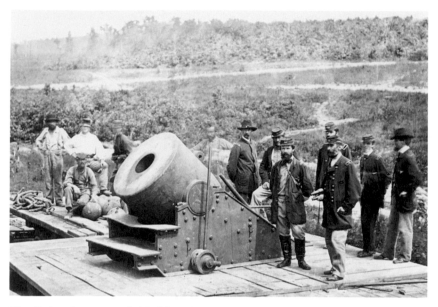

The Union forces used this 13-inch mortar, known as the "Dictator," during the siege of Petersburg to shoot large shells over the defensive works. *(Library of Congress)*

and new types of ammunition. Some shells had studs on them to engage the rifling. Some Confederate gunners tried to use smooth-bore cannons as if they were rifled by fitting their shells with tailfins to make them spin. The most successful system, the one still used, was to circle the shell with a softer metal such as brass, which could take the rifling. Shells of this type intended for muzzle-loaders had bands that would expand on firing, like the base of the minié bullet.

One advantage of rifling was that the gun could fire an elongated projectile, because it would always travel nose-first. Naturally, an elongated projectile was heavier than a round one and could carry a larger bursting charge. That changed the designation of artillery ammunition. A three-inch gun that had been known as a six-pounder, for example, became a 12-pounder.

Rifling in small arms and artillery forced a change in cavalry tactics. John S. Mosby, a Confederate cavalry guerrilla, said his men always fought mounted and relied entirely on revolvers. But Mosby did not have to hold territory nor guard the flanks of an infantry outfit. He stayed hidden and attacked with the advantage of surprise. He never attacked infantry prepared to resist. Commanders of regular cavalry

CIVIL WAR AIRCRAFT

On July 18, 1861, Thaddeus Sobieski Constantine Lowe piloted the bal-loon *Enterprise* while a telegraph operator tapped out the first message to be sent from an aircraft to the ground. On October 1, 1861, Lowe became the Chief Astronaut of the Army of the Potomac's Balloon Corps. The corps consisted of seven balloons, which observed artillery fire and gave directions to gunners. During the Peninsular campaign, the balloons were based on a converted coal barge that synchronized its movements with those of the army.

General McClellan's Balloon Corps was the original ancestor of the U.S. Air Force, but an even more spectacular aircraft was rejected by the federal government during the Civil War.

On September 5, 1862, while the residents of Washington, D.C., were terrified that the Confederate army of Stonewall Jackson might attack the capital, an inventor was trying to get word to President Lincoln and Secretary of War Stanton that he had an invention that might save the Union. The inventor was Solomon Andrews, a physician from Perth Amboy, New Jersey, who had served three terms as mayor of Perth Amboy and was president of its board of health. Andrews had made a fortune with a string of successful inventions.

(continues)

At the Battle of Fair Oaks, Virginia, on May 31, 1862, Union forces used a tethered balloon—here seen in the distance—in an early attempt to engage in aerial observation of an enemy's actions. *(Library of Congress)*

(continued)

Interviewed by an official at the Bureau of Topographical engineers, Andrews explained that his invention was a flying machine—a balloon that could be steered and could climb, descend, turn, and fly into the wind. Such an aircraft had been the dream of inventors for centuries, but until then the closest anyone had come was a Frenchman, Henri Giffard. In 1852, Giffard flew a balloon with a steam engine, basically a dirigible that could be steered, but its top speed was six miles per hour, and any wind stronger than that would blow it backwards.

The official asked Andrews what would power his balloon.

"Gravitation," the doctor answered.

The official decided that, in spite of Andrews's successes, he was dealing with a nut. The inventor heard no more from him. Undaunted, Andrews decided to build the aircraft himself and show it to the government. The project cost him $10,000.

On June 1, 1863, Andrews climbed into a wicker basket suspended below three cigar-shaped balloons. There seemed to be hundreds of ropes on the contraption, including some to a huge rudder at the rear. Andrews's associates on the ground released the balloon, and it swiftly rose in the air.

Onlookers said the balloon was merely blowing in the wind. Then it turned into the wind and headed back toward them while climbing to 200 feet.

Andrews was not satisfied. He made several more improvements in the craft and conducted further trials. At one, he invited two prominent citizens of Perth Amboy who had expressed skepticism about his invention. Basically a dirigible called *Aereon* by Andrews, it climbed high into the sky, flew over the shore, and returned "faster than a cannon ball," according to one witness.

Andrews wrote to President Lincoln, requesting that he appoint two people with scientific credibility to witness the next trial. There was no reply. (Much later, he learned that the letter had been misplaced and never reached the president.) Andrews had been warned not to make a proposed flight from Perth Amboy to New York City because Confederate spies might see him, and the enemy might learn the secret of flight.

units found that mounted men armed with revolvers and sabers had no chance against infantry riflemen, especially if the foot soldiers were backed up with rifled artillery. Cavalry usually functioned as mounted infantry—riding into battle, then dismounting to fight.

So, on August 26, 1863, Andrews again wrote to President Lincoln, announcing that he would make one more test. He would remove all ballast from *Aereon* to see how fast it could fly. Then he would destroy the craft so that Confederates could not copy it.

On September 4, 1863, *Aereon* made its last test flight. This time, it drew a crowd of spectators, including a reporter from the *New York Herald*. Andrews took his dirigible up to 1,000 feet and at various speeds flew with the wind and into the wind.

"I never saw any vessel, railroad car, or any other thing of magnitude go so fast," said Ellis C. Waite, an architect present at the demonstration. The *Herald* reporter estimated *Aereon*'s speed at 120 miles an hour. Andrews then released *Aereon,* and it flew away never to be seen again (presumably crashing somewhere).

But the matter of the government's acquisition of Andrews's dirigible had not been resolved. Andrews finally obtained an interview with Lincoln. The president asked him to send testimonial letters from four or five witness, after which he would take action. Andrews sent the letters, but that was the last he heard of the matter. Once again, the letters never reached the president.

In January 1864, Andrews sent a petition to both the Senate and the House of Representatives. He got a chance to demonstrate a four-foot model of *Aereon* to members of the military committees of both houses. They recommended that the secretary of war appoint a commission to investigate the airship. After a further demonstration, the commission sent a glowing report to Stanton recommending an immediate appropriation to build an airship. But after a series of bureaucratic mix-ups, nothing happened, and on March 22, 1865, Andrews received a letter from a military committee saying the military had lost interest in his aircraft. The war was almost over, and the committee decided that any money spent on the flying machine would be wasted.

Andrews wrote a book, *The Art of Flying,* but few could understand it. He went into business giving rides in a new flying machine, but in the postwar depression, business was not brisk. The Aerial Navigation Company went bankrupt, and Andrews went back to practicing medicine.

This modernization of weaponry was not reflected in infantry tactics, however. Tactics had changed little in the previous 100 years, and not much more in the previous 300 years. In attack, men shouldered their weapons and marched shoulder-to-shoulder in long, straight lines toward the enemy in time with the beating of a drum. When they were about 100 yards from the enemy, they stopped, leveled their rifles and fired a volley, then charged with bayonets.

But in the Civil War, defensive riflemen began firing on those long, solid lines when they were a half-mile away. Shrapnel (*spherical case, in the language of the day*) shells began exploding over the marchers from even farther. Few attackers reached bayonet range. Whole ranks of attackers were cut down, in some cases leaving rows of dead bodies still in formation.

The attacker's artillery, of course, played its traditional role, laying barrages on the enemy position to shatter the defender's infantry or at least force them to keep their heads down. But before the war had gone on very long, defenders on both sides learned to build field fortifications that rivaled those of World War I or the last half of the Korean War. Barbed wire had not yet been invented, but access to trenches was blocked by a variety of traditional obstacles. These included the *abatis*—French for "felled," as in trees cut down—trees and bushes laid on the ground with their branches sharpened and facing the enemy;

As part of their defensive works around Petersburg, the Confederates had erected stakes known by a French term, *chevaux de frise* ("horses of the Frisians," a Germanic people who did not have cavalry), a log frame set with long spikes to impale advancing horses or troops. *(Library of Congress)*

the *trous de loup*—French for "wolf's hole"—interlocking pits, each containing a sharpened spike; the *cheval de frise*—French for "Frisian horse"—a log set with long spikes; and *caltrops*—a plant with sharp spikes—four iron spikes arranged so that one was always pointing up to pierce the foot of an attacker. The use of French for such devices, by the way, reflects France's traditional position as the predominate land power on the European continent.

Troops under Robert E. Lee, who was originally an engineer officer, built especially formidable field fortifications. But in 1864, Colonel Henry Pleasants, a mining engineer in civilian life, tried to out-engineer the Confederates. His regiment, the 48th Pennsylvania, was made up almost entirely of ex–coal miners. With the permission of General Ambrose Burnside, he and his men dug a tunnel under a Confederate strongpoint outside of Petersburg. Most of Burnside's troops were worn out after the prolonged and bloody Wilderness campaign, but he got fresh troops who were eager to get at the enemy. They were eight regiments of the 4th Division.

When Pleasant set off the 8,000 pounds of gunpowder under the Confederate fort, the 4th Division troops were supposed to rush around the crater resulting from the explosion, rout the shell-shocked survivors, and open the way to Petersburg so that the Federal troops could take Lee's army from the rear and probably end the Civil War. Burnside trained his fresh new regiments incessantly. But at the last minute, Burnside's superiors changed the plan.

Their reason: The eight regiments training to exploit the explosions were African-American freemen. General George Meade had no confidence in the ability of black troops to fight. Instead of spearheading the assault, the 4th Division was placed at the rear of the attacking column. Leading the assault were untrained and war-weary white troops who did exactly the wrong thing. They dove into the crater, from which they could not escape. The Confederates brought up reinforcements while the Union troops were trying to climb out, and the Union troops behind the blunted spearhead could not get forward in time to exploit the destruction of the rebel fort. The Battle of the Crater was a Confederate victory—one of the few the Southern forces had at this stage of the war.

The Civil War saw the introduction of a number of ingenious multi-shot weapons that would have increased the firepower—and the casualties—of both sides even more if the military authorities had not been so conservative. One was the Billinghurst and Requa "battery gun"—named after its inventors, actually two dentists—which had 25 breech-loading .52 caliber rifle barrels on a carriage. All barrels could be loaded with one motion by a frame that held 25 cartridges. One percussion cap ignited a powder train that fired all the barrels, which could then be instantly reloaded. A Confederate gun of this type, perhaps a copy, was used to defend Charleston Harbor.

Then there was the Agar "coffee mill," which was patented in Britain before the Civil War. It was offered to Abraham Lincoln, and he had the Union army purchase some 50 Agar machine guns. The gun was not adopted as a standard weapon, however, because of opposition by the Army Ordnance Department. The Agar fired steel-cased cartridges, which were dropped into a hopper. Turning a crank loaded the cartridges, fired them, ejected the cases, and loaded new cartridges into the single barrel. Another machine gun was the Williams, invented by Captain R. S. Williams of the Confederate army. The Williams was a single-barrel, hand-cranked automatic cannon that fired one-pound projectiles at the rate of 65 a minute. Captain Williams was a member of Pickett's Brigade, a unit that used several of his guns.

The most successful of all machine guns was the Gatling, but the U.S. government refused to adopt it because Richard Jordan Gatling was born in the South, and some thought he might be a Confederate sympathizer. A number of Gatlings were used in the Civil War, but they had been privately purchased by such people as General Benjamin Butler. The Gatling had a bundle of barrels, 10 or six, depending on the model, that rotated when an operator turned a hand crank. As the bundle turned, the barrels were loaded and fired, and cartridges were ejected. A strong crank-turner could make it fire at the rate of 1,000 rounds a minute.

Seagoing weaponry was as innovative as that designed for land warfare. Everyone has heard of the battle between the *Monitor* and the *Merrimack*—the latter renamed the *Virginia* after the Confederates raised and restored the vessel after it was sunk. Although this was the first battle between ironclad warships, these were not the first of their kind. That distinction belongs to the French *La Gloire*. The second iron warship was the British *Warrior*. But during the Civil War, both the Union and Confederacy turned out numerous ironclads, and either navy probably could have wiped out the combined navies of the rest of the world.

The battle between the USS *Monitor* and the CSS *Virginia* (better known as the *Merrimack,* the name of the original Union navy's ship) signaled that the future of naval warfare lay with iron ships. *(Library of Congress)*

The Union navy was especially endowed with ironclads. They ranged from armored side-wheel steamboats for river duty to monsters such as the *New Ironsides,* an oceangoing ironclad carrying 16 heavy guns. In 1863, the *New Ironsides* and eight other ironclads began to systematically pulverize the forts in Charleston Harbor. Confederate cannons had no effect on the monster. Two Confederate torpedo boats attacked it. The second, a semisubmersible, the CSS *David,* was successful. The *David* pushed a bomb on the end of a pole, known as a torpedo in those days, under the ironclad and exploded it. It slightly damaged the *New Ironsides,* but the big ship remained on station, blockading Charleston.

The Confederates turned to H. L. Hunley, a marine designer experimenting with submarines. Hunley was killed while testing his submarine, but the boat later sank the USS *Housatonic,* history's first sinking of a ship by a submarine. However, the *Hunley*, as the submarine was known, also sank with all eight crewmen trapped. (It was raised in 2000.) Both navies continued to use submarines and semisubmersibles for combat in harbors and shallow coastal waters.

The Union blockade of Confederate ports slowly became more effective, especially as amphibious operations began closing the biggest ports, one after another. Monitors, a class of ships named after the original *Monitor*, were especially effective in these operations. Monitors, carrying one or two rotating turrets, presented small targets, and shot that hit the round armored turrets tended to glance off. Other navies adopted the monitor, and the low, shallow draft vessels were still being used in World War I. (In that war, British monitors destroyed the German cruiser *Konigsberg*, hiding in Africa's Rufiji Delta.)

The Confederate navy also introduced a new class of warship, the ram. Rams, low-lying ships with sloping iron sides, were patterned after the *Virginia* (the converted Union frigate *Merrimack*). The biggest ram, the CSS *Tennessee*, was captured at Mobile Bay after the monitor *Chickasaw* got behind it and pounded one spot with shot after shot. The *Tennessee* filled with smoke, and one shot cut the big ram's tiller chain so that she could not be steered, and another injured Admiral Franklin Buchanan, who had been the *Virginia*'s captain during the fight with *Monitor*.

There were few battles on the high seas during the Civil War. Rather, most of the sea battles involved raids on merchant ships. The most famous was the fight between the Confederate commerce raider *Alabama* and the USS *Kearsarge* outside the French port of Cherbourg. The *Alabama* was the most successful of the Confederate commerce raiders and had built up an impressive roster of ships defeated and captured—mostly merchantmen. The *Alabama* was being repaired at Cherbourg when the *Kearsarge* arrived. The *Alabama*'s captain, Raphael Semmes, sent a challenge to the *Kearsarge*'s captain, John Winslow, begging him not to retreat before he could bring the *Alabama* out to fight. When Semmes did so, it took the *Kearsage* only about an hour to turn the *Alabama* into a sinking wreck. The Union ship sustained little damage.

More important than any commerce raiders were the many ironclad Union steamboats that landed and supported troops at strategic points on the Mississippi and other rivers, cut the Confederacy in half, and ended the commercial river traffic so vital to the Confederacy. They,

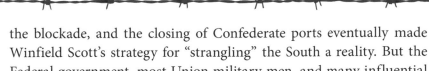

the blockade, and the closing of Confederate ports eventually made Winfield Scott's strategy for "strangling" the South a reality. But the Federal government, most Union military men, and many influential civilians had scoffed at this, calling it the "Anaconda Plan," a reference to the snake. However, if the Union had earlier depended more heavily on the Anaconda strategy, neither side might have had to employ all the weapons and tactics that led to such an effusion of blood.

GRANT AND LEE

Sherman's triumphs in 1864 were in brilliant contrast to what looked like a deadlock in the Virginia theater. After a hungry winter, the Confederates under Robert E. Lee prepared for the spring campaign with fewer than half the forces available to Ulysses S. Grant, the overall Union commander, and George G. Meade, commander of the Army of the Potomac. President Lincoln had put Grant in charge with the hope that Grant would defeat the main rebel armies in Virginia and Georgia and end the war. In May 1864, Grant instructed Sherman to advance against Joseph E. Johnston in north Georgia. At the same time, Grant would move across the Rapidan River with Meade's army in pursuit of Robert E. Lee.

Grant meant to strike early and hard, for he faced the prospect of seeing his army's best and most experienced regiments turn and march for home. Many of the three-year enlistments were to expire in mid-1864, and Lincoln had decided not to extend them by executive order. Instead, the government offered $400 cash bounties and immediate 30-day furloughs to encourage veterans to reenlist. "They use a man here just as they do a turkey at a shooting match," a Massachusetts veteran complained, "fire at it all day and if they don't kill it raffle it off in the evening; so with us, if they can't kill you in three years they want you for three more—but I will stay."

Many soldiers chose to do the same, and in some cases entire regiments rejoined. Even so, the reenlistment rate in the Army of the Potomac ran no better than 50 percent. Conscripts, bountymen, and substitutes took the places of seasoned veterans. As a group, these indifferent soldiers were welcomed neither by Grant nor by the men in the ranks. "Such another depraved, vice-hardened and desperate set of human beings never before disgraced an army," a New Hampshire infantryman wrote, speaking for many veterans. Confederate leaders

Gen. U.S. Grant, Cold Harbor, Virginia, June 1, 1864 *(National Archives)*

believed the enlistment expirations would seriously weaken the Army of the Potomac, making it possible for Lee to hold off the depleted Yankees through the summer. Then, in November, a war-weary North might vote to replace Lincoln with a peace Democrat who would negotiate Southern independence.

Lee had his own manpower problems—he faced greater difficulty making up the losses in his 61,000-man Army of Northern Virginia than Grant did in the 122,000-strong Army of the Potomac. And Lee's supply problems seemed impossible to solve. "There is nothing to be had in this section for man or animals," he wrote President Davis on April 12, 1864. The troops were "lousy and almost naked," one veteran wrote. They lived, wrote another, on "dry cornbread and a combination of spoilt bones and fat which the commissary calls bacon."

In the end, however, Lee's toughest problem would prove to be Ulysses S. Grant. For the first time, Lee would meet an opponent of equal ability. Everyone who knew Grant remarked on his force of will. He would set an objective, they said, and keep pushing forward until he reached it. "He habitually wears an expression as if he had determined to drive his head through a brick wall and was about to do it," one of his officers wrote. His orders to Meade were a model of clarity and singleness of purpose. "Wherever Lee goes," Grant told him, "there you will go also." When Lee's ablest lieutenant, Gen. James Longstreet, learned that Grant had been given the supreme Union command, his assessment sounded like a death sentence for the Army of Northern Virginia: "That man will fight us every day and every hour until the end of the war."

Federal forces began crossing the Rapidan River west of Fredericksburg on May 4. Grant wanted to push southeast through the dark, overgrown region of the Wilderness—the scene of Lee's Chancellorsville victory one year before—and beyond the Confederate right. The armies would then meet in open country, where Grant believed his chances of bringing off a decisive battle were good. Lee forestalled him, however, sending strong forces forward to strike the Federals in the flank before they could clear the Wilderness.

The armies collided on the morning of May 5, touching off the Battle of the Wilderness. Battle lines soon broke down, and isolated groups met and fought one another in the pine thickets and brambles. "Closing with the enemy, we fought them with bayonet as well as bullet," recalled Capt. H. W. S. Sweet of the 146th New York. "Up through the trees rolled dense clouds of battle smoke, circling about the green of the pines and mingling with the white of the flowering dogwoods. Underneath, men ran to and fro, firing, shouting, stabbing with bayonets, beating each other with the butts of their guns. Each man fought on his own resources, grimly and desperately."

The first day of fighting ended inconclusively. That night, front-line troops felled trees and scooped up the soft earth to fashion rough fortifications. Parties moved though the woods in search of the wounded. Little fires burned here and there in the undergrowth. Scouting for stragglers, Maj. Abner Small of the 16th Maine stumbled and pitched forward. "My outflung hands pushed up a smoulder of leaves," Small

In the Battle of the Wilderness, May 5–7, 1864, one of the most decisive engagements was on May 6 along the Orange Plank Road. The battle, which raged all day, went back and forth but ended with no clear victor and heavy casualties on both sides. *(Library of Congress)*

remembered. "The fire sprang into flame, caught in the hair and beard of a dead sergeant, and lighted a ghastly face and wide open eyes." Scattered firing continued into the night. The wounded let out terrible cries as the fires burned nearer. At his field headquarters, Grant resolved to renew the advance at dawn.

The next morning the battle took up where it had left off the previous day, along the Orange Plank Road near Wilderness Tavern. In the late afternoon Lee launched a strong assault on the right of the Union line north of the tavern. Advancing rebels under Jubal Early took several hundred prisoners and caused a temporary panic among some senior Federal officers. As the Union right crumpled, one general reported to Grant that Lee seemed about to repeat his Chancellorsville victory. But Lee had not mesmerized Grant as he had Hooker and the others. "I am heartily tired of hearing what Lee is going to do," he scolded the frightened general. "Some of you always seem to think he is suddenly going to turn a double somersault and land on our rear and both flanks at the same time. Go back to your command and try to think what we are going to do ourselves, instead of what Lee is going to do."

Thinking it over himself, Grant decided to break off the battle that night. The Wilderness encounter had cost the Army of the Potomac 17,500 casualties, double the Confederate total. In the past a Union retreat would have followed such a bloodletting. Now, though, instead of turning back to the Rapidan the army continued its advance. Grant put his columns on the road to the southeast, around the Confederate right, toward the crossroads village of Spotsylvania Courthouse.

Inevitably, there were delays. Not even Grant could change the sluggish ways of the Army of the Potomac overnight. Divisions started late; some even got lost. Lee, alert as ever, detected the move, and his fast-moving infantry actually reached Spotsylvania first. By the morning of May 9, strong rebel forces were entrenched in Grant's path. A Federal assault on May 10 failed at a cost of 3,000 killed, wounded, and missing. Grant promptly ordered a renewal of the attack for May 12. "I propose to fight it out on this line if it takes all summer," he wired Halleck, the Union chief of staff, on May 11.

A dead Confederate soldier, one of the casualties at the scene of Ewell's attack, May 19, 1864, near Spotsylvania *(Library of Congress)*

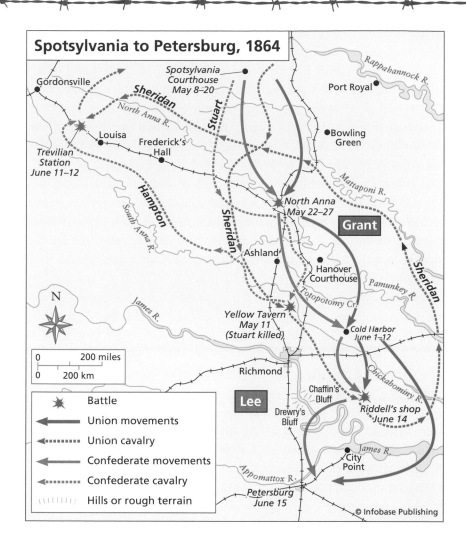

Spotsylvania to Petersburg, 1864

Gordonsville

Spotsylvania Courthouse
May 8–20

Sheridan

North Anna R.

Stuart

Port Royal

Rappahannock R.

Louisa

Frederick's Hall

Trevilian Station
June 11–12

Hampton

Sheridan

South Anna R.

North Anna
May 22–27

Bowling Green

Mattaponi R.

Grant

James R.

N

Ashland

Yellow Tavern
May 11
(Stuart killed)

Hanover Courthouse

Pamunkey R.

Totopotomy Cr.

Sheridan

Cold Harbor
June 1–12

0   200 miles
0   200 km

Richmond

Chaffin's Bluff

Lee

Drewry's Bluff

Chickahominy R.

Riddell's shop
June 14

✷   Battle
◄   Union movements
◄·······   Union cavalry
◄   Confederate movements
◄·······   Confederate cavalry
\\\||||| Hills or rough terrain

Appomattox R.

City Point

James R.

Petersburg
June 15

© Infobase Publishing

At dawn on May 12, Gen. Winfield Scott Hancock's II Corps advanced in massed ranks, 20,000 strong. The assault cut gaps in a bulge in the rebel line known as the Mule Shoe, and Hancock's troops captured 2,000 prisoners and 20 guns before a counterattack halted their progress. Then, in the action that would be known as the Bloody Angle, Federal forces attacked both flanks of the Mule Shoe. All through the day, in fog and rain, the armies struggled for possession of a few hundred yards of trenches. "Men mounted the works, and with muskets rapidly handed them, kept up a continuous fire until they were shot down, when others would take their places and continue the deadly work," recalled Brig. Gen. Lewis A. Grant of the Vermont

Brigade. By nightfall, the survivors had fired hundreds of rounds. "Our lips were encrusted with powder from biting cartridge," G. Norton Galloway of the 95th Pennsylvania wrote. "Our shoulders and hands were encrusted with mud that had adhered to the butts of our rifles. When darkness came on we dropped from exhaustion."

Exhausted too, the rebels abandoned the Bloody Angle in the night. At daybreak the Federals took possession of trenches in which bodies lay eight deep. The rate of fire had been the heaviest of the war. Lt. Col. John Schoonover of the 11th New Jersey remembered looking over the captured rebel parapet at a scoured landscape. "The trees . . . were stripped of their foliage, and it looked as though an army of locusts had passed," he wrote. "The brush between the lines was cut and torn into shreds, and the fallen bodies of men and horses lay there with the flesh shot and torn from the bones."

Spotsylvania had cost more than 11,000 Union casualties. In one week's continuous fighting, the Army of the Potomac had lost 32,000 killed, wounded, and missing. Lee's casualties, about 18,000, were roughly in proportion to Grant's. "The world has never seen so bloody and protracted a battle as the one being fought," Grant wrote his wife, "and I hope never will." Thousands more were soon to fall, for Grant kept up a relentless pressure. The Federals abandoned the Spotsylvania trenches and again moved out around the Confederate right. Lee followed, the armies skirmishing for several days along the North Anna River northwest of Richmond. Then Grant moved yet again, a wide swing 20 miles farther to the southeast. Lee kept pace, marching hard by day and digging by night. By June 1, the armies faced each other across several miles of trench lines near the hamlet of Cold Harbor. Grant ordered an attack for June 3.

The Cold Harbor lines were formidable, and the soldiers of the Army of the Potomac had become respectful of the Confederate ability to build strong works on short notice. When Horace Porter, one of Grant's aides, toured the front-line positions on the evening of June 2, he noted that many men had taken their coats off and seemed to be mending them. As it turned out, said Porter, they were "calmly writing their names and home addresses on slips of paper and pinning them on the backs of their coats." They wanted the burial details to be able to identify their corpses. They did not intend to die unrecognized and unmourned.

By 3:30 A.M. on June 3, the assault brigades had formed up. "The hopeless look which many of the soldiers wore was quite noticeable," recalled Capt. W. S. Hubbel of the 21st Connecticut. "They did not expect to succeed." The advance into the center of the rebel line began at 4:30. In 30 minutes it was over, and 7,500 Federals were dead, wounded, or captured. "It seemed like murder to fire upon you," a Confederate officer told a New Hampshire prisoner. Grant must have felt the same. "I regret this assault more than any one I have ever ordered," he said that night.

Grant did not grieve for long. By June 12, he had the Union army on the march again, heading south for the James River and, beyond, to the crucial railroad center of Petersburg below Richmond. The move caught Lee by surprise, and when leading elements of the Federals' XVIII Corps reached Petersburg on June 15 the rebels had only 2,500 militia to man the defenses. However, the Federal commander, Gen. W. F. Smith, hesitated before attacking, and when he finally did strike that evening, he failed to press his advantage. By June 16, rebel reinforcements had arrived, and the energetic P. G. T. Beauregard had taken charge of the Petersburg lines. Federal attacks on June 16 and 17 failed to break into the city. By June 18, Lee, finally alerted to the danger, ordered the Army of Northern Virginia to Petersburg.

By then the Federal attacks had slackened. "The men feel at present a great horror and dread of attacking earthworks again," Gen. Francis H. Barlow, one of the army's best divisional commanders, said. "The

Federal gun emplacements at Fort Brady, in the Siege of Petersburg, Virginia (National Archives)

Wounded soldiers rest under trees at Marye's Heights, Fredericksburg, after the nearby Battle of Spotsylvania, 1864. *(National Archives)*

men went in, but not with spirit," reported one of Meade's aides. "You can't strike a blow with a wounded hand."

Meade's army no longer had the strength to force the issue. It had been bled away on the killing grounds of the Wilderness, Spotsylvania, and Cold Harbor. The four days of the Petersburg assaults had cost the Union another 12,000 casualties. Since the campaign opened on May 4, the Federals had lost 65,000 killed, wounded, and missing—60 percent of the *total* casualties in the Army of the Potomac during the previous three years. "For thirty days it has been one funeral procession past me," V Corps commander Gouverneur K. Warren lamented, "and it has been too much."

Grant, some said, had destroyed the army's offensive power. The fighting undeniably had taken its best officers and men. John Gibbon's II Corps division, one of the army's most efficient fighting formations, crossed the Rapidan with 6,799 men. In two months, the division suffered 7,970 casualties—more than 70 percent of the original complement as well as thousands of replacement troops. Gibbon lost an astonishing 40 percent of his regimental commanders to death or wounds. Even Grant recognized that the army could do no more, at least for now. He ordered the troops to entrench and prepare for a siege. "We must rest the men and use the spade for their protection until a new vein can be struck," he told Meade.

So the offensive stalled in front of Petersburg. As a result, Lincoln faced serious political challenges, in his own party and from the peace Democrats. In the North, the war's end seemed more distant than ever. "Patriotism is played out," a Democratic newspaper announced. "Each hour is but sinking us deeper into bankruptcy and desolation." The president, his confidence temporarily shaken, came down to see Grant in late June. The general reassured him. "I am just as sure of going into Richmond as I am of any future event," he told Lincoln. "It may take a long summer day, as they say in rebel papers, but I will do it."

In fact, Grant did hold important advantages. Although his losses had been heavy, Lee's were proportionately as great. Moreover, Grant had done what no other commander had been able to do: He had taken the initiative from the Army of Northern Virginia. Lee remained penned in the Petersburg and Richmond defenses, his army's strength slowly draining away.

Grant kept up a moderate pressure by reaching around Lee's right to raid the two railroads that carried supplies up from the Deep South. Both armies worked industriously on their defensive lines, building fortifications, digging parallel lines of trenches, and fabricating bomb-proof shelters. Federal engineers built a rail line from the main base at City Point on the James River, so the troops could be supplied with fresh food and other luxuries. As the weeks wore on, siege routines were established. In the heat and dust of an abnormally dry summer, the days passed by monotonously.

Then, on July 30, a tremendous explosion rocked the center of the Confederate line, creating the infamous Crater. A regiment of Pennsylvania coal miners had dug a 511-foot-long tunnel under the rebel works and packed the end of it with four tons of gunpowder. The detonation created a chasm 170 feet long, 60 feet wide, and 30 feet deep, buried an entire rebel regiment, and stupefied the survivors. "Some scampered out of the lines," recalled Col. Fitz William McMaster of the 17th South Carolina. "Some, paralyzed with fear, scratched at the counterscarp as if trying to escape." For a brief moment, the way into Petersburg lay open.

The assault forces were also confused. Worse still, they were badly led. Gen. James Ledlie, commander of the leading division, remained safely behind in a bomb shelter, dosing himself with surgeon's rum. Some of the attackers actually climbed into the Crater and milled about there, collecting souvenirs and helping to dig out half-buried rebels. The initial shock soon wore off, however. The defenders began pouring artillery fire into the Crater, then launched a vicious counterattack. After several hours of aimless fighting, the Federals withdrew. The casualty list totaled 3,800, including a handful of black soldiers who had been murdered by rebels when they tried to surrender. "It was the saddest affair I have witnessed in the war," Grant wired Halleck. "Such an opportunity for carrying fortifications I have never seen, and do not expect again to have."

If the Crater saddened Grant, the burning of Chambersburg, Pennsylvania, the next day angered him. A 10,000-man rebel force under Jubal Early had swept up the Shenandoah Valley in early July, crossed the Potomac, raided in Maryland, and threatened the Washington defenses. Federal forces chased after Early unsuccessfully, and Grant had to send an army corps north to calm the nervous capital. Early found Washington too strong to assault, so he turned north in late July and set fire to Chambersburg on July 31.

This, however, would be the last time the Confederates used the Shenandoah as an invasion route, or even as a source of supply. Grant moved to close off the valley once and for all. He established a new Army of the Shenandoah, gave the command to Gen. Philip H. Sheridan, and ordered Sheridan to catch and destroy Early.

Sheridan, 33 years old in 1864, a short, dark, belligerent Ohioan with a flaring black mustache, pursued Early like the Furies. "Smash 'em up, smash 'em up!" Sheridan liked to say, and the phrase neatly expressed his attitude toward the job. By late September, he had routed Early in battles at Winchester and Strasburg and cleared the valley of rebels. In early October, he began clearing the Shenandoah Valley itself, stripping the countryside of food, livestock, and forage. "The people must be left nothing," he said, "but their eyes to weep with over the war."

Sheridan, with cold efficiency, carried out his assignment to leave nothing of use to the enemy. Luman H. Tenney, a trooper in the 2nd Ohio Cavalry, set down in his diary a talk he had with an old man whose home lay in the army's path. "He owned a farm, sterile and poor, of 200 acres in among the hills," Tenney wrote. "Moved there 34 years since when all was wilderness. Had never owned a slave. Had cleaned up the farm, built a log house and made all the improvements with his own hands. It made him almost crazy to see all going to destruction in one night—all his fences, outbuildings, cattle, sheep and fowls. . . . Only wished that God would now call him, that he might be with his many friends in the church yard."

By late autumn, the Federals were closing in everywhere. Sherman had taken Atlanta and started for Savannah. His successes assured Lincoln's reelection, and with the vote all chance of a negotiated settlement passed. Continued pressure from Grant forced Lee to extend his thinly held lines, which now stretched 35 miles in an arc from northeast of Richmond to south of Petersburg. Lee's troops were hungry, tired, and discouraged. "Some of the men have been without meat for three days," Lee wrote War Secretary John C. Breckinridge, "and all are suffering from reduced rations and scant clothing, exposed to battle, hail, cold and sleet."

As the winter advanced, they began deserting in increasing numbers. In February 1865, Lee reported that hundreds of men were deserting nightly. By then, Federal forces had taken Wilmington, North Carolina, the last open Confederate Atlantic port, and Sherman's

Union soldiers sit in the trenches before Petersburg in December 1864.
(National Archives)

sweep northward through the Carolinas had closed out the last major source of rebel supplies.

In early March 1865, Lee resolved to attack in a last effort to break out of Petersburg. He hoped to join Johnston in North Carolina, defeat Sherman there, and turn on Grant with the combined armies. His attack of March 25 failed to crack the Yankee line. It failed, too, to delay Grant's spring offensive by even a day. The Federal drive opened at the end of March when Sheridan, with cavalry and infantry, swung out to the southwest around Lee's right flank. He broke up a rebel force at Five Forks on April 1. The next day Meade followed with a powerful assault that pierced Lee's main defenses at several points. As the rebels

THE RUINS OF RICHMOND

At the end, Southerners turned on themselves. They set their capital city of Richmond afire as they withdrew just ahead of advancing Union forces.

Word that the enemy had pierced Richmond's defenses reached the Confederate president, Jefferson Davis, in Saint Paul's Church on the morning of Sunday, April 2, 1865. Gen. Robert E. Lee, commanding a disintegrating Army of Northern Virginia, recommended withdrawal. Davis ordered the immediate evacuation of the capital, then gathered his family and fled on a special train with his cabinet and a fortune in Confederate gold reserves.

Anarchy reigned in the stricken city. The rear guard could not control the mobs and the small groups of whiskey-fueled vandals that prowled the streets, breaking windows, plundering stores, breaking into liquor stocks, and setting fires. From time to time explosions rocked the city as the flames detonated stocks of powder.

Confederate forces, acting on orders, deliberately set the most destructive fires. They put the torch to important buildings in the city, including two large tobacco warehouses fired to keep the valuable commodity from falling into Yankee hands. Soon the wind-assisted fires were burning out of control, a stiff breeze from the southeast carrying the blaze from building to building. The last of the Confederates withdrew over the James River bridges by the flickering light of the flames.

Federal forces entered Richmond unopposed and eventually brought the fires under control. Union general Godfrey Weitzel accepted the formal surrender of the Confederate capital, now smoking and desolate, from Mayor Joseph Mayo at City Hall.

withdrew into Petersburg's inner lines, Lee wired Davis that Richmond could no longer be held. That night, the Confederate government evacuated Richmond, setting some of its buildings on fire, while pillaging mobs added to the arson. With most of central Richmond in flames, the army retreated westward toward the village of Amelia Court House.

Federal troops, including the all-black XXV Corps, entered Richmond on the morning of April 3. Lincoln arrived in one of Adm. David D. Porter's gunboats the following day. With an escort of 10 sailors he walked the streets of the fallen Confederate capital, holding his 12-year-old son Tad by the hand. Freed slaves crowded around the president,

"We took Richmond at 8:15 this morning," a jubilant Weitzel wired General Grant on April 3.

The "Burnt District" of Richmond, Virginia, in April 1865 *(Library of Congress)*

touching him to prove to themselves he really existed. "Thank God I have lived to see this," he told Porter. "It seems that I have been dreaming a horrid dream for four years, and now the nightmare is gone."

Southwest of Richmond, the Army of Northern Virginia continued its weary retreat. Federal cavalry, driven hard by the tireless Sheridan, raced alongside the rebels. "Flankers and scouting parties of cavalry were constantly bringing in scores of prisoners from the woods on either side," wrote Lt. Col. Frederic C. Newhall of Sheridan's staff. "They were hungry and tired, and if there was a Confederacy to sustain, they could not find it in the woods."

Lee had expected to find rations in Amelia Court House, but there were none. Again the army took to the roads, footsore, hungry, and continually harassed by Sheridan's troopers. On April 6, Lee reorganized the dissolving army's remnants into two corps, under Longstreet and John B. Gordon, and ordered them to concentrate at Farmville on the Appomattox River, where a final effort might be made to break out toward the south. Now Sheridan, forcing the pursuit, could sense the end. "If the thing is pressed I think Lee will surrender," he wrote Grant after breaking up the rebel rear guard at Sayler's Creek on the route to Farmville. Grant forwarded the message to Lincoln, now back at the City Point base. "Let the thing be pressed," the president replied.

Sheridan permitted the rebels no rest, chasing them out of Farmville before they could regroup and reprovision. By the evening of April 7, Lee's survivors were staggering westward toward the railroad depot of Appomattox Station, where food and forage had been stockpiled. However, Sheridan beat them there. On April 8, Brig. Gen. George A. Custer's cavalry captured four freight trains loaded with supplies, then took up defensive positions between the rebels and the railroad. Meanwhile, Federal II and VI Corps infantry were closing in from the east. Lee could see their campfires burning that night. He, Longstreet, and Gordon agreed to try a breakout attack in the morning, but Federal infantry units, marching all night, arrived before dawn to reinforce Custer's cavalry. Grant had nearly closed the trap on Lee. "He couldn't go back, he couldn't go forward, and he couldn't go sideways," a Federal officer exulted.

Lee could see the end. "There is nothing left for me to do but go and see General Grant," he told his staff, "and I would rather die a thousand deaths." That morning, Palm Sunday, April 9, 1865, Lee sent

Before Union troops entered Richmond on April 3, Confederates set fire to many buildings. These ruined buildings are near the Tredegar Iron Works, the Confederacy's major manufacturer of heavy-duty artillery and other military supplies. *(Library of Congress)*

a messenger into the Union lines with a request to meet with Grant to discuss surrender terms.

Grant, in the meantime, had been riding a long circuit around the Federal lines to join Sheridan at Appomattox Station. The tension of these climactic days had produced in him what he called a "sick headache"—a migraine. A courier finally caught up with him at about 11 A.M. and delivered Lee's message. "The moment I saw the note, I was cured," he said. Headache gone, Grant pushed forward toward the battlefront. He met Sheridan along the roadside near the village of Appomattox Court House.

"Is Lee up there?" Grant asked, motioning toward the village.

Sheridan said he was.

"Very well," said Grant. "Let's go up."

EPILOGUE

Touched with Fire

Grant and Lee met in Wilmer McLean's red-brick, colonnaded house in the village of Appomattox Court House. This turned out to be McLean's second appearance in the long war. By chance, Confederate forces had used his farmhouse near Manassas as a headquarters on July 21, 1861, during the First Battle of Bull Run. Not long afterward, he moved his family to southern Virginia to escape the fighting. On April 9, 1865, Lee surrendered the Army of Northern Virginia in McLean's parlor.

Grant arrived at about 1:30 P.M., his plain blue uniform mud-spattered, trousers tucked into his high boots. Lee, who had been waiting for about 30 minutes, wore his full dress uniform with sash and sword. Grant apologized for the contrast in their appearances. Possibly because of it, he seemed ill at ease, reluctant to come to the point. When Lee reminded him of the purpose of the meeting, Grant offered his terms. They were generous. Rebel officers and men could go home, and would not be prosecuted for treason so long as they obeyed the law. Lee signed his formal acceptance just before 4 P.M., and the main Confederate army passed out of existence.

"I felt . . . sad and depressed at the downfall of a foe who had fought so long and valiantly," Grant wrote later. Lee did not leave a record of his feelings, and Grant said Lee's expression and manner had given no hint of them. In the lines, Federal troops sent up cheers and fired cannon salutes. Grant brusquely ordered a stop to the noisy celebration. "The war is over," he said. "The rebels are our countrymen again." The armies soon commingled, the well-fed Yankees sharing their rations with Lee's soldiers. "There was nothing that resembled guard duty that night. It resembled a picnic rather than a picket line," wrote Pvt. Charles Dunn of the 20th Maine. "Success had made them good-natured," a rebel soldier remarked.

This 1865 Currier and Ives lithograph, which depicts Generals Lee and Grant at the signing of the surrender in the farmhouse at Appomattox Court House, provided many Americans with their first image of this epochal event. *(Library of Congress)*

Grant had insisted on a formal surrender ceremony for the surviving 28,000 soldiers of the Army of Northern Virginia. On the cool, rainy morning of April 12, a long Confederate column paraded past Federal troops to stack their arms and colors. As they passed, Gen. Joshua L. Chamberlain, in charge of the ceremony, ordered a salute. John B. Gordon, leading the rebel column, had it returned. "On our part," wrote Chamberlain afterward, "not a sound of trumpet more, nor roll of drum; not a cheer, nor word, nor whisper of vain-glorying, nor motion of man standing again at the order, but an awed stillness rather, and breath-holding, as if it were the passing of the dead."

Three Confederate armies remained in the field after Appomattox. On April 26, Joseph E. Johnston surrendered to Sherman in North Carolina. Two weeks later, Gen. Richard O. Taylor's army surrendered in Alabama. On May 10, the day Federal cavalry captured the fleeing Jefferson Davis in Irwinsville, Georgia, a presidential decree declared the war "virtually at an end." The last rebel army, Gen. Edmund Kirby Smith's in Texas, surrendered on June 2.

General Lee after Appomattox with Maj. Gen. George Washington Custis Lee and Col. Walter Taylor, C.S.A., April 1865 *(Library of Congress)*

President Lincoln did not live to see the final capitulation of the Confederacy. The pro-Confederate actor John Wilkes Booth shot and fatally wounded him in the presidential box at Ford's Theater on the night of April 14. Earlier that day, Lincoln had told Grant and others of a dream he recalled from the night before—one he had had several times on the eve of great battles or disasters. In the dream, he was aboard some "singular, indescribable vessel . . . floating, floating away on some indistinct expanse, toward an unknown shore." The dream, the president had said hopefully, might anticipate news of Johnston's capitulation to Sherman.

Instead, it foretold his assassination. The shot rang out at 10:15 P.M. as Lincoln watched the beginning of the second scene of the third act of an English farce called *Our American Cousin*. "His wound is mortal," said an army surgeon in the theater who had rushed into the box to examine the president. "It is impossible for him to recover." Lincoln died at 7:22 the next morning in the small, seedy back room of a boarding house across the street from the theater.

Thus the president became one of the last of the Civil War's 1 million casualties. Some 10,000 actions were fought during the four years of the war, including 76 full-scale battles, 310 engagements, and 6,337 skirmishes. These left, on both sides, more than 200,000 dead and 469,000 wounded. In the North, one of every 10 men of military age died or was wounded in battle; in the South, the ratio was one in every four. Disease and other causes claimed twice as many lives as battle did—421,000 Yankees and rebels.

The armies soon melted away. By the end of 1865, 800,000 soldiers had been mustered out of the Union army. For nearly all these men, most of them young, the war, with its high purpose and drama, would be the defining event of their lives. Many had trouble settling down to the old ways. "I do feel so idle and lost to business that I wonder what will become of me," an Iowan wrote in his diary in May 1865. "Can I ever be contented again?"

Defeated rebels returned to poverty and ruin, and where the armies had fought a blight lay upon the land. In South Carolina, Sherman's army had left "a broad black streak of ruin and desolation," Republican politician and journalist Carl Schurz reported in July 1865. Wide areas of Tennessee, Georgia, and Virginia had been stripped by advancing Union forces. The Southern transportation system, especially the railroads, had been wrecked. In some places, returning rebels outdid the worst of the Yankees in rapaciousness. "Villages [were] sacked in Yankee style by lawless mobs, and every man returning from the army on mule or horse had to guard his animals and himself with loaded weapons," South Carolinian Emma Holmes reported.

Gradually the North imposed order in the defeated states of the Confederacy. Grant's surrender terms were liberal, but they left no doubt that the immense power of the Union had prevailed.

Historians still debate the reasons for the Union victory. Size, wealth, and industrial capacity were crucial factors: The North had more soldiers, and they were better armed, equipped, and fed than the rebels. Moreover, the Federal blockade prevented the South from exporting cotton to pay for the imports of arms and munitions its factories failed to produce in sufficient quantities.

Some historians believe internal divisions and lack of will to continue the fight hastened the Confederacy's collapse. States' rights had helped to bring on the war, and some state governments, such as Georgia's, refused to place the Confederacy's interests ahead of their own at critical times. Men, money, and materiel were withheld; in North Carolina and elsewhere, some politicians openly encouraged the desertions that increasingly weakened the rebel field armies.

Finally, superior political and military leadership assured a Union victory. Lincoln proved to be a great war leader, his strategic vision and political ability far superior to that of Jefferson Davis. Davis had failed to hold his nation together, while Lincoln succeeded in restoring his. From 1863 onward, Grant and Sherman gave the Union a significant edge in generalship. They seemed bound to win. While Lee, the South's finest commander, could not see beyond the Virginia theater—he never left its environs, except for the two brief incursions into Maryland and Pennsylvania—the western campaigns of Grant and Sherman brought the Union control of the Mississippi Valley, Tennessee, and Georgia. By early 1865, Federal forces occupied vast areas of the Confederacy and were poised for the final offensive that would crush rebel resistance.

What did it all mean? What did the great war accomplish? The conflict began over slavery, and by late 1862, its abolition had become a key Union war aim. By 1865, there could be no doubt that slavery in America had been destroyed, and the Thirteenth Amendment to the Constitution formally ratified its end. The war invalidated the idea of secession too. The states, with their own rights and duties, were nevertheless part of an indissoluble whole. Finally, the war established, for the first time, the principle of the federal government as the guarantor of individual freedom.

For black Americans, freedom could be a hollow word. "The emancipated slaves own nothing, because nothing but freedom has been given them," one Southern planter said. For millions of former slaves, little seemed to change. Within a few months after the war's end, white officials were setting curfews for blacks, segregating trains and steamboats, and making interracial marriage illegal. "The negroes are no more free than they were forty years ago," Tennessee politician Emer-

Text of the Emancipation Proclamation. Two U.S. flags and an eagle over a portrait of Abraham Lincoln are flanked by the allegorical figures of Justice and Liberty. *(Library of Congress)*

son Etheridge declared, "and if anyone goes about the country telling them that they are free, shoot him."

Still, African Americans made important advances for some years after the Reconstruction Act of 1867, by which Congress sought to guarantee economic and political power for freedmen. Some gains, especially in educational opportunity, were preserved even after the collapse of Reconstruction in 1877 and the imposition of a rigid system of white supremacy that would last for nearly a century. For most blacks, even sharecropping, or working on the old plantation for pittance wages, represented something better than slavery.

The veterans, Union and Confederate, returned home and tried to adjust to peace and to the commonplace disciplines of family, farm, and workshop. In time, the older leaders began to pass from the scene. Robert E. Lee died of a heart ailment in October 1870 in Lexington, Virginia, where he had accepted the presidency of Washington College. The triumphant Grant served two terms as president of the United States, from 1869 to 1877. He managed to complete his memoirs before a painful throat cancer claimed him in 1885. Sherman served as commander in chief of the army from 1869 to 1883. In his hard, uncompromising way, he refused all offers of political power. He died in 1891. His old adversary Joe Johnston helped carry the casket at his funeral.

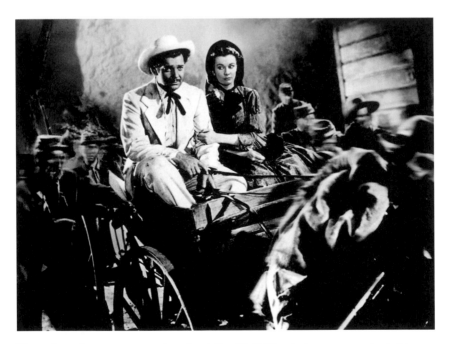

There have been many movies about the Civil War, but none can compete with *Gone With the Wind* (1939), which continues to rank as one of the greatest movies of all time. Although most people probably now enjoy it as a romantic drama, it actually presents an idealized view of the South before and during the Civil War. *(Photofest)*

Veterans of the Civil War at a reunion in Grand Rapids, Michigan, in 1927 *(National Archives)*

Standing bareheaded in the rain with the other pallbearers, Johnston caught a chill and died a few weeks later.

George Thomas, the Rock of Chickamauga, died in 1870; Henry Halleck and George Meade died in 1872; George McClellan, the Little Napoleon, a postwar governor of New Jersey, died a few months after Grant in 1885. James Longstreet, who ordered Pickett's charge at Gettysburg against his better judgment, died in 1904. Jefferson Davis spent two years in prison after his capture in Georgia. Federal authorities never brought him to trial and he lived on, writing memoirs that attempted to justify secession, until December 1889.

Not long after the war the custom spread from state to state, in both the North and South, of setting aside a day to honor the dead. The observance became institutionalized as Memorial Day, celebrated for many decades on May 30. Once a year, in innumerable town squares, wreathes were laid, flowers strewn, crepe hung, and orations given. No speech better expressed the mystic claims of the war upon those who had fought it than one by former captain Oliver Wendell Holmes, Jr.—a three-times-wounded veteran of a Massachusetts infantry regiment and, eventually, chief justice of the United States—in Keene, New Hampshire, on Memorial Day 1884.

"The generation that carried on the war has been set aside by its experience," Holmes told the crowd gathered around the war memorial there. "Through our great good fortune, in our youth our hearts were touched with fire. It was given us to learn at the outset that life is a profound and passionate thing. While we are permitted to scorn nothing by indifference, and do not pretend to undervalue the worldly rewards of ambition, we have seen with our own eyes, beyond and above the gold fields, the snowy heights of honor, and it is for us to bear the report to those who come after us."

The last surviving Civil War veteran carried the report down to 1959. Now successive generations, imagining the past, must create the war's meaning for themselves.

Glossary

abolition movement   A program that called for an immediate end to slavery, as opposed to the desire of most Northerners, including Lincoln, for the restriction of the institution of slavery to states where it already existed. Abolitionists were a distinct minority in the antebellum era.

army   A large operational military force. Some 16 Union and 23 Confederate units were given the designation of "army." Civil War armies generally were named for a geographical region (Army of Tennessee, Confederate) or a feature of a region (Army of the Shenandoah, Federal).

Army of Northern Virginia   The main army of the Confederacy, commanded from June 1862 by Robert E. Lee.

Army of the Potomac   The main eastern army of the Union. George Gordon Meade assumed command of the army near Gettysburg in June 1863 and proved to be the most successful of its four commanders.

battery   A set of heavy weapons, guns, howitzers, or mortars, and/or the men who served the weapons. A battery is the basic unit of an artillery formation, equivalent to an infantry company.

bivouac   A nightly halt, differing from an encampment in that soldiers sleep with their arms (weapons) at their side and thus are in a state of readiness to move.

blockade   Isolating a port, city, region, or nation by surrounding it with ships or troops to prevent the passage of traffic or supplies. Lincoln banned maritime trade with the seceding states in April 1861 and eventually some 600 U.S. naval vessels were on blockade duty, sealing off the Confederacy's 3,500-mile coastline.

border states   Slave states along the U.S. midsection that formed a divide between the North and the South. Virginia and Tennessee joined the Confederacy. Federal troops kept Delaware, Maryland, Kentucky, and Missouri within the Union, although men from these states fought on the Confederate as well as the Union side.

bounties   Cash awards, ranging from $25 to $400, to stimulate voluntary enlistments in the Union and Confederate armies. Various branches
of government paid out some $750 million in bounties during the Civil
War.

brigade   A unit of military organization, composed of two or more
regiments. Two or more brigades made up a division. Union brigades,
which averaged around 2,000 men, were styled by arabic numerals. Confederate brigades, slightly smaller than their Union counterparts, bore
the names of their commanders.

conscription   The compulsory enrollment of troops, also known as the
draft. The first Confederate conscripts were raised in the spring of 1862;
the U.S. Congress passed the Union's first conscription act in March
1863. Service could be avoided by paying a fee of $300 or by hiring a
substitute. Only around 50,000 conscripts were actually forced to serve
in the Union army.

Copperhead   A pejorative name (in reference to the poisonous snake)
applied to Northerners, mostly Democrats, who supported the South by
advocating a negotiated end to the war.

corps   A large body of troops, usually two or more divisions, composed
of all the elements—infantry, cavalry, and artillery—that make up an
army. Union corps were designated by Roman numerals. Confederate
corps were known informally by the name of the commanding general
(for example, Longstreet's corps).

division   A large formation of infantry or cavalry. A division was
formed when two or more brigades were linked together. At full strength,
a federal division mustered around 6,200 men; Confederate divisions
were slightly larger.

flag of truce   A flag, usually white, carried when a peaceful communication or message is to be delivered to an enemy.

flanking move   A move along the sides of an enemy's force, it is usually
made to seek a position without being exposed to all of an enemy's fire.

foraging; forage   The act of searching for and gathering food and provisions for troops or animals; *forage* refers solely to food for the army's
mounts and draft animals.

fortress   A set of strongholds designed to protect a place from attack
and capture; a fortified place. Confederate forces fortified Vicksburg in
1862 and 1863; Fortress Monroe in Virginia was a strongly defended
military base.

habeas corpus   From the Latin; meaning "you have the body," it refers
to a court order requiring that a person being held by the authorities be

brought before the court. This is regarded as a fundamental right under American law. Citing his emergency powers, Lincoln controversially suspended the writ of habeas corpus during the war.

impressment   During the Civil War, the practice of taking supplies or livestock for an army's use, usually with some form of a written promise to pay.

invest   To surround an enemy's position with troops or ships; to place under siege.

monitor   Generic designation for an armored, shallow-draft warship with a flat deck and carrying one or two great guns in a revolving turret. John Ericsson designed the first of these vessels and named it the USS *Monitor*, conveying the notion that the ship would "admonish" Confederate leaders.

peculiar institution   A reference to the institution of slavery as practiced in the United States. The phrase first appeared in writing in 1842 in James S. Buckingham's *The Slave States of America*. The word *peculiar* here does not mean "strange" but "distinctive" or "special."

rations   An allowance of bread, meat, and coffee or tea distributed to soldiers.

regiment   A basic unit of military organization. An infantry regiment contained 10 companies. Volunteer regiments were recruited by state and so designated (for instance, the 20th Massachusetts). A regiment's authorized strength was about 1,000 men. In practice, regimental numbers declined sharply as the war advanced, as new regiments were created for volunteers and casualties in veteran regiments were not replaced.

salient   The section of a line of battle that extends closest to the enemy's position. The salient at Spotsylvania (Virginia) saw heavy fighting in May 1864.

sap   A trench, often covered, sometimes tunnelled, leading at right angles from the main line of field works toward an enemy's entrenchments.

secession   A claimed right to leave the union of the United States. Southerners defending slavery and state's rights argued the union was a voluntary compact among the states. South Carolina in December 1860 became the first state to secede.

sectionalism   A parochial concern for the interests or well-being of one part of a country, sometimes at the expense of other parts. A tariff designed to protect Northern industry was an example of a sectional dispute between North and South before the Civil War.

shoddy   Inferior woolen yarn made from reused fibers and spun into cheap fabric. Union uniforms made of shoddy tended to fall apart quickly. Of unknown origin, the word later passed into generic use as an adjective for anything poorly made.

siege   An army's painstaking sealing off of a town or a fortress from all outside contacts and supplies for the purpose of bringing its occupants to surrender without requiring the force of arms. Grant's siege of Vicksburg in 1863 lasted more than two months.

strategy   The science of planning and directing large-scale military movements designed to bring about the defeat of an enemy.

substitution   During the Civil War, the hiring of a willing man to take a conscript's place in the army.

tactics   The arranging, deployment, and maneuvering of troops in battle, usually in pursuit of a short-range objective such as capturing a position.

theater   A large geographic area in which military operations are conducted, usually with some strategic coordination or goal. The actions of the Civil War are traditionally, and somewhat arbitrarily, assigned to either the eastern theater or the western theater.

volley   The simultaneous and orchestrated discharge of a number of firearms or other weapons.

Further Reading

NONFICTION

Alcott, Louisa May. *Hospital Sketches.* Bessie Z. Jones, ed. Cambridge, Mass.: Belknap Press of Harvard University, 1960.

Alexander, Edward Porter. *Military Memoirs of a Confederate: A Critical Narrative.* New York: Charles Scribner's Sons, 1910.

Barrett, Jenny. *Shooting the Civil War: Cinema, History and American National Identity.* London: Tauris paperback, 2009.

Blount, Roy, Jr. *Robert E. Lee: A Penguin Life.* New York: Lipper/Viking, 2003.

Boritt, Gabor S. *The Gettysburg Nobody Knows.* New York: Oxford University Press, 1997.

Brumgardt, John R., ed. *Civil War Nurse: The Diary and Letters of Hannah Ropes.* Knoxville: University of Tennessee Press, 1980.

Burkhardt, George S. *Confederate Rage, Yankee Wrath: No Quarter in the Civil War.* Carbondale: Southern Illinois University Press, 2007.

Burlingame, Michael. *Abraham Lincoln: A Life.* Baltimore: Johns Hopkins University Press, 2008.

Burns, Ken. *The Civil War.* Florentine Films/PBS Video, VHS, 9 vols., 1989.

Carhart, Tom. *Lost Triumph: Lee's Real Plan at Gettysburg—and Why It Failed.* New York: G. P. Putnam's Sons, 2005.

———. *Sacred Ties: From West Point Brothers to Battlefield Rivals. A True Story of the Civil War.* New York: Berkeley, 2010.

Catton, Bruce. *Glory Road.* Garden City, N.Y.: Doubleday, 1954.

———. *Grant Moves South.* Boston: Little, Brown, 1960.

———. *A Stillness at Appomattox.* Garden City, N.Y.: Doubleday, 1953.

Cornelius, Steven. *Music of the Civil War Era.* Westport, Conn.: Greenwood Press, 2004.

Davis, David Brion. "The Enduring Legacy of the South's Civil War Victory." *New York Times,* 26 August, 2001, sec. 4, p. 1.

Davis, William C. *Jefferson Davis: The Man and His Hour.* New York: HarperCollins, 1991.

DeKay, James Tertius. *Monitor.* New York: Walker and Company, 1997.

Donald, David Herbert. *Lincoln.* New York: Simon & Schuster, 1995.

Eicher, David J. *The Longest Night: A Military History of the Civil War.* New York: Simon & Schuster, 2001.

Fellman, Michael. *Citizen Sherman: A Life of William Tecumseh Sherman*. New York: Random House, 1995.

———. *The Making of Robert E. Lee*. New York: Random House, 2000.

Flood, Charles Bracelin. *Grant and Sherman: The Partnership That Won the Civil War*. New York: Farrar, Straus and Giroux, 2005

Foner, Eric, ed. *Our Lincoln: New Perspectives on Lincoln and His World*. New York: W. W. Norton & Co., 2008.

Foote, Shelby. *The Civil War: A Narrative*. 3 vols. New York: Random House, 1990.

Franklin, John Hope, and Loren Schweniger. *Runaway Slaves: Rebels on the Plantation*. New York: Oxford University Press, 1999.

Furgurson, Ernest. *Ashes of Glory: Richmond at War*. New York: Alfred A. Knopf, 1996.

Glatthaar, Joseph T. *Forged in Battle: The Civil War Alliance of Black Soldiers and White Officers*. New York: The Free Press, 1990.

———. *General Lee's Army: From Victory to Collapse*. New York: Free Press, 2008.

Golay, Michael. *A Ruined Land: The End of the Civil War*. New York: John Wiley & Sons, 1999.

———. *To Gettysburg and Beyond: The Parallel Lives of Joshua Lawrence Chamberlain and Edward Porter Alexander*. New York: Crown, 1994.

Goodwin, Doris Kearns. *Team of Rivals: The Political Genius of Abraham Lincoln*. New York: Simon & Schuster, 2005.

Grant, Ulysses S. *Personal Memoirs of U. S. Grant*. New York: Library of America, 1990.

Griffith, Paddy. *Battle Tactics of the Civil War*. New Haven, Conn.: Yale University Press, 1989.

Grimsley, Mark. *The Hard Hand of War: Union Military Policy toward Southern Civilians, 1861–1865*. New York: Cambridge University Press, 1995.

Guelzo, Allen C. *Lincoln's Emancipation Proclamation: The End of Slavery in America*. New York: St. Martin's Press, 2004.

Higginson, Thomas W. *Army Life in a Black Regiment*. New York: Collier Books, 1962.

Holzer, Harold. *Lincoln President-elect: Abraham Lincoln and the Great Secession Winter*. New York: Simon & Schuster, 2008.

Jones, Virgil C. *The Civil War at Sea*. New York: Holt, Rinehart, 1960.

Kemble, Fanny. *Journal of a Residence on a Georgia Plantation in 1838–1839*. Edited by John A. Scott. New York: Alfred A. Knopf, 1961.

Keneally, Thomas. *American Scoundrel: The Life of the Notorious Civil War General Dan Sickles*. New York: Nan A. Talese/Doubleday, 2002.

Lankford, Nelson D. *Cry Havoc! The Crooked Road to Civil War*. New York: Viking, 2007.

Lewin, J. G., and P. J. Huff. *Political Cartoons of the Civil War*. New York: Collins, 2007.

Linderman, Gerald. *Embattled Courage: The Experience of Combat in the Civil War*. New York: Free Press, 1987.

Marszalek, John F. *Sherman: A Soldier's Passion for Order*. New York: Free Press, 1993.

Marvel, William. *Mr. Lincoln Goes to War.* Boston: Houghton-Mifflin, 2006.

McDonough, James. *Shiloh—In Hell before Night.* Knoxville: University of Tennessee Press, 1977.

McFeely, William S. *Grant: A Biography.* New York: Norton, 1981.

McGovern, George S. *Abraham Lincoln.* New York: Times Books, Henry Holt Co., 2009.

McPherson, James M. *Battle Cry of Freedom: The Civil War Era.* New York: Oxford University Press, 1988.

———. *Crossroads of Freedom: Antietam.* New York: Oxford University Press, 2002.

———. *This Mighty Scourge: Perspectives on the Civil War.* New York: Oxford University Press, 2007.

———. *Tried by War: Abraham Lincoln as Commander-in-Chief.* New York: Penguin, 2008.

Miller, William Lee. *President Lincoln: The Duty of a Statesman.* New York: Knopf, 2008.

Mitchell, Reid. *Civil War Soldiers.* New York: Viking, 1988.

Nolan, Alan. *Lee Considered: General Robert E. Lee and Civil War History.* Chapel Hill: University of North Carolina Press, 1991.

Olsen, Christopher J. *The American Civil War: A Hands-on History.* New York: Hill & Wang, 2006.

Redkey, Edwin S. *A Grand Army of Black Men: Letters from African-American Soldiers in the Union Army, 1861–1865.* New York: Cambridge University Press, 1992.

Robertson, James I., Jr. *Soldiers Blue and Gray.* Columbia: University of South Carolina Press, 1988.

——— . *Stonewall Jackson: The Man, the Soldier, the Legend.* New York: Macmillan, 1997.

Royster, Charles. *The Destructive War.* New York: Alfred A. Knopf, 1991.

Sears, Stephen. *Chancellorsville.* Boston: Houghton Mifflin, 1996.

———. *Landscape Turned Red: The Battle of Antietam.* New Haven, Conn.: Ticknor and Fields, 1983.

Sherman, William T. *Memoirs of General W. T. Sherman.* New York: Library of America, 1990.

Simpson, Brooks D. *Ulysses S. Grant: Triumph over Adversity, 1822–1865.* Boston, Mass.: Houghton Mifflin, 2000.

Stampp, Kenneth M. *The Peculiar Institution: Slavery in the Antebellum South.* New York: Alfred A. Knopf, 1956.

Striner, Richard. *Father Abraham: Lincoln's Relentless Struggle to End Slavery.* New York: Oxford University Press, 2007.

Swanson, Mark. *Atlas of the Civil War Month by Month: Major Battles and Troop Movements.* Athens: University of Georgia Press, 2004.

Thomas, Benjamin P. *Abraham Lincoln.* New York: Alfred A. Knopf, 1952.

Thomas, Emory M. *Robert E. Lee: A Biography.* New York: Norton, 1995.

Thomas, William G., and Alice E. Carter. *The Civil War on the Web: A Guide to the Very Best Sites.* Wilmington, Del.: Scholarly Resources, 2000.

Trudeau, Noah Andre. *Like Men of War: Blacks Troops in the Civil War.* Boston: Little, Brown, 1998.

Wagner, Margaret E. *The American Civil War: 365 Days.* Vincent Virga, picture editor. New York: Abrams in association with the Library of Congress, 2006.

Ward, Geoffrey C., with Ric Burns and Ken Burns. *The Civil War: An Illustrated History.* New York: Alfred A. Knopf, 1990.

Weigley, Russell. *A Great Civil War: A Military and Political History, 1861–1865.* Bloomington: Indiana University Press, 2000.

Wert, Jeffry D. *Cavalryman of the Lost Cause: A Biography of J. E. B. Stuart.* New York: Simon & Schuster, 2008.

Wheeler, Tom. *Mr. Lincoln's T-mails: The Untold Story of How Abraham Lincoln Used the Telegraph to Win the Civil War.* New York: Collins, 2006.

Wiley, Bell I. *The Life of Billy Yank.* Baton Rouge: Louisiana State University Press, 1951.
———. *The Life of Johnny Reb.* Indianapolis: Bobbs-Merrill, 1943.

Williams, T. Harry. *Lincoln and His Generals.* New York: Alfred A. Knopf, 1952.

Wills, Garry. *Lincoln at Gettysburg: The Words That Remade America.* New York: Simon & Schuster, 1992.

Wilson, Edmund. *Patriotic Gore: Studies in the Literature of the American Civil War.* Boston: Northeastern University Press, 1984.

FICTION AND POETRY

Auchincloss, Louis. *Watchfires.* Boston: Houghton Mifflin, 1982.

Banks, Russell. *Cloudsplitter.* New York: HarperCollins, 1998.

Bierce, Ambrose. *The Complete Short Stories of Ambrose Bierce.* Garden City, N.Y.: Doubleday, 1970.

Crane, Stephen. *The Red Badge of Courage.* New York: Norton, 1976.

DeForest, John. *Miss Ravenel's Conversion from Secession to Loyalty.* New York: Harper & Brother, 1867. Reprint, New York: Penguin, 2000.
———. *The Unvanquished.* Drawings by Edward Shenton. New York: Random House, 1965.

Faulkner, William. Faulkner, William. *Absalom, Absalom!* New York: Random House, 1936.

Foote, Shelby, ed. *Chickamauga, and Other Civil War Stories.* New York: Delta, 1993.

Frazier, Charles. *Cold Mountain.* New York: Atlantic Monthly Press, 1997.

Mitchell, Margaret. *Gone with the Wind.* New York: Macmillan, 1936.

Shaara, Michael. *The Killer Angels.* New York: McKay, 1974.

Stowe, Harriet Beecher. *Uncle Tom's Cabin.* 1852. Reprint, New York: Library of America, 1982.

Whitman, Walt. *Poetry and Prose.* New York: Library of America, 1982.

Wicker, Tom. *Unto This Hour.* New York: Viking, 1984.

WEB SITES

The American Civil War. URL: http://www.history.com/content/civilwar
The American Civil War Homepage. URL: http://sunsite.utk.edu/civil-war

The American Civil War Rare Map Collection, Hargrett Rare Book and Manuscript Library, University of Georgia. URL: http://www.libs.uga.edu/darchive/hargrett/maps/civil.html

Civil War History. URL: http://etext.lib.virginia.edu/civilwar

Civil War Women. URL: http://library.duke.edu/specialcollections/binghamd/guides/civilwar.html

National Park Service Civil War Website. URL: http://cwar.nps.gov/civilwar/

The United States Civil War Center. Special Collections, Louisiana State University Libraries. URL: http://www.cwc.lsu.edu/cwc.edu/cwc

Index

Page numbers in *italic* indicate a photograph or illustration. Page numbers followed by *m* indicate maps. Page numbers followed by *g* indicate glossary entries. Page numbers in **boldface** indicate box features.

A

abatis 212
Abbott, E. G. 165
abolition/abolition movement 2, 7–8, 243*g*
    British support for 96
    John Brown 19
    Kansas-Nebraska Act 14, 16
    purpose of war 80
    and recruitment of blacks 120
    "Secret Six" 20
    Thirteenth Amendment 238
Acton, Edward 49
Adams, Charles Francis, Jr. 130
Adams, Henry 150
advances on Vicksburg 153–155, 157
Aereon (dirigible) **210, 211**
aerial observation 202, **209**
African Americans *113. See also* free blacks; freed slaves; slaves
    acceptance of blacks in military 116
    Emancipation Proclamation 112
    in military services 79–80, 116–122
    Northern hostilities toward 100
    postwar advances for 239–240
    risks for, as soldiers 120
    as Union army volunteers **117**
aftermath of war viii, ix, 237–242
Agar "coffee mill" 214
aircraft **209–211**

Alabama, CSS 216
Alabama, secession of 28
Alcorn, James 107
Alcott, Louisa May 171, 172
Alexander, E. Porter 127, 148
American Anti-Slavery Society 7
American Missionary Association 115
amnesty, for deserters 104
"The Anaconda Plan" 38, *38,* 217
Anderson, Richard 143, 146
Anderson, Robert 33, 34
Andersonville, Georgia *199,* 200
Andrews, John 120, 127
Andrews, Solomon **209–211**
Antietam, Battle of 85–93, *87,* **88,** *90, 92*
antislavery. *See* abolition/abolition movement
Appomattox Court House 233, 234
Appomattox Station 232–233
Archer, James 140
Arkansas, secession of 35
Armory Square Hospital 172
army, Confederate 41. *See also specific battles*
    black soldiers in 203–204
    combat with black soldiers 119–120
    demise of 237
    desertions 102–105
    militiamen **39**
    mobilization of 36–37, **39**
    move into Maryland 82, 83
    near Washington 43
    physical condition of troops 83, 102, 219–220, 229, 232
    railroads **180**
    ratio of Union troops to 202, 203

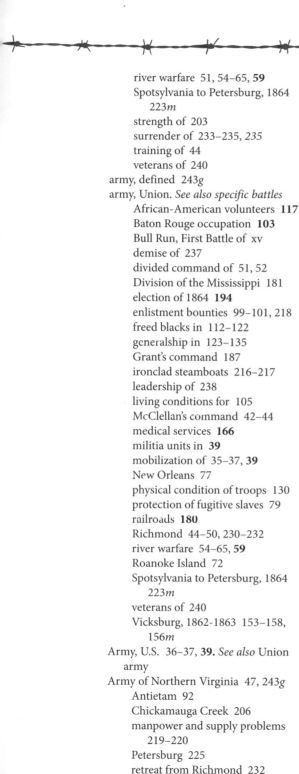